NEWS FROM SOMEWHERE
A Reader in Communication
and
Challenges to Globalization

edited by
Daniel Broudy, Jeffery Klaehn,
and James Winter

News from Somewhere: A Reader in
Communication and Challenges to Globalization
Copyright © 2015, Wayzgoose Press

ISBN-10: 1938757092
ISBN-13: 978-1-938757-09-9

1. globalization 2. neoliberalism 3. militarism 4. hegemony
5. post-colonialism 6. intercultural communication 7. language
8. security 9. education 10. environment 11. identity politics
12. Inequality

The content of this collection has been peer reviewed.

Printed and bound in the United States of America
by Wayzgoose Press, Eugene, Oregon
http://wayzgoosepress.com

Set in Garamond

Edited by Daniel Broudy, Jeffery Klaehn, & James Winter
Copy Editing by Dorothy E. Zemach
Cover Design by D. J. Rogers

CONTENTS

PART V. ENERGY POLICIES, EXTERNALITIES, AND RESISTANCE

Acknowledgments

The editors wish to thank Makoto Arakaki, Christopher Valvona, David Ulvog, and Suh Yuna for critical comments on this project, the initial proposal, and the process of its development.

Note: The editors respect the varieties of English and spelling used by the authors throughout this volume.

FOREWORD

Some twenty years ago, when I was teaching in Tokyo, the college inaugurated a class in Intercultural Communication. The school had a long history of training young people in the skills of promoting international understanding, beginning, of course, with foreign languages but also including the study of other people's cultures and customs, the causes of misunderstandings, and the ways of overcoming them. The new class in Intercultural Communication seemed to align well in this educational environment.

Thus, it was a surprise when one of the students in my seminar, a sharp and sensitive woman, told me that the class had driven her to outrage. Her father's company had stationed him in the US, as a result of which she had spent a number of years there before entering the college. With this background, the contents of the textbook amounted to a challenge to her identity, and a personal insult. Again and again, she was told by the textbook and the teacher, Japanese behave like this, Japanese think like that, Japanese have these feelings. "I don't think like that" she would say. "Does that mean I'm not Japanese?"

It seems that the textbook—and the entire notion of "Intercultural Communication" out of which it had grown—had been developed in the US. Because she had lived there, the distortions that resulted from the book's development were more visible to her than they were to other students. Claiming to have overcome stereotyping, the book in fact piled one American stereotype on top of another. Claiming to teach students to see things from the other's point of view, the book relentlessly stuck to the American point of view, and by multiplying stereotypes locked people of other cultures into the inescapable category of Other. Moreover, the American point of view was built into the very structure of the book. That is, its stated purpose was to enable "us/we" to improve communication with "them." Reading through the book, one gradually would come to understand that "us/we" meant white, middle class, mostly male, college-going Americans.

In short, it was a very strange textbook to assign in a country outside the US.

As presented in that text, the field of Intercultural Communication had built within it another ideological presupposition: This was the notion that friction among people of different cultures mainly results from misunderstanding and miscommunication. If people could only understand each others' cultural background a little better, we should all be able to get along. Of course, anything that helps us to get along better is welcome. But there are some issues about which the clearer our understanding becomes, the angrier we get. And, it is also true that difference in culture is not the only thing that can distort communication among peoples; it can also be distorted by difference in power.

The world we have inherited has grown out of a history of slavery, colonialism, imperialism, class exploitation, gender exploitation—I will not attempt to complete this list. This tale is not over, and wild differences in wealth and power exist today—and in some cases are increasing. It would be nice if we could make all this go away by pretending that it is not so, and that we all came into the world with equal wealth, power and status, so that the only thing left to interfere with our perfect communication is "culture." In the field of Intercultural Communication—intentionally or unintentionally—there seems to be an underlying tendency to promote this illusion.

The present volume seeks to reverse this trend. That is, as communications and communication theory can be used to conceal the real world of injustice, unequal power, and maldistributed wealth, so can the critical analysis of communications and of communication theory be used to make that world visible once again. Of course, this project is not aimed at increasing the friction among peoples, but is based on the belief that only when the true situation is clearly understood can we begin to work toward a true solution. Papering things over with words will not help.

The essays in this volume may seem to be on a wide variety of topics. I hope this foreword will help you to see the larger project in which they are joined.

C. Douglas Lummis
Professor Emeritus, Tsuda College
January 2015

INTRODUCTION

Where globalization means, as it so often does,
that the rich and powerful now have new means
to further enrich and empower themselves
at the cost of the poorer and weaker,
we have a responsibility to protest
in the name of universal freedom.

—*Nelson Mandela*
(November 22, 2000)

In the modern era, with the final obstacles to global capitalism cleared by the fall of the Berlin Wall, the forces of globalization were able, at long last, to prevail upon markets around the world. What the anticipated, indeed hoped for, peace dividend accomplished in the wake of the Cold War, though, was not stability and reconciliation between East and West but unsurpassed corporate access to markets long closed by warfare waged on ideological fronts. Alex Carey crystallized the importance of this curious confluence of political and market freedom in observing that the 20th century has "been characterized by three developments of great political importance: the growth of democracy, the growth of corporate power and the growth of corporate propaganda as a means of protecting corporate power against democracy,"[1] In what may be described as a subsequent tsunami of colonialism, neoliberalism has widened the control by elites, extending it from resources and labour to the privatization of public industries and structures. As Chomsky notes, "Power is no longer in the hands of the 'merchants and manufacturers,' but of financial institutions and multinationals."[2]

In the 21st century with neoliberalism's expanding influence, which carries the message that free market forces are both democratic and objective forces for good on earth, global capitalism has enlisted peoples across the world in the service of annihilating the environment and erasing long-cherished concepts of human rights, relations, and dignity in the interest of development as understood by transnational corporate powers. The spread of this ideology, note Michael Hardt and Antonio Negri, has appeared to be "irresistible and irreversible"[3] to the owners of capital who have invested in its promises of economic freedom and control beyond the entanglements of government regulation.

This volume recognizes the inequities, tensions and injustices produced by these purportedly appealing and permanent processes, and examines the resulting conditions and language used by the elite to rationalize these processes. It comes out of a November 2013 lecture given by Professor C. Douglas Lummis for the Graduate School of Intercultural Communication at Okinawa Christian University, an institution committed to applying the liberal arts in the spirit of making and preserving peace among peoples and nations.

As a region of extreme devastation and horror during the waning months of World War II, Okinawa, by the reckoning of many official sources, saw more than one-third of its population killed in the cross-fire between the invading American forces and forces of the Imperial Japanese military. This final campaign was also an immense clash of cultures, languages, and ideologies and yet a conflict that endures in sundry forms of intensity today where the forces of militarization and globalization remain arrayed against people intent on preventing the conditions that had wrought such grief and destruction in the previous century.

If intercultural communication represents a real effort to breach the cultural boundaries and mores that impede peaceful relations and understanding among peoples, why is the field so subsumed by assumptions that both inform and emanate from a largely North American outlook on the world? With this question in mind, Lummis deconstructed portions of a popular communications textbook featuring some intriguing presuppositions. Among them, the perplexing use of the deictic "we," to an international audience, presumes that readers already know why it might be important to understand local customs before entering a home in occupied war zones. In the 2009, *Communication Between Cultures*, Larry Samovar et al. observe that, "A U.S. military patrol entering a home in Iraq or Afghanistan would be well served by a knowledge of local cultural etiquette." Not always, but all too often, the members of the "we" group, observed Lummis, are pictured as being in a position of power over the people with whom they are communicating, and "the study of international communication" is useful in helping them (the power holders) to achieve their goals.

The authors of the 2009 textbook suggest as much, pointing out that such knowledge would serve rather well U.S. military patrols maneuvering in these areas for control and stability. Yet, "we" would seem somewhat strange (if not inexplicable) to an international audience, since the plural pronoun implies those who already have access to the sort of social, economic, and military power the authors refer to throughout the text.

This collection was proposed initially as a critical reader, which we had intended to assemble as an appeal to reason over the hyper-rational forces now shaping the practices and processes of neoliberal globalization. As editors of this volume, we are concerned about how the developed world has devolved in the hands of the neoliberal corporate elite in light of our observations, studies, and experiences in cultures around the world. To be a credible counterbalance to the globalization bandwagon that many nations have boarded, we felt that the voices reflected herein should meet the wide range of students, researchers, and academics at a level that engages them clearly with language and content grounded in unique lived experiences.

This is a central reason why elements of each author's narrative style—woven into critically reflective exposition—are key features of the pieces we have brought together. Thus, the book takes a global view but tells the unfolding story of globalization and its consequences from the perspective of individuals who have taken care to carefully observe its effects firsthand and who intend to make sense of (or explain) those effects by way of some overarching theory. Academic jargon we, therefore, asked authors to keep to the bare minimum while vivid language, instead, was encouraged.

In its contemporary guise, globalization as an economic force behind transnational business practices owes its current successes and failures to foundations laid long ago under industrialism and colonialism. Globalization today reflects an unfair battle between countries of the North which were bolstered by the immense wealth taken from colonial victims, versus relatively newlyindependent nations weakened by centuries of plunder and exploitation. Initially, newly independent countries pursued economic sovereignty through protectionism, while global corporations fought to maintain their colonial privileges.[4] The neoliberal phase, beginning in the 1970s, consisted of major counterattacks by global corporate interests, under the auspices of the IMF, WTO, and the World Bank. This forced many countries to surrender much of their economic sovereignty. While the Latin American Revolution, for example, has since reversed this

Part I

Education and Civilization

CHAPTER ONE

INSPIRATIONS FOR CRITICAL LITERACY ACROSS CULTURAL AND MEDIA STUDIES

Katarzyna Molek-Kozakowska

Introduction

My experience as a tutor and supervisor of undergraduate research projects in Cultural and Media Studies in a public Polish university is that many students are not prepared to include a *critique* of their objects of study, be they popular media representations, conventions in public discourse, or routine communicative practices. One explanation of why their papers are not sufficiently critical might be that interrogation of everyday cultural practices and media uses must be exceedingly difficult for young people raised in the digital age without the awareness of the cultural constructedness of consumerism and ideological preponderance of globalization. Another explanation could be that the dominant schooling model in Poland requires students to absorb views that are handed down to them by the curriculum rather than to learn how to deconstruct meanings and power relations in canonical texts and institutional discourses. No matter what the causes are, my taking notice of this shortage of critical skills has led me to an observation that my students need not only a functional literacy—proficiency in comprehending and producing academically viable papers—but also a certain degree of critical literacy.

I understand critical literacy as an ability to grasp the social, institutional, ideological, even economic contexts of discourse production and to identify how texts (including one's own) may be used to re-affirm or resist dominant discourses. To many, some linguistic and rhetorical forms (e.g. speech styles, stereotypical representations, argumentative conventions or narrative sequences) are perceived as "common sense"—the natural way to communicate meaning—even though these forms are mostly culture-specific constructs that privilege some meanings over others. By problematizing the conventions of language use that are taken for granted by my students, I wish to refresh, for example, their experience of corporate and public communication in order to encourage them to reflect on cultural constructedness and ideological provenance of certain "common-sensical" meanings. Thus, for me, critical literacy is not only a set of analytic skills but also a particular frame of mind that students should adopt in order to develop in-depth insight in discourse.

Critical literacy is also a notion conducive to educational practice, though I admit it is hard to be critically literate in an educational context that discourages challenging the status quo. However, my reading of the literature on criticality suggests that something akin to my notion of critical literacy has already been addressed by researchers of diverse backgrounds and interests.[1] This essay is devoted to reviewing some intellectual currents and strands of research within Cultural and Media Studies that have contributed, in the long run, to my isolating critical literacy as a social ideal. I try to re-examine them here to focus on their potential for the establishment of critical literacy as an educational paradigm and to validate my own interventionist agenda.[2]

Early Strands of Cultural Critique

The pursuit to describe and evaluate cultural practices and texts has been a major preoccupation in Cultural and Media Studies, particularly as regards the popular forms. I admit that the enhancement of critical literacy has been implicit in many theoretical and empirical strands of Cultural Studies, and it is criticality that delimited it as a scholarly discipline established to improve the quality of social life. Paradoxically, the idea of criticality may be said to have sprung from the conservative Leavisite tradition, with its rigid distinction of high and popular culture. Although considered as elitist and reactionary, the postulates of "close readings," "discrimination" and "upholding standards" against the forces of "leveling down" made by F.R. Leavis and Denys Thompson[3] in 1977 were aimed at increasing public awareness of the impoverishing nature of many forms of mass culture, particularly advertising. Among other things, Leavisites advocated close analyses and critical evaluation of popular press, film, fiction and other mediated cultural products to expose their reliance on the "lowest common denominator." This might be, I suspect, a good departure point for students to reflect on the characteristics and actual value of many cultural products and discursive encounters around them.

Another vein of criticism in Cultural Studies was informed by Frankfurt School philosophers, particularly Theodor Adorno, Max Horkheimer, and Walter Benjamin. Their form of Critical Theory is predicated on exposing how the class system is perpetuated by culture industries. They claim that the masses are being pacified with various forms of cultural and media products: by offering temporary satisfaction and escapism, popular culture keeps the masses ever more depoliticized and impoverished intellectually, emotionally and, above all, economically. Adorno's critique is directed at how culture industries have been profiting from once radical or original forms of cultural expression by turning them into palatable formulas that are mass-produced to appeal to the general public.[4] In this framework, youth rebellion, for example, can be said to have been turned into a saleable commodity by the culture industry, which treats it as a useful construct helping to sell more films, records, clothes or accessories. Critical theory is most helpful to critical literacy acolytes to become aware of *why* cultural products are like they are.

By contrast, most of Raymond Williams's work has been devoted to complex relations between communication technologies and institutions on the one hand and cultural practices and textual meanings on the other. Using his method of tracing cultural "keywords,"[5] students could register the "emergent" cultural forms, not in order to condemn them, but to explore them as materially grounded cultural change. Williams insists on the need to resist the negative influence of the cultural markets, but at the same time he sees new technological advances as potential tools for informing "an educated and participatory democracy."[6] Cultural critique consists here in exploring the ways meaning is produced out of material means available (complementary to scholarship within the political economy of the media as developed by Edward Herman and Noam Chomsky)[7] and Williams's writings could be an important inspiration for students.

Neo-Marxist Ideological Critique

Although it is difficult to refer to Marx's writings in Poland without invoking at least a silent form of resistance (as he was appropriated by the former communist regime to empower itself), critical literacy education cannot avoid including this strand of critique. For example, for the neo-Marxist philosopher Louis Althusser, the notion of ideology is of special merit.[8] For him, it is a largely unconscious mode of operation, which offers false, although seemingly true, interpretations of the real conditions of existence. He regards ideology—a system of representations such as images, myths, ideas, concepts or discourses—as a mental practice through which individuals live their relation to the social formation.

Althusser also introduces the notion of "a problematic," which is characterized as the underlying assumptions, motivations and ideas by which the practical form of any cultural product, and especially text, is performed. An important task of a critical analyst of ideology is thus to deconstruct the problematic: if students are to understand a cultural text, they have to be aware not only of what is in this text, but also the assumptions which inform it—its ideology, especially if their aim is to expose the implicit relations of dominance and subjection. Also Althusser's notion of interpellation explains how people, despite generally having the feeling of being free and independent, are actually positioned in certain social roles against their will. The cultural system requires people to take assigned positions, such as those of receivers of political propaganda or consumers of commodities, for example. I argue that, through raising awareness of interpellating practices, students can better see through means of subordination and manipulation.

A similar point about social subordination through symbolic practice can be taken from the reading of Antonio Gramsci's theory of cultural hegemony.[9] Hegemony relies on cultural practices through which those in power exercise their "intellectual and moral leadership" in modern capitalist democracies, where despite the unequal and often exploitative conditions of existence, there is a high degree of consensus and stability. In this theory what matters is the fact that civil institutions (e.g. family, school, media) reproduce the elite's values, beliefs and representations—its ideology. In practice, students might want to see how hegemony uses various symbolic processes for the constant winning of consent of non-elites to the system, often in the form of practices that naturalize the elite ideology as "common sense," or how social conflicts, should they arise, are contained by negotiation and appropriation.[10] Recognizing the hegemonic arrangements of the society is, for me, an indispensable element of critical literacy.

Media Criticism

Despite radically different political groundings represented by the above strands, they can be seen as important precursors of contemporary critical literacy projects, particularly with respect to media discourse. Mediascape, according to Stuart Hall,[11] is envisioned as "a realm of articulations" that should be elucidated in order to "make a difference" in the world. My claim is that the ideals of critical literacy are best implemented in fine ideological analyses of mediated meanings and forms. Previous studies[12] could be informative here: media scholars demonstrated empirically how public media can promote the interests of business and power elites, rather than presenting diverse views and agendas, including anti-consumerist ideologies. Examples of ideological studies of media representations include news, war reportage, horoscopes or cartoons.[13] Media scholars have been promoting criticality, which has been regarded as an audience's capability of negotiating, adapting, even resisting hegemonic meanings, despite the rhetorical power of some mediated forms.

For Stuart Hall, the construction of media content—what is selected, how it is edited, with what it is combined, how it is narrated and what legitimacy it is given—is not a "technical question" but a question of "the politics of signification." Since no significations are interest-free, "the power involved here is an ideological power: the power to signify events in a particular way."[14] Interestingly, Hall does not conceive of criticism as identifying a set of propositions about what things mean, or a set of concepts/images that dominate, but rather as delineating the rules that guide the organization of meanings, images and concepts into certain constellations (discourses).[15] Just as a native speaker of a language produces grammatical utterances without the awareness of an elaborate system of syntactic rules that organize them, media outlets reproduce conceptual frameworks and ideological inventories of their societies fairly automatically. Students' critical attention should thus be devoted to how media discourse is likely to sustain society's ideological inventories (rather than to modify them), because, according to Hall, it is when such significations are historicized that they start operating as frames of reference—the common sense.[16]

In one way, media criticism can be said to have contributed to criticality with its theory, motivation and methodology of questioning dominant forms and practices. And yet, it can be noted that it has considerably neglected the need to devise critical pedagogies and concrete interventions that would promote critical media literacy. As put rather bluntly by Douglas Kellner:

> Cultural Studies has often underplayed the importance of developing pedagogies for promoting critical media literacy. While the Frankfurt School believed that the culture industries were overwhelmingly manipulative and overwhelmingly ideological, some versions of Cultural Studies argue that the media merely provide resources for use and pleasure. (...) Yet mindless celebration of media culture, without cultivation of methods to promote critical media literacy, is equally pernicious. (...) It is important to be able to perceive the various ideological voices and codes in the artifacts of our common culture and to distinguish between hegemonic ideologies and those images, discourses, and texts that subvert the dominant ideologies.[17]

That is why I turn to discourse analysis for some inspiration on how to enhance critical literacy skills.

Critical Discourse Analysis

The notion of signification as a product of social practice implies awareness, criticism, alternatives and choice. In the same vein, media do not offer one, unalterable, dominant signification, but open the society's ideological inventories to "struggle over meaning."[18] This underlines the need for students to look at how precisely ideologies tend to be articulated in discourse.

Discovering the ideology underlying a message is currently at the root of many forms of textual analysis. One very specific field of such ideological criticism is critical discourse analysis. This multidisciplinary field of research investigates text and talk in socially situated contexts, paying particular attention to public, or institutional, discourse practices. No wonder media discourse is of specific interest to CDA practitioners. This is because even in the most advanced and egalitarian societies there is much of symbolic (and social) oppression. This oppression is often masked with discourse-driven ideological operations that need to be brought to awareness, subjected to criticism and, hopefully, corrected. Teun Van Dijk spells out the main principles of CDA insisting that its aim is to critique social inequality by attending to the role discourse plays in the reproduction (i.e., representation, legitimation, mitigation or concealment) of elite dominance.[19] CDA is concerned with exposing which "structures, strategies or properties of text, talk, verbal interaction or communicative events" tend to be applied in these modes of reproduction and how they could be brought to the critical awareness of non-elites.[20] That is why I suggest that CDA is a toolkit my students need to master to exercise their criticality.

Media discourse, along with other public discourses, is instrumental to reproducing ideologies both at the stage of media production (with expression and legitimation of dominance) and at the stage of media reception (with interpretation, justification and acceptance of dominance).[21] However, ideologies may be challenged, contested or resisted, if active and critical positions are taken at the reception stage. The role of CDA is to facilitate this by identifying the insidious discursive practices in the media that impede criticality. Also, doing ideological criticism requires analysts to be "activists" and to acknowledge their ideological positions, rather than pretending that they operate "outside ideology."[22]

Van Dijk observes that the relation between language and social inequality is complex, cumulative and mediated. The intervening factors range from pragma-linguistic principles, interaction patterns, cultural norms, cognitive dispositions to psychological variables and social representations. These are important interfaces between discourse and social inequality, which need to be integrated in non-reductionist, methodologically oriented frameworks for criticism, such as for example van Dijk's socio-cognitive model of ideology,[23] or Fairclough's categories of media discourse analysis.[24] That is why I suggest incorporating these frameworks into critical literacy interventions.

Conclusion

In my practice of teaching, tutoring and supervising, I try to foster critical literacy as a particular frame of mind and to equip students with some conceptual tools they might apply to their own criticisms of the ideologies that shape their ideas and perspectives, particularly those naturalized by globalizing corporate communications. I encourage students to resort to CDA analytic categories and research procedures to produce insightful descriptions and critical assessments of various objects of study within the scope of Cultural and Media Studies. I argue that practicing theoretically well-grounded ideology-oriented critiques of media discourse can help students not only to prepare better research papers, but also to use media resources for their own self-expression.

The attempts at raising awareness of hegemonic discourse patterns in order to overcome the naturalized, accepted, common-sensical ideological concepts are not easy in the current circumstances but nevertheless worth undertaking. In the long run, critical awareness of media production/reception modes, media rhetorics and hegemonic/counter-hegemonic discourse practices can result in students' engaging in "politics of signification," their resisting of disempowering practices of globalization, and, hopefully, their interest in the sort of direct democratic action that challenges them.

Questions for Critical Reflection

1. In the opening paragraph, the author offers some possible explanations for why writing produced by students tends not to be "sufficiently critical." Do the author's explanations sufficiently capture the problem? From what you have observed in your own experiences, what other factors might hamper young people from developing sufficient (or useful) critical perspectives on issues that touch their lives?

2. The author discusses various models of cultural critique but admits that it is, "hard to be critically literate in an educational context that discourages challenging the status quo"—an observation that reflects Florian Zollmann's point about the Propaganda Model (PM), a theory of mass media performance that critiques the corporate media status quo. If the PM has been marglinalized, as Zollmann observes, in "contemporary academic

curriculum and debates," how, as the author urges, can young people who lack access to the academy begin to develop important critical perspectives on their own?

3. The author suggests the use of "critical literacy interventions," which call up images of a need for urgent clinical care. A so-called intervention suggests a systematic (or orchestrated) effort to identify and treat a critical mental, physical, or psychological problem that others are contending with. Why might the author have used such language to describe the need for critical literacy?

4. How might the author's overall argument be useful to understanding the forces of globalization presently at work in the world?

References

[1] Paulo Freire, *Education for Critical Consciousness*, trans. David Goulet (London: Sheed and Ward, 1974); Norman Fairclough, ed., *Critical Language Awareness* (London: Longman, 1992); William Stanley, *Curriculum for Utopia: Social Reconstructionism and Critical Pedagogy in the Post-modern Era* (Albany, NY: SUNY Press, 1992); Douglas Kellner, *Media Culture: Cultural Studies, Identity and Politics between the Modern and the Postmodern* (London: Routledge, 1995); Hillary Janks, *Literacy and Power* (London: Routledge, 2010).

[2] Katarzyna Molek-Kozakowska, "Theory and Practice of Media Education: A Case for Critical Media Literacy," in *Language, Cognition, and Society*, edited by Jan Zalewski (Opole: Wydawnictwo Uniwersytetu Opolskiego, 2009), 55–70; Katarzyna. Molek-Kozakowska, "A Knowledge Society or a Knowledgeable Society? The Role of the Humanities in the Fostering of Knowledge through Critical Literacy," *Polish Journal of Philosophy: Conference Proceedings Series* 1(2010): 33–46; Katarzyna Molek-Kozakowska, "How to Foster Critical Literacy in Academic Contexts: Some Insights from Action Research on Writing Research Papers," in *Language in Cognition and Affect*, edited by Ewa Piechurska-Kuciel and Elżbieta Szymańska-Czaplak (Heidelberg: Springer, 2013), 95–110; Katarzyna Molek-Kozakowska, "Design and Style of Cultural and Media Studies Textbooks for College Students," in *New Media and Perennial Problems in Foreign Language Learning and Teaching*, edited by Liliana Piasecka. (Heidelberg: Springer, 2015).

[3] F.R. Leavis and Denys Thompson, *Culture and Environment: The Training of Critical Awareness* (Westport, CT: Greenwood Press, 1977).

[4] Theodor W Adorno, *The Culture Industry: Selected Essays on Mass Culture*, edited by James. M. Bernstein (London: Routledge, 1991).

[5] Raymond Williams, *Keywords: A Vocabulary of Culture and Society* (London: Flamingo, 1983).

[6] Raymond Williams, *The Long Revolution* (London: Hogarth, 1992).

[7] Edward Herman and Noam Chomsky, *Manufacturing Consent: The Political Economy of the Mass Media* (New York: Pantheon Books, 1988).

[8] Louis Althusser, *Essays on Ideology* (London: Verso, 1984).

[9] Antonio Gramsci, *Selections from the Prison Notebooks*, trans. and edited by Quintin Hoare and Geofferey Nowell Smith (London: Lawrence and Wishart, 1971).

[10] Gramsci, *Selections*, 108–110.

[11] Stuart Hall, "The Rediscovery of 'Ideology': Return of the Repressed in Media Studies," in *Culture, Society and the Media*, edited by Michael Gurevitch, Tony Bennett, James Curran and Janet Woollacott (London: Routledge, 1982), 56–90.

[12] Glasgow University Media Group, *Bad News* (London: Routledge and Kegan Paul, 1976); Glasgow University Media Group, *Really Bad News* (London: Routledge and Kegan Paul,1982); James Curran and Jean Seaton, *Power without Responsibility. The Press and Broadcasting in Britain* (London: Routledge, 1991).

[13] Jane Stokes, *How to Do Media and Cultural Studies* (London: Sage, 2003), 77–78.

[14] Hall, "The Rediscovery of 'Ideology'," 69.

[15] Stuart Hall, ed., *Representation: Cultural Representations and Signifying Practices* (London: Sage, 1997).

[16] Hall, "The Rediscovery of 'Ideology'," 75–76.

[17] Kellner, *Media Culture,* 335.

[18] Jonathan Potter, *Representing Reality: Discourse, Rhetoric and Social*

[19] Teun van Dijk,"Principles of Critical Discourse Analysis," *Discourse and Society* 4.2 (1993): 249-283.

[20] Van Dijk, "Principles of Critical Discourse Analysis," 251.

[21] Van Dijk, "Principles of Critical Discourse Analysis," 256–257.

[22] Van Dijk, "Principles of Critical Discourse Analysis," 252.

[23] Teun van Dijk, *Ideology: A Multidisciplinary Approach* (London: Sage, 1998).

[24] Norman Fairclough, *Media Discourse* (London: Longman, 1995).

CHAPTER TWO

WHAT ARE SCHOOLS FOR, EXACTLY? COMPARING THEN AND NOW

Charlotte V.T. Murakami

Introduction

In some ways, I think of myself as a child of Margaret Thatcher, former Conservative Party Prime Minister in the UK. In the year I was born, she was the Education Secretary, busy approving the creation of comprehensive schools across the country—a policy she eagerly sought to reverse later on. When I was six and in my second year of primary school, she became Prime Minister. I even became a teacher in a comprehensive school system during the final days of her administration as led by John Major.

In the upper playground, the children used to call this coiffured woman in a blue skirt suit the Milk Snatcher. As she always seemed to be telling people off on the news, she was in many ways the Headmistress of the country. Unlike former Prime Ministers, Thatcher had a very keen interest in education. Thus, the abolishment of free school milk was not the only change in the school system that she initiated. In fact, historically, the eighteen years of this Conservative Party administration proved to be some of the most tumultuous that the English and Welsh state schooling system had ever seen—setting the precedent for all subsequent governmental interference.

Prior to Thatcher, British governments had rarely paid much attention to what went on in classrooms across the country. The 1944 Butler Act overhauled England's school system making secondary education a universally free provision and a civil right, but its actual governance changed little. The responsibility of what was taught was simply entrusted to teaching colleges as well as local boards of education that, in turn, largely left matters down to school heads and the class teachers.

There was a trust held by many in those days that these people would act in the best interests of the pupils. There was no national curriculum; no large-scale system monitoring the performance of teachers and/or pupils; and no publication of league tables comparing schools.

From the 1960s, local authorities also used a catchment area system to decide who went to what school. Children went to schools with children from their neighbourhood and often played with them afterwards cementing community life. In general, most parents were not overly concerned as to how well their children were doing at school unless they received a bad report card, or a letter home from the teacher. More often than not, the parents also supported the teacher's views.

Thatcher, however, changed the very ecology of the schooling system. Until her premiership, members of the Conservative party had been wondering how it could successfully disassemble the comprehensive school system. At the time, party member Szamuely insisted the party needed an ideology that would counter the political principles underpinning comprehensivisation. To understand what the comprehensive school system was, we will have to take a few steps back in time.

Comprehensivisation

After World War II, social democrats—such as Robin Pedley (Professor at Leicester University), H.C. Dent (Editor of the Times Educational Supplement), Harold Shearman (Vice-Chairman of the London County Council Education Committee), Eric James (High Master of Manchester Grammar School)—began to argue that England, Wales and Northern Ireland needed to dissolve its tripartite schooling system.

In the British tripartite system, the authorities administered psychometric intelligence testing to eleven-year-old children in order to allocate them to one of three different types of schools. Initially, this form of testing was considered a fair and square way of checking a pupil's ability, and one that ignored their financial resources.

Top scorers, approximately 5-10% of the pupils, went to grammar schools where they would focus on attaining 'A' grades that would hopefully grant them entry into the university system. Going to university would in most cases grant them access to the professional and cultured classes. Another 10 to 15 percent went to a secondary technical school that specialized in scientific and mechanical subjects preparing them for commercial or industrial vocations. The rest went to an ordinary secondary modern school. Outside this system, the private independent schools continued to provide an education, similar to that given in grammar schools, to the children of the affluent, the religious, and the powerful.

Pedley and others called into question the validity of this system. What is this IQ test testing exactly? What about the late bloomers? Why is the socioeconomic future of the country being decided through the testing of eleven year olds? Pointing to the common schooling systems operating in the United States of America and Russia, they argued in favour of a school framework where children would learn and rub shoulders with peers from all walks of life before making their own way. Comprehensivisation, they argued, would be a fairer and squarer way to tap the potential that lay within the country's populace. It would cut across the class system reducing social differences that created social biases. It would provide the basis for a healthier democracy and promote the growth of the economy.

It is this facet of 'democracy' that is the most vital feature of this educational picture, and it is this matter to which we now turn by making some bigger leaps back in time into England's educational past.

Education as a Cornerstone of Democracy

Historically, the idea of a national education system was long resisted in England. The Puritans lobbied for it in the sixteenth century under the pretext that every man, woman, and child should be able to read the Bible for themselves. At the time, the Crown, Church and Oxbridge resisted their efforts.[1] In the seventeenth century, the Dissenters (Christians who were separated from the Church of England) and the King's Head Society man-

Those who benefitted from child employment complained bitterly about the provision of any schooling. Others echoed Corbett's view that schools would teach the working poor to dislike their lot in life. 'It would render them factious and refractory' complained Conservative politician, Davies Giddy, to Parliament. 'It would enable them to read seditious pamphlets, vicious books and publications against Christianity; it would render them insolent to their superiors...It would go on to burden the country with a most enormous and incalculable expense'.

As 'self-interest' wormed its way deeper into the Victorian psyche, interactions between people became ever more strained and complex as the socio-economic gap widened. Once again, workers began to reorganize their efforts to protect their interests, and the first Trade Unions were legalized in 1864, whereupon two workingmen were elected to Parliament in 1874. Now that the rights of workers were recognized in this official capacity, interest in the purpose of schooling grew.

It is at this point in history that Matthew Arnold took his cue. Education was in Arnold's blood. The son of a famed private school Headmaster, he served 35 grueling years as a school inspector during which he visited over a hundred schools each year to assess their quality of education. On account of his vast experience, Arnold was also sent by various commissions to inspect educational institutions of France, Holland, Switzerland, Italy, and Prussia, so as to report back with recommendations.

Arnold saw great wrong in schools staffed with poorly trained teachers that merely sought to prepare pupils for working life. When we treat work and wealth as the end goals of life, he argued, we simply degrade human existence.

In Arnold's view, the purpose of the school curriculum should be to expand the soul, liberalize the mind, dignify the character of each pupil.[6] It was a matter of cultivating intelligence. It must be understood that until now, the humanities were the preserve of expensive, private schools, but Arnold argued all pupils should have access to 'the best that has been said and thought', be it in books, in music, and art. This is because such learning will help pupils to find their 'best selves'. One's best self, however, is not self-centred. The goal is to teach children and youths to be socially responsible, by way of helping them to create life goals that are not just self-satisfying but socially beneficial. Collectively, he argued, such acts form the basis of 'good democracy'.

England's Establishment of Universal Education

Guided by the writings of the educational philosopher, John Dewey, the United States of America had already established a public school system based on a principle of providing a common education for all citizens by the 1830s. In Britain, Arnold advanced the idea that the state should subsidise the school system as was the case in France and Prussia. Following serious debate, England and Wales followed suit in the 1870s with the Elementary School Act. A key difference was its emerging tax-funded school system was highly selective, complementing Britain's rigid class structure.

The eventual acceptance of universal education can be seen, in part, as a response to industrialisation that required greater numbers of people to be literate. Britain needed both a literate and more educated workforce to maintain its place in the world market; a need that intensified following the loss of hundreds of thousands of men and women in the First and Second World War. However, it is important to see that the steps towards realising universal education walked hand in hand with the growth of democracy in the 19th and 20th centuries.

After the Second World War, numerous countries around the world began abandoning their selective education systems. The principle concern in Scandinavia, Japan, Canada, Israel, New Zealand, and Eastern Europe was that this school system was inherently unfair. It served certain social biases and reproduced social inequalities. These biases, in their view, had simply become an economic and socio-cultural threat to the democracy of their country. In the UK, the Labour Party finally reached the same conclusion in the 1960s, and set about reorganising secondary education along more comprehensive lines. The central aim was to cut across and reduce social differences between people—to level the scholastic and social mobility playing field so to speak.

Comprehensivisation brought with it many challenges. It was no mean feat for a teacher to teach large mixed ability classes at the secondary level. Nevertheless, these were exciting times for educators, and many embraced or tackled these challenges with an informed enthusiasm.

In addition to trying to cultivate pupils' ability to articulate their views and exposing them to the very best of what has been written, many English teachers also saw their educational mission as one that must protect and assure the liberty of the people. In their view, education was also a matter of cultivating pupils' ability to reflect critically on what newspapers report, companies advertise, and politicians say, and the like. It was a matter if preparing them to be discerning participants in the political framework. Their choices in life would be informed, and not misguided.

Changing the Purpose and Culture of Schooling

Margaret Thatcher, as I said before, then changed the very ecology of schooling. She offered the ideological counter to comprehensivisation that Szamuely said the Conservative Party needed. Thatcher embraced a deep belief in 'the survival of the fittest' as adapted by neo-liberal economist and philosopher, Friedrich Hayek. In brief, it is a theory that sees 'stepping on people' as a natural process in sorting out who should come out on top. Being of this persuasion, Thatcher was far more concerned with the relationship between liberty and private enterprise than liberty and democracy. Indeed, unlimited democracy was considered a threat to governance, because it may undermine needed consensus.

Thatcher's party was unable to do away with comprehensive schools in one fell policy swoop due to their widespread acceptance and support by the public. Thus, it became a matter of destroying the comprehensive system from within. Step by step, Thatcher's government set about obtaining control over what could be taught and how by setting up the National Curriculum. Great battles ensued in the 1980s as teachers tried to resist governmental interference in the classroom. The press also took to portraying teachers as pseudo-professionals who were ruining the schooling of children with 'progressive' teaching methods and political agendas.

Another important step was the 'marketisation' of schools. The Conservatives introduced school choice, and in so doing stimulated competition and contestability. It was a matter of enhancing the differences between institutions and people. League tables were introduced so that the public could compare one school with another, and parents began to compete with each other for spots in better schools. In a sense, there was no turning back as all scrambled to serve their own self-interests—at least those who could afford options. Subsequently, schools began to 'cheat' in subtle but detrimental ways to move up the tables.

While these parents were not paying any school fees, they invariably saw themselves as educational consumers having certain rights over schooling. Parents began to place an increasing amount of pressure upon teachers to conform to their uninformed wishes about schooling. Pupils too became more demanding and hostile, requiring the introduction of 'security staff' to patrol corridors. Teachers were weighed down with a growing number of policies that required them to document their practice. On top of this, teachers began to be routinely monitored by inspection agencies. In short, the very breath of the state schooling system was slowly squeezed out.

Swiftly, schooling in England was transformed into a business. Schools were expected to be enterprising by the government. Teachers began to have 'line managers' who are in charge of their accountability. Principals, in schools that opted out of local governmental control, became answerable to 'boards' that seated affluent parent and business owner trustees. Recently, it transpired that taxpayer-funded Academy schools are paying out millions to businesses linked with their board Directors or trustees.[7] Curiously, such practice is not illegal. Even more curiously, the number of schools silently converting to academy status leapt from just 203 in 2010, under the new Conservative Coalition government, to just under 2,500 in 2013.

Dismantling Education as a Cornerstone of Democracy

The argument is, of course, that schools run as enterprising businesses will improve standards of education. The simple fact is that such a practice has little or nothing to do with social justice or improving outcomes for children. It has everything to do with what Conservative Education Minister, Michael Gove, called a 'supply side revolution': privatisation and deregulation of the school system without public debate.[8] It is the completion of the destruction of the comprehensive system initiated under Thatcher. Moreover, it has a lot to do with social segregation by way of producing a lot of people who are supposedly educated, but who are in fact not. These are people who are not able to fully process varying proportions of information from employers, news reporters, priests, advertisers, politicians and pressure groups. These are people who do not have the ability to discuss, evaluate, and make sense of what they are told. In addition, they are not able to take effective action in the democratic framework due to the narrowness of their education.

Comprehensivisation, for all its woes, sought to equip pupils with the tools so that they could realise their stake in society. The purpose was to produce more competent and empathetic humans who could play a beneficial role in the family, community, and society. The focus also was upon realising 'similar to' social relations—an attempt to make society a fairer and squarer experience.

The marketisation and diversification of the state school system allows only a few to realise their stake in the democratic and economic framework. Schools are, in a sense, the very opposite of what Arnold called for at the end of the nineteenth century. The educational philosophy underpinning the schooling experience is now extremely limited—one oriented on test outcome. Schooling is too often about 'getting a good job', causing the gradual demise of subjects that have long enriched and bettered humankind.

In this competitive climate, too many students will merely create life goals that are designed to satisfy their own self-interests with little regard for others in their communities. Educated in such limited terms, too many are emerging from England's school and university system ignorant of who they are and the world around them. They are uninterested in the value of being human and the possibilities of being humane. They shun democratic obligations, and struggle to fulfill its purpose. Most importantly, where genuine participation fails, there is only the imposition of ideas of those who run the country, run the companies, and run the schools. This is the picture of modern hegemony: not a mass of illiterate individuals but a mass of falsely educated individuals. It was far more than milk that Thatcher snatched. It was her government's marketisation of the school system that snatched away our democratic well-being. The question is: 'How do we get it back?'

Questions for Critical Reflection

1. The author observes that Margaret Thatcher had had a "very keen interest in education," and offered evidence of this with a reference to her abolishing the "free school milk program" (among other changes) to the English and Welsh state schooling system. To what extent does the author seem to be ironic about Thatcher's "keen interest"? To what extent can we take the author's description as literal?

2. What particular cuts in education enacted by the state have you seen in the name of economic progress or austerity measures?

3. The author refers to a series of critical questions that William Cobbett posed to the people as regards the use of taxes to pay for schooling for the young. Of these sorts of questions, which still seem to appear in the public discourse in your community, state, or nation? What kind of language is used to criticize efforts to fund education? What kinds of public or private figures are voicing the criticism?

4. To what extent have media or education systems preached (or promoted) the virtues of maintaining a "new faith" in the "free market economy"?

5. In what way does the "survival of the fittest" ideology inform educational practices or theories in your community, state, or country?

6. Discuss practical ways in which you might answer the author's final question.

References

[1] "Oxbridge" refers to Oxford and Cambridge University.

[2] William Cobbett, *Political Register: From April 4 to June 27, 1835 (1835)*, London: Printed and published by the author, pp. 28-30.

[3] Charles Dickens, *Hard Times for these Times* (1854). Cambridge: Houghton.

[4] Monitorial System (Lancastrian System) was conceived by a London teacher by the name of Joseph Lancaster. In these schools, a master or mistress would oversee the schooling of a hundred children or more. The class was split into smaller groups in which more advanced pupils taught and disciplined the others. The philosophical pretext was this: *Qui docet, discit*—He who teaches, learns. In short, it was a form of low cost schooling, and one that was highly influential between 1798 and 1830. It is said that the system inspired Frederick Taylor's conception of the assembly-line method.

[5] Davies Giddy, Tory MP, Hansard, House of Commons, Vol. 9, Col. 798, 13 July 1807.

[6] Matthew Arnold, *Higher Schools and Universities in Germany* (1882), 154-156.

[7] Hayley Dixon, 'Academies paying millions to businesses linked to their directors', *The Telegraph*, January 13, 2014. For example, one 'chain of schools', the Grace Academy, paid over £1 million directly and indirectly to companies, like International Motors Ltd, for consultancy work, which us owned by the school's founder and donor, Lord Edmiston, as well as his relatives.

[8] Tory Party Manifesto, 2009.

CHAPTER THREE

COUNTERING THE HEGEMONIC ENGLISH CURRICULUM: INTERCULTURAL COMPETENCE THROUGH POETRY

Daniel Xerri

A Reader's Discovery

I discovered world literature at the age of 16. Despite always having been a bookworm, my literary diet up to then had been restricted to novels penned by American and British writers. My family travelled to England every summer on holiday and I remember badgering my parents for cash to spend on the stacks of second-hand books at the charity shops we passed by whilst visiting towns and villages in Devon and Cornwall. My parents could only afford to spare me one or two pounds but luckily the books were dirt-cheap and so I worked my way through writers as diverse and uniform as Enid Blyton, Jeffrey Archer, Mark Twain, Charles Dickens and many others. My literary sensibility was not sufficiently refined to allow me to discriminate between Archer and Dickens; all I was after was a good story.

Those writers kept me up till the early hours of the morning and I could not get enough of them. My parents were proud that I loved books so much but not being great readers themselves they failed to realise how our yearly jaunts to the West Country were limiting my exposure to the rest of the world's literature. Just as the summer holiday always consisted of a fortnight spent in Devon and Cornwall, reading always consisted of British and American authors. In Malta, a former colony of the British Empire, my weekly trip to the village public library allowed me to stock up on more of the same, especially since the librarian took an interest in guiding my reading by making recommendations that did not venture far from her taste in Anglo-American literature.

At secondary school, studying English literature was compulsory. I remember enjoying the line-by-line analysis of *Macbeth* while half the class were given permission to go play soccer so as to avoid disrupting the lesson. At the age of 16, I enrolled in a postsecondary school and this time round the class was expected to study *Othello*, Philip Larkin's *The Whitsun Weddings*, Graham Greene's *The Power and the Glory*, Muriel Spark's *The Prime of Miss Jean Brodie*, and Thomas Hardy's *The Mayor of Casterbridge*. During literary criticism seminars, the teacher stuck to a limited range of poets from the Anglo-American tradition; we analysed their work in search of the holy grail of poetry, the hidden meaning behind every elliptical poem.

At 16, however, I also started working as a waiter, serving drinks every single weekend at a bar named after the 1966 Bob Montgomery song 'Misty Blue'. The money I earned allowed me to add dramatically to the library I had been building since the first book I received as a toddler. At a small bookshop in Valletta, I discovered the range of titles published by Wordsworth Classics. Even though many of these consisted of familiar names, I also stumbled upon Dostoyevsky, Tolstoy, Cervantes, and Rousseau. In a way, these translated authors enabled me to realise that literature was a much vaster galaxy of culture than I had previously imagined. The books were cheap and I took pleasure in seeing my library expand beyond what I could possibly read in a year let alone in between each one of my regular shopping sprees. The range of countries and cultures represented by the names on the book spines gradually increased; my own inner journeys as a reader became more varied and enriching.

I enjoyed collecting books but I still visited public libraries, in particular the national public library in Floriana. On its dust-covered shelves I discovered Naguib Mahfouz, Amos Oz, Osvaldo Soriano, Gabriel Garcia Marquez, Gao Xingjian and so many others. The books I was able to purchase by waiting tables in combination with those I borrowed during my occasional visits to public libraries meant that I was reading more literature in translation than literature originally written in English.

In the summer immediately before I enrolled on a Bachelor of Arts degree course in English, I had read a total of 52 books. I kept a reading log and marvelled at the diversity of cultures and voices represented by their authors. Once at university, I intentionally opted for study-units that would give me the possibility of studying world literature, but these were few and far between. I remember reading Patrick White and Thomas Keneally, Ngũgĩ wa Thiong'o, Chinua Achebe, and Ayi Kwei Armah.

A Dissatisfied Educator

Once I became a teacher of English at the same postsecondary school where I had once been a student, I realised that most of the young people in my classes relied on the curriculum for contact with literature, not sharing the same passion for reading I had at their age. At the beginning of an academic year, I always discussed reading interests with them and most of my students reported that they were not really inclined to read anything else apart from what formed part of the curriculum. Together with my students' lack of interest in reading literature in general was the complete absence of enthusiasm for poetry. If their knowledge of English literature was severely limited, their knowledge of poetry written in or translated into English was almost non-existent.

What disillusioned me most as a teacher, however, was the fact that the reading list prescribed by the curriculum was almost exclusively comprised of the same body of Anglo-American literature I had been expected to read when I was my students' age. Due to Malta's colonial heritage, English is one of the country's two official languages. The majority of the population is deemed to be bilingual; most people value their ability to speak the global language fluently since this will allow them to participate in the world of commerce and industry. One of the effects of Malta's colonial history has been that the study of English in Maltese schools has for many decades emphasised the importance of a literary education that is for the most part centred on the Anglo-American literary tradition.

The curriculum I was expected to teach contained no acknowledgement of cultural diversity, no indication that English literature transcended the strictly white canonical writers who had been a staple part of the curriculum for decades after Malta's independence from the British Empire. The curriculum was giving my students a very narrow perspective of English literature together with a complete lack of awareness of literature translated into English from a wide range of languages. My students were only studying texts that represented the hegemonic presence of Anglo-American literature in English curricula all over the world.

Ascribing my adult curiosity in exploring the world's diverse cultures to my broad reading experiences as an adolescent, I resolved to redress the curriculum's debilitating influence on my students. I did not have the power to change the set titles prescribed by the curriculum, however, for the purposes of my weekly literary criticism seminars I had the dispensation to choose whichever poems or prose passages I wanted to discuss with my students. I decided that it was best to start small and yet achieve something that was highly rewarding. For this reason I opted to vary as much as possible the range of poetry that my students came into contact with. I did so because I was aware that my students had practically no exposure to multicultural poetry and, hence, its potential to develop in them a higher intercultural competence remained unharnessed.

The poetry I encouraged them to read consisted of a medley of poems written in English as well as works translated into English from a variety of languages. Through my seminars students discovered such poets as John Agard, Pat Mora, Imtiaz Dharker, and Moniza Alvi, all of whom use English in order to explore the rich complexity of their cultural background. I also provided students with the opportunity of reading poetry in translation and in this case they discovered the works of Toeti Heraty, Pedro Serrano, Mohan Rana, and Caasha Lul Mohamud Yusuf. By critically engaging with poetry from different cultures, my students were able to shatter stereotypes and develop an appreciation of contemporary society's vibrant cultural variety. For example, Caasha's poem 'The Sea Migrations' managed to galvanise their empathy for the hundreds of Somali immigrants who cross the Mediterranean Sea each year hoping to start a new life in Malta and the rest of Europe. The critical reading of the poem allowed them to question their prejudices in relation to immigrants by paying heed to a voice that is usually stifled in Maltese society.

Countering Hegemony

The classroom is one of the most sensitive sites where the hegemonic forces of globalisation find their manifestation. In fact, Spring goes so far as to identify Western societies as typical of a "globalised educational security state."[1] According to Santos globalised localism is one of the ways through which globalisation is engendered. This is "the process by which a particular phenomenon is successfully globalised."[2] He mentions the emergence of English as *lingua franca* as an example of this; however, the prevalence of Anglo-American literature in curricula aimed at foreign or second language learners of English could also be seen as typifying the process of globalised localism.

Despite the small-scale nature of their efforts, educators can play an important role in countering hegemonic practices. In fact, countering hegemony consists of "grassroots initiatives, community innovations and popular movements that try to counteract social exclusion, thus opening up spaces for democratic participation, for community building, and for alternatives to dominant forms of development and knowledge."[3] Bailey maintains that, "education can certainly be dangerous and destructive but, by the same measure, can also be a generative and dialogic site for the cultivation of alternative knowledges and counter-hegemonic strategies."[4] The simple act of varying the kind of poetry that my students read and discussed in class could be interpreted as a counter-hegemonic act since it enabled them to critically engage with voices that are usually silenced by the curriculum.

As I argue elsewhere, multicultural poetry is typically associated with ethnic minorities and other socioeconomically marginalized and under-represented groups.[5] Usually their literature is as sidelined in the curriculum as it is in the globalised world and this means that in an increasingly multicultural society students might find it difficult to engage with texts that are completely alien to the multicultural reality of which they are already an integral part. Like many other Western societies, Maltese society is becoming increasingly multicultural and in most classrooms the need to move away from an exclusive focus on the cultural manifestations of the dominant group is becoming ever more significant. The agents of change in this sense are educators such as myself.

Agents of Change

In order not to risk colluding with the homogenising forces of globalisation, teachers need to embrace the responsibility of making careful reading choices and avoid perpetuating practices that manifest a complete disregard for multiculturalism. Dong posits that, "there is an urgent need for English teachers to increase their sensitivity to cultural differences and develop teaching skills to conduct classroom discussions that promote cross-cultural understanding and culturally varied ways of living and knowing."[6] Nault affirms that "English educators should adopt and promote a more cosmopolitan outlook that recognises and accepts other ways of life, modes of thought, and styles of English usage beyond Great Britain and the United States."[7]

Teachers need to "integrate world cultures into their materials and lessons to promote true linguistic/cultural awareness and international understanding among themselves and their students."[8] For this to happen, teachers require the sort of training that would not only equip them with the necessary knowledge and skills but also develop their beliefs and attitudes in relation to intercultural education. Oikonomidoy argues that there is a need for "critical spaces in teacher education for the renegotiation of the local and the global and for sharpening prospective and in-service teachers' understanding of their professional roles."[9] Such training "could sensitise all educators to the multiple spaces that they occupy and could provide the meeting places for the development of informed responses to the pro- and counter-globalisation forces."[10] Lanas believes that

> Intercultural education in teacher education is not simply a forum for teaching the skills needed to imagine new possibilities for social justice, but a forum where that imagination can occur, where both teacher educators and student teachers encounter multiple others, engage in difficult knowledge and explore the zone of discomfort to reimagine the world in which they live.[11]

My own teacher training certainly did not consist of such a forum. If it were not for my own appreciation of multicultural literature, I might never have sought ways of enabling my students to critically engage with it. Teacher education is fundamental as it ensures that the instruments of change in the classroom can resist the hegemonic practices of globalisation by enabling their students to develop the necessary intercultural competence.

Developing Intercultural Competence

Intercultural communication is the communicative exchange that occurs amongst people belonging to different social and cultural groups. The forces of globalisation affect individuals both directly and indirectly, and highlight the necessity for intercultural communication. According to Sorrells, "The context of globalisation is characterised by an increasingly dynamic, mobile world and an intensification of interaction and exchange among people, cultures, and cultural forms."[12] For this reason, developing young people's intercultural competence is fundamental. Intercultural education should not be seen as a trivial accessory but as a crucial component of every student's ability to function in a multicultural society. Coulby explains that "Interculturalism is a theme, probably the major theme, which needs to inform the teaching and learning of all subjects."[13] Portera agrees with this and claims that inter-cultural education "represents the most appropriate response to the challenges of globalisation and complexity. It offers a means to gain a complete and thorough understanding of the concepts of democracy and pluralism, as well as different customs, traditions, faiths and values."[14]

Such outcomes are only possible if there is "a commitment to communicative action which reaches towards the discourse of the other."[15] In demonstrating this kind of commitment in the English classroom, I was aiming to effect change in my students. Language learning within the paradigm of inter-cultural communicative competence possesses a transformative potential because "as learners explore their identities and come to understand their social situatedness, they will soon perceive the connections between themselves, their native cultural practices, alternative cultural practices, and the wider world."[16] Through the critical reading of multicultural poetry my students were able to augment their knowledge of cultural differences and similarities, question cultural stereotypes, and adopt the voice of the 'other'.

My classroom experience leads me to believe that by engaging students with multicultural poetry, teachers of English can help them become intercultural communicators. This is possible because "literature and the arts contribute to the formation of a convivial culture, one that is tolerant and spontaneously at ease with its rich diversity."[17] The fact that poetry can help develop intercultural competence is highly significant given that this is a crucial aspect of any twenty-first century student's repertoire of communicative skills in a globalised world. For this reason, teachers need to demonstrate a willingness to contribute to the process of countering the hegemonic English curriculum.

Questions for Critical Reflection

1. The author refers to his local public library as a rich source of literature, but what sort of case can be made for seeing the library he describes as a reflection also of cultural or literary hegemony?

2. Summarize how the author's use of poetry in the classroom could serve as an effective tool to deconstruct dangerous or unfair stereotypes.

3. If the current forces of globalization are guarded and guided by Anglo-American economic interests, what benefits does the "globalised security state" reap from the status quo? What are the detriments?

4. Create a shortlist of author or poets whose names should also appear in the academic canon. Discuss and list their contributions to the cultural literature.

5. Why do the most vocal advocates of economic globalization appear to resist (or fear) multiculturalism or efforts to deepen intercultural communication?

References

[1] J. Spring, "Pedagogies of Globalisation," *Pedagogies: An International Journal* 1, no. 2 (2006): 118.
[2] B. S. Santos, "Globalisations," *Theory, Culture & Society* 23, nos. 2-3 (2006): 396.
[3] J. E. Diniz-Pereira, "'Globalisations': Is the Teacher Research Movement a Critical and Emancipatory Response?" *Educational Action Research* 10, no. 3 (2002): 376.
[4] P. L. J. Bailey, "Globalising Knowledges," *British Journal of Sociology of Education* 34, no. 4 (2013): 623.

[5] D. Xerri, "Multicultural Poetry in ELT: Benefits, Challenges and Strategies," in *Plurilingualism: Promoting Co-operation between Communities, People and Nations*, ed. P. Díez, R. Place, and O. Fernández Vicente (Bilbao: University of Deusto, 2012), 65-66.

[6] Y. R. Dong, "Bridging the Cultural Gap by Teaching Multicultural Literature," *The Educational Forum* 69, no. 4 (2005): 367.

[7] D. Nault, "Going Global: Rethinking Culture Teaching in ELT Contexts," *Language, Culture and Curriculum* 19, no. 3 (2006): 324.

[8] *Ibid.*, 325.

[9] E. Oikonomidoy, "Reinventing Aspects of Multicultural Education under the Shadow of Globalisation," *Pedagogy, Culture & Society* 19, no. 3 (2011): 341.

[10] *Ibid.*

[11] M. Lanas, "Failing Intercultural Education? 'Thoughtfulness' in Intercultural Education for Student Teachers," *European Journal of Teacher Education* 37, no. 2 (2014): 173.

[12] K. Sorrells, *Intercultural Communication: Globalisation and Social Justice* (Thousand Oaks, CA: SAGE Publications, 2013), xiv.

[13] D. Coulby, "Intercultural Education: Theory and Practice," *Intercultural Education* 17, no. 3 (2006): 246.

[14] A. Portera, "Intercultural Education in Europe: Epistemological and Semantic Aspects," *Intercultural Education* 19, no. 6 (2008): 488.

[15] L. Bash, "The Globalisation of Fear and the Construction of the Intercultural Imagination," *Intercultural Education* 25, no. 2 (2014): 83.

[16] M. Pegrum, "Film, Culture and Identity: Critical Intercultural Literacies for the Language Classroom," *Language and Intercultural Communication* 8, no. 2 (2008): 145.

[17] L. López Ropero and A. Moreno Álvarez, "Multiculturalism in a Selection of English and Spanish Fiction and Artworks," *Social Identities: Journal for the Study of Race, Nation and Culture* 17, no. 1 (2011): 102.

Chapter Four

Shooting a White Elephant in the Heart of Darkness: How English has Gone the Way of McDonald's and Starbucks

Christopher Daniel Melley

Introduction

Originally, when considering how to begin my personal experience with the ubiquity and pervasiveness of English as part of a globalized world, I imagined describing some acutely ambiguous personal narrative such as Hemingway's "Hills Like White Elephants," using the camera-like lens of his terse narrator to display characters who describe hills that betoken some singular epiphany looming in the distance. I could find no one experience in particular.

I imagined mimicking the narrator that George Orwell depicts so well, in his enduring story "Shooting an Elephant."[1] Since the voice was probably Orwell's own, I imagined that I could shadow the master writer, if only I were a policeman using only good English words—something even Orwell instructs English writers to do[2]—but, thankfully, did not practice[3] in a foreign land where my culture and its economy leaned heavily and pressed itself and its wordy world. I wondered in my drafts if I could find one definitive event, one big agitated elephant 'in musth'[4] that had mashed some hapless native into the mud.

If I too could find some gaggles of Buddhist monks and resentful villagers to glare at me from every street corner, then, I thought, I would have something to say about how I have witnessed the atrocities of empire and globalization, leading to a highly polarized planet of a billion or so haves and six or so billion have-nots. What singular event would color my view of cultures such as the one Orwell's bitter and conflicted constable describes, in his self-revealing way, showing an event, a time, a clash of cultures that captures some beastly or benign imperialism or some oddity of contemporary life that leaves the reader thoughtful and captured by the thought itself? In another context, Orwell mentions that, "there is often a need of some concrete incident before one can discover the real state of one's feelings."[5] I could find no particular incident. For me, the object is not an elephant gone mad, but a language that won't leave me alone; it is not one sentence or word, but the global nature English seems to have attained.

I haven't visited any heart of darkness, literal or figurative, to record and impart the tale of what imperial adventures and financial interests have done to distant and remote places and peoples. I am no Marlow and certainly no Kurtz, from Joseph Conrad's imagination. What could I say about the distribution and use of English as part of an increasingly globalized community? My own experience is severely limited. After all, my start in life was decidedly monolingual, with some small inkling of other languages.

Having grown up in a sea of North American English, the first non-English words I remember were from the Catholic Mass. Like millions of others, in church, I mimicked the Latin words, but did not understand the words. "*Dominus vobiscum*," "*Et cum spiritu tuo*." [The Lord be with you, and with your spirit.] The foreign words from the start were, for me, something ethereal, wholly other, confusing, and yet entirely sanctified. The first living language I heard was Arabic, thanks to my friend Nick Haddad's Lebanese grandmother and his parents who also spoke Arabic with all three of their children. I heard for the first time another language being used with great animation and passion. In idle times, my friend Nick and I would listen to his family's old radio in his basement. Slowly turning the big dial on the illuminated display of the bulky wood-framed, vacuum-tubed transmitter, we would troll the static expanse, crossing time-zones and cultures, listening, through the crackling, for the sounds of other languages. We wondered where all these people were and what they were saying.

After college, I left for Germany, first in *Freiburg im Breisgau*, then later, near *Saarbrücken*. Though I had learned German at school, I had forgotten much and basically knew little when I arrived, nearly illiterate. I learned German at university and on the job, studying scientific German with a gaggle of pretty Finnish coeds, deciphering the tabloid *Das Bild* on rainy days with my proletariat comrades, learning the rough and ready language of building sites. Back at university, I listened to but did not understand lectures on Nietzsche and practiced writing sentences, talking mostly with other non-native German-speaking students from Poland and Turkey. In the *Wohngemeinschaften*[6] of my student days, I learned, word by word, experience by experience. The entire stint was a monumental failure, and one I would not replace for anything.

A few years later, I returned to Germany and succeeded in breaking through to a higher level, completing my doctorate in philosophy at the University of Saarbrücken, close by the French border. I remained and worked for an American school attached to the U.S. military, as well as taught ESL at several German universities, language schools and company training facilities. Nearly half my life, I have spent in a language other than my native language, and that has made all the difference for me. Living among other languages has gotten me thinking more deeply about language, as I moved here and there across Europe to Italy, then Greece and beyond, to Japan, where I presently live.

While in Europe, I was able to see a few of the worn limestone and marble temples of the long gone Greek empire, from Athens to Delphi, from Brindisi to Taranto, from Syracusa to Agrigento, from Iraklion to Kos; in Kos, I watched young graduating Greek medical students standing in the ruins of the Asklepieion, as they recited the Hippocratic Oath in their native Greek. I touched the bleached marble of the Temple of Poseidon, tried to count the names of sailors and travelers whose names and dates are etched roughly into the bleached and massive marble columns, noticing Lord Byron's literary graffiti. At the Parthenon, I looked for Socrates and watched for a priestess at Delphi, amid the tour buses and trinket stores featuring the philosopher on a refrigerator magnet. In Agrigento, before the Temple of Concordia, in the slanting remnants of a white-hot day, I wondered how far the Athenians had come, thinking how Sicily was their

Afghanistan or their Iraq or their Vietnam. Words follow wars. I wondered about the words in the ruins.

In the ruins of the temples, in the rubble of history, inscriptions still read to people long since gone. Greek and Latin inscriptions, chiseled for the ages, have gone silent to many or most. With the ebb of Greek and then Roman culture, the languages receded as well to smaller territories or morphed to something else or survived by hiding in another language. With the implosion of an earlier empire, the Roman language bloomed into yet other, related languages, spawning entire traditions of French, Spanish, Portuguese, and Romanian, to name a few. Though Latin has gone into hiding, it lives beneath the veneer of newer languages. Aramaic, once the *lingua franca* of everyday life, trade, and worship in the Middle East and beyond, the language Jesus most likely spoke, the language of some of the Dead Sea scrolls and Talmud, has now frayed to tiny threads, in multiple dialects, in Syria, Turkey, and Iraq,[7] having been rented by Arabic with the rise of Islam. Other languages have either added themselves or replaced others.

Fledgling English too did indeed eventually put the kibosh on Irish Gaelic and left only smidgens of Scottish Gaelic and Welsh, leaving pockets of each and contemporary efforts, through public programming and education, to recapture what was lost. Japanese has displaced Ainu and Ryukyuan languages, perhaps for good.[8] A language lives, flourishes, dominates; other languages languish, become moribund and, eventually, die; the process is continual and with multiple, related causes too complex to consider here. We know that the number of human languages is dissipating at a murderous rate, about 25 per annum.[9] "The last speakers of probably half the world's languages are alive today," penned K. David Harrison, in English.[10]

An exception to the general trend is the revival of Hebrew. Once a dead or moribund language, Hebrew has experienced a significant comeback. Having been made the official language of Israel, Hebrew is now spoken by over 6 million people in Israel and more around the world. Welsh, despite vigorous and varied funding and educational initiatives, is declining, with Welsh literacy hovering around 20 percent of Wales.[11] The Maori language is worse off, with only five percent of New Zealanders are today able to converse in Maori.[12]

Maori language advocates are fighting the disbandment of their language by creating language nests where language immersion within several generations is practiced. Let's see if new generations of Maori speakers hatch—I hope so, since every language is a picture of reality reflected through a particular culture, time and place. Unfortunately, the writing for many languages with limited numbers of speakers is already on the wall. If something is written on the wall, chances are that it will be written in some form of English.

Wherever I have visited, English seems to have established itself. After six years of living and working in Japan, as an ESL instructor, I cannot help but pause and wonder if all this English is always a good thing. Of course, it would be ludicrous to critique all the many benefits that knowledge of English affords. Robert McCrum, author of *Globish: How the English Language Became the World's Language*, stated "One of the phenomena we have to deal with at the moment, which is absolutely new in the history of the planet is that for the first time in recorded history it is possible for the English languages to be both transmitted and received anywhere in the world."[13] Today, one in three people alive can speak some form of English or globish, a term coined in 1995, by Jean-Paul Nerriere, to refer to a dressed down English of 1,500 words sans nuance, sans metaphor, sans idiom, with basic syntax, to be used by the increasing number of speakers whose first language is something other than English for everyday, simple business transactions, tourism.[14]

Yet one of the negative effects of the globalization of English, or 'globish', is also the spread of my native language, English, the very words I am using at the moment. As with McDonald's and Starbucks, everywhere I have gone, in one form or another, I have found English, on billboards, public instructions, even at the supermarket and in car lots. *Wasei-eigo* [和製英語] (English made in Japan) or pseudo-anglicisms printed on clothing and accessories are words whose meanings have little or nothing to do with the wearers' own beliefs or outlook but which link wearer with words as a form of branding by association.[15] Yet more English is found in graffiti, in lyrics and videos.

School English advocacy is pressing for more study time with middle and now primary school children in Japan so much so that serious critics in Japan are concerned that their children are not learning their own language sufficiently deeply to think more profoundly. This is a well-intentioned, but misguided educational reform. Linguist Robert Phillipson notes that English is really "the language of power" and "the language of the elite"[16] of many non-native English-speaking cultures. This is precisely one of the main motivators of why so many governments, such as those of Singapore, and, I would add, Japan, are pushing English at early stages of child development.

English seems pervasive, at least according to my personal experience, but English in fact is not pervasive in much of Latin America, southern Europe and wide swaths of Asia.[17] As well, in contrast to common assumptions, English is actually slipping in its percentage of text on the Internet. In 1996, over 80 percent of web materials were in some form of English, while today, English sites comprise less than 30 percent of the world total. Web readers are also generators of web materials, and with the ease of reading and generating web materials, localization and a rise in the use of smaller languages is being experienced.[18]

Aside from the effects of English on the non-English-speaking communities, I think of the deficits of living in and enjoying use of a deeper facility with this dominant language when that language is one's only language. I think of the legions of otherwise highly educated people, monolinguals with English as a first language, particularly in the US, finding it either superfluous or too much of a bother to learn another language, even as their own culture is diversifying and betraying the old melting-pot metaphor for one of a stitched quilt of multiple language communities co-existing and flourishing. In studied monolingualism, I sense a certain insolence or smugness that can come only from an elite vantage point of power, in this case, being able to wield the power of English.

I have only a small experience of how much is being missed by allowing oneself the easy option of letting the rest of the hungry language world access the language of power, the language of the elites. In order to learn, I have to consciously leave behind the comfortable confines of English, in order to make place for another language, at the moment, Japanese.

In corporate boardrooms, on college campuses, at conferences, in international governing bodies and venues, the English language dominates, and those with native proficiency at least appear to have the upper-hand and are able to talk circles around the others. The world for English-speakers is cushy and requires the others to conform to the dominant language. How many academic conferences in Europe I have attended, all (or mostly all) were in English. English is, of course, the default language of convenience when those in 'language power' convene. However, with words and phrases and categories come values, beliefs and culture.

When English in effect replaces a less powerful language group, where power is defined by control of financial systems, economic resources, military hardware and personnel, rather than adds to and enhances a given language community, then we see that the beliefs are not far behind the words. These larger issues do not pop out at a conference or conversation or meeting; rather, English has become the default setting for much discourse. The language of 'flat world' described by American author Thomas Friedman is this default setting. Linguist Robert Phillipson suggests that, "A lot of the thrust behind global English at the moment is connected with globalization, with Americanization, and with consumerist values."[19] If Phillipson is correct, then, as humble ESL instructor, I wonder if I am "one of the unwitting stooges"[20] in this much larger movement.

The complacency of the monolingual native English speaker is misplaced. Monolingual native English, supercharged with idiom, subtle nuance, culture-specific allusion, complicated syntax, extensive vocabulary, and regionalisms, can easily lose all but the most gifted of non-native English speakers. Anyone who has studied another language in order to use the language will note at some point that speaking the studied language with other non-native speakers of more or less the same level is much easier, transparent, more immediately informative. We non-native language learners of a given language share a discrete set of grammatical structures and similar vocabulary, far fewer than the native speaker, hence the popularity and appeal of globish, in the case of English.

Further, the solitary complacent English speaker who compels everyone within earshot to speak English must feel a certain superiority in the quick manner of comprehension and sophisticated phrases he or she can employ, in contrast to the non-native English speakers struggling to accommodate and adapt to the one-way cross-cultural situation; where the monolingual continues in English, others either adapt or fall silent. The silence is a form of exclusion and shows that English as a dominant language invoked by the monolingual speaker does help some, but not others and also not the situation in which communication is taking place in the nexus of differing languages. Further, the complacency of the native English speaker is wrecked when we notice that those non-native speakers of English know more about the native English speaking counterpart than the native speaker knows about his Japanese or German or Slovenian counter-parts struggling with English.

Wherever I have gone, I have found my language—or it has found me. And so have millions of others in scores of countries where English was impressed or willingly imported, first as a foreign language, then adopted it as a second language, such as in Sweden and Belgium[21] Much of my linguistic life has been spent speaking in English to others who have picked it up and made it their own, so many, in fact, that half of those speaking a form of English are non-native speakers and upwards of 80 percent of communication taking place today is among non-native English speakers.[22]

English is ubiquitous, alive, growing, merging with other languages and is itself being changed, infiltrated, and globalized. As Englishes soar, other languages falter and decline. Reactions differ. The French and Quebec Canadians have fought on different fronts and have either acquiesced or lost, despite government funding. By contrast, in Japan, learning English has taken on religious intensity. In the test-taking culture of *juku* (or cram school) Japan, English ranks as the number one language of study, eclipsing all others, perhaps Japanese as well. The Japanese Ministry of Education has increased the exposure of English to the Japanese curriculum to start at middle school or earlier.

The fervor for English in Japan has an incessant, nearly religious intensity that makes evading my language all the more difficult. Still, beyond the smattering of fixed phrases in very narrow contexts requiring a discrete and quickly repeatable vocabulary, many Japanese speakers of English just as quickly find themselves in new linguistic territory, giving the *gai-koku-jin* [外国人] (foreign person) a chance to speak Japanese. In order to learn German as a graduate student in Germany, I had to consciously avoid expatriated native English speakers and avoid Germans with strong skills in English; I am doing the same with Japanese. I wonder if someday this method will be possible in Japan.

Conclusion

Is it time to invoke my juggernaut metaphor, where I imagine English as the image of Krishna drawn in a huge wagon, as hundreds of languages throw themselves under the massive jeweled wheels of the celestial chariot? But the metaphor is overblown and misleading, though colorful and even a bit true. Today, new devotees of English are not compelled to memorize their irregular verbs; people choose to learn English for a multitude of reasons, and I have yet to meet those who think that by learning English, they are willingly diminishing chances for their native language to thrive and live a deep life in the people who live with and in the native language in the fullness and variety of its native forms.

The spread of English is both an effect and expression of globalization, as banal and benign as the growth of McDonald's and Starbucks franchises and as tragic for all the linguistic worlds that have already and are already being nudged out by English, partly as a result of the overzealous and unwitting application of English. A byproduct of this displacement by English may lead to dissolution of other languages, displacement, or creative integration that involves everyone, regardless of their proficiency in the dominant language—globish. Slavoj Zizek wrote that, "The true victory...occurs when the enemy talks your language."[23] If Zizek is correct, English has won, at least for now, but only at certain privileged levels of the cultures it presently occupies. *Ite missa est.* [Go forth. The Mass is ended.] *Tschüss*! [Goodbye, informal] sayonara! [さようなら].

Questions for Critical Reflection

1. To what extent does the author use allusion in the title to call attention to colonialism?

2. Select ten words found in this essay and show, through etymology, how English is related to other languages. What do these word origins say about the English language?

3. Is the use of English throughout much of the world a partial cause or result of globalization? How so?

4. Should we strive to speak more than one language? Why? Why not?

References

[1] Orwell, George. "Shooting an Elephant." 1936. Accessed December 16, 2014 at http://www.orwell.ru/library/articles/elephant/english/e_eleph

[2] Orwell, George. "Politics and the English Language." *Fifty Essays*. Accessed December 16, 2014 http://gutenberg.net.au/ebooks/03/0300011h.html#part31

[3] Orwell, George. "Revenge is Sour." 9 November 1945. *Fifty Essays*. http://gutenberg.net.au/ebooks03/0300011h.html#part31

[4] An alternate spelling is 'must' or rut.

[5] *Op. cit.*, Orwell, "Revenge."

[6] college dormitory

[7] Adams, Sam. "Race to save the language of Jesus: Aramaic in danger of becoming extinct as number of speakers of ancient tongue plummets." MailOnline. 25 January 2013. http://www.dailymail.co.uk/sciencetech/article-2268204/Race-save-language-Jesus-Aramaic-danger-extinct-number-speakers-ancient-tongue-plummets.html

[8] Mufwene, Salikoko S. "Colonisation, Globalisation, and the Future of Languages in the Twenty-first Century." *International Journal on Multi-Cultural Societies*, v. 4, nr. 2, 2002.

[9] "Are dying languages worth saving?" BBC News. 15 September 2010. http://www.bbc.com/news/magazine-11304255

[10] Harrison, K. David. *When Languages Die: The Extinction of the World's Languages and the Erosion of Human Knowledge.* Oxford: Oxford University Press, 2008.

[11] Roderick, Vaughan. "Census 2011: Number of Welsh speakers falling." BBC News. 11 December 2012. http://www.bbc.com/news/uk-wales-20677528

[12] Mason, Cassandra. "Bid to keep Maori language alive." Bay of Plenty Times. 21 July 2014. http://www.nzherald.co.nz/bay-of-plenty-times/news/article.cfm?c_id=1503343&objectid=11296844

[13] Phillipson, Robert and Robert McCrum. Interview with Riz Khan. Linguistic Imperialism? (Episode 155). Al Jazeera. October 21, 2010 https://www.youtube.com/watch?v=c3TJe4jnqFocom/watch?v=c3TJe4jnqFo

[14] Lavelle, Peter. "English vs. Globish." Cross Talk interview, RT. Uploaded 6 May 2011. https://www.youtube.com/watch?v=CjXn3lW5wQ4

[15] Sargeant, Phillip, editor. "The Symbolic Meaning of Visual English in the Social Landscape of Japan," in *English in Japan in the Era of Globalization*, 2011.

[16] *Op. Cit.*, Phillipson and McCrum, "Interview." [17] Phillipson, Robert. "English vs. Globish." *Cross Talk*, with Peter Lavelle, interview. Moscow, Russia. May 2011.

[18] Zuckerman, Ethan. "English is no longer the language of the web." Quartz. 20 June 2013. http://qz.com/96054/english-is-no-longer-the-language-of-the-web/

[19] Phillipson, Robert. *Linguistic Imperialism*. Oxford: Oxford University Press, 1992.

[20] Honisz-Greens, John. "To What Extent is it Socio-politically and Socio-linguistically Acceptable to Promote Native Speaker Language Norms in Expanding Circle Countries?" *Memoirs of the Osaka Institute of Technology,* Series B, Vol. 51, No.2 (2006) pp.1 - 8. https://www.oit.ac.jp/japanese/toshokan/tosho/kiyou/jinshahen/51-2/01JHG.pdf

[21] Zizek, Slavoj, quoted in "China: Lost in translation," by Thorsten Pattberg. 24 July 2012. http://www.atimes.com/atimes/China/NG24Dj02.html

[22] Op. cit., Honisz-Greens, John.

[23] Zizek, Slavoj, quoted in "China: Lost in translation," by Thorsten Pattberg. July, 24 2012. http://www.atimes.com/atimes/China/NG24Dj02.html

PART II

WHO ARE YOU? A GLOBALIZED POLITICS OF IDENTITY

CHAPTER FIVE

NON-REGULAR WORKERS, NEOLIBERALISM AND NATIONALISM IN JAPAN

Noriko Layfield

Introduction

In Autumn 2005, I finished my four-year-long Ph.D. studies in England, and returned to my hometown in Okinawa, Japan. The degree was conferred the following year. Travelling halfway across the world to attend a university is probably not so unusual in this day and age of globalization, so when I left Japan, I was genuinely hoping (and was still hopeful for a few years) that, one day, I might be able to secure myself a very good, if not spectacularly wonderful, career, with the extra knowledge and experience that I would have gained from working abroad.

I was, however, soon to be disappointed by the harsh realities of the job market. The only work I could find which was more or less reliable was part-time teaching at local universities. Part-time posts at Japanese universities are often considered a stepping-stone to a fully-fledged profession in academia, but, in reality, there are many more obstacles to overcome. With a relatively late start in an academic career and a young child to look after, the demands of pursuing a full-time academic post seemed to me too daunting to meet. Although I considered searching for a non-academic job, it was equally difficult, because many jobs are also temporary, and still beset by age or gender biases. Besides, with a postgraduate degree, I was often considered overqualified for most jobs and, thus, forced to endure some extended periods of soul-searching, self-reflection, and occasional attempts at justifying the situation I was thrown into.

As a postdoc already in her late thirties, my experience was probably unique in some ways, but it is undoubtedly true that, nowadays, people in Japan are increasingly facing a similar problem; they are unable to find steady, regular employment. For instance, in 2006, the year when I was awarded my degree, approximately one in two graduates who completed their Ph.D. went on to find full-time employment in Japan. The figures for those in the humanities and social science fields were even worse, and only 35% managed to find a full-time job.[1] Many postdocs look for a permanent academic post, while teaching or researching on temporary contracts for a few years, but they are likely to face severe competition in the job market. It is not only that permanent jobs are in short supply; as wages are often set considerably lower for part-time teachers, a number of part-timers end up juggling a couple of different jobs to make ends meet. It needs to be stressed, however, that it is by no means only those with high academic qualifications that are disadvantaged in the job market. One thing that has become evident with the deepening influences of globalization is a definite change in the pattern of employment: we are now increasingly forced to choose between two rather undesirable alternatives of either being unemployed or taking on unstable work in temporary jobs.

Japan was long renowned for its "lifetime employment," although there is some debate concerning the actual extent of this practice. Nevertheless, it was more or less assumed a few decades ago that new graduates (usually male) would find a job with a company or in a public office, and continue working in the same workplace until they retired. This system is said to have begun crumbling around the end of the 1990s and the early 2000s.[2] Employers began to replace more permanent, regular workers (*seiki*) with temporary, non-regular workers (*hi-seiki*), who could be made redundant more easily. In Japan, non-regular workers are called by a variety of names, such as "haken," "pāto," "shokutaku," etc., but what is common to all is that they are hired for a fixed term and the conditions of their work remain insecure; also, they tend to work very long hours for wages that are often not sufficient to cover living expenses. The problem of this differential wage treatment arises partly because Japanese workers' pay is usually set by their status, i.e., being *seiki* or *hi-seiki*, and not by the content of their work.[3] Non-regular workers are also often denied the benefits and entitlements that permanent employees regularly receive. What seems to be even more worrying is the large increase in the number of such non-regular employees over the last few decades. According to a survey by the Japanese government, regular workers constituted 87.3% of the total workforce in 1981, while non-regular workers 12.7%.[4] In 2013, the proportion of the latter nearly tripled to 36.6% (the percentage is even higher for women, with 55.8% being non-regular).[5] In the same year, though the official unemployment rate in the country stood at 4%,[6] around 60% of the new jobs advertised at public job placement centers were, in fact, non-regular jobs (it was as high as 70% in Okinawa).[6] These facts do suggest that, while older generations may still be receiving the benefits of the "job for life," more and more young people are obliged to accept unstable, non-regular jobs.

Global economic competition and the drive among employers to look for cheap and flexible labor are behind this growth of the non-regular workforce. The Japanese government expedited the process by deregulating the labor market in the 1990s in an attempt to improve the competitiveness of domestic businesses. The current government led by Prime Minister Shinzo Abe intends to "flexibilize" the labor market further, vowing to reduce labor costs and, thus, make Japan "the most favorable location for businesses in the world."[8]

Nevertheless, the detrimental social and economic impact of non-regular employment has been well documented.[9] Wages in contemporary Japan are often so low that if the workers try to stand on their own feet, they would "have to work to death." [10]In addition to low wages, non-regular workers generally have to deal with the insecurity and anxiety over maintaining a job, which hardly allows them to develop a long-term vision of the future. It is not surprising, therefore, that the increase in non-regular work leads to a fall in domestic consumption, and declining marriage and birth rates. As Japan suffers an acute demographic challenge, these declines have very serious implications. Ultimately, the expansion of non-regular jobs encourages the bifurcation of workers; it entrenches inequality, and is likely to undermine citizens' sense of stability and thus the continued cohesion of society in the long term.

Neoliberalism and Nationslism

The problem of non-regular employment seems to reinforce the view that the purported benefits of economic globalization are not extended to a rather large part of society. Despite this, the current government, rather than seeking to protect workers in vulnerable positions, is aiming to push for more pro-market, i.e., neoliberal, reforms. What is also worrying is its appeal in part to nationalistic sentiments among the public to galvanize support for these policies.

Prime Minister Abe, personally, has long been a conservative politician and cultural nationalist, and was never oblivious to catering to his right-wing power base. When he first served at the helm of government in 2006, the government revised the Fundamental Education Law. It is well known that Mr. Abe then insisted on having the word "love of country" inserted in the law (although the expression was later somewhat modified). In December 2013, one year after returning to office as Prime Minister, he visited the controversial Yasukuni Shrine, which honors the spirits of Japan's war dead, including some war criminals from the Second World War. His revisionist reflections on the war also provoked tensions with neighboring countries in the past.

The nationalism that the Abe government appeals to is not always as blatant but, nonetheless, visible. It might seem odd that neoliberalism, an ideology that relies on open markets and internationalism, is to be coupled with nationalist politics. However, the point here is not to argue that these two are really theoretically compatible.[11] Rather, it is to point out that the Japanese government, whilst carrying out its neoliberal economic reforms, also appears to invoke nationalism, sometimes in an overt way (such as with periodic visits to Yasukuni), and at other times in less direct ways (such as the rhetoric used in policy proposals). It seems to arouse the nationalistic sentiments of the public, partly to win broad support for potentially divisive policies, despite the fact that the beneficiaries of neoliberal policies tend to be a small minority of corporate and political elites and not the whole nation.

The government's economic growth package, "Japan Revitalization Strategy" (subtitled "Japan is back"), is an illustrative example. It contains a plan for deregulation, intending to make Japanese companies (and academic institutions) "winners" in the global race toward sustained economic growth. The document contains a number of expressions that attempt to reawaken Japanese people's nationalistic spirit. Just as our Olympic athletes aim for the top medal, our companies must aim to be the world's top medalists, and so the entire nation is goaded to rally behind this notion. To reinforce the importance of the government's concept of progress, slogans such as "development of…a workforce that can win in the world stage,"[12] "[aiming for] the top in the world's ranking,"[13] "regulatory reforms to achieve the world's top level,"[14] "reviving the manufacturing industry that can win through the global competition," etc.[15] echo in the public discourse.

In fact, words such as "winning," "race," and "competition" are increasingly becoming part of the common parlance. Tatsuru Uchida suggests that such words are probably necessary for citizens to accept the "story that [the global economic race] is comparable to a 'war'."[16] He argues that, although today's global Japanese businesses are actually "stateless," they are unwilling to let go of the national badge of "Japanese," while their advocates keep posing the question: "how is it possible for Japanese businesses to win?"[17] For them to "win," there must be some concerted effort, and perhaps some sacrifice, on the part of the general public. Uchida argues:

> Competitive global corporations are "flagships of the Japanese economy." So, it is said that we, the nation of a hundred million people, must support their business activities in unison.… Thus, the people have to accept low wages, the collapse of local economies, English as the official language of a company, unpaid overtime work, a rise in the consumption tax, the demise of agricultural, forestry, and fishing industries caused by TPP [Trans-Pacific Partnership Strategic Economic Agreement], and the restart of nuclear power. To have the nation "swallow" these essentially anti-democratic demands, fanning of their emotion is by all means necessary, for instance, by saying, "otherwise, Japan cannot win."[18]

It may be no coincidence that the *Keidanren*, a Japanese federation of businesses, advocated school education that places emphasis on the nation's traditions, culture, history, as well as fostering a love of country and respect for the anthem and flag.[19] It is sometimes argued that neoliberalism may need nationalism to bind ordinary people together and goad them on for a particular purpose. Colin Crouch, for example, suggested that neoliberalism, which tends to favor a minority of privileged class and is therefore not a popular creed, has to be allied with another political force, such as nationalism, to gain measurable influence in society.[20]

It has been said that the government's economic war rhetoric, in fact, camouflages who the true beneficiaries are of neoliberal reforms. Heightened nationalism would also risk Japan's relations with neighboring countries, which have already been strained over the disputed territories and the question of Japan's wartime guilt. It risks breeding further tensions, hatred, and misunderstandings among different ethnic groups. In recent years, Japan has seen a rise in the number of cases of "hate speech" directed at ethnic minorities. Although it is beyond the scope of this essay to analyze the background to this trend, it is possible to speculate that the general anxiety reflecting increasing competition and job insecurity may be playing a part in generating this exclusionary atmosphere. If so, the government's turn to neoliberalism and nationalism would only help exacerbate the situation.

Towards Cross-National Solidarity

Currently, the governing parties occupy a majority of the seats in the Japanese Diet (Parliament), and there are no effective opposition parties. The neoliberal tendency in national politics will, therefore, likely continue for the time being. Nevertheless, efforts are continuing to resist the effects of globalization and government policies that give priority to corporate profits over the lives of ordinary people. Citizens are raising their voices in protest, as witnessed by the mass demonstrations held against the proposed restart of nuclear power plants, some of which brought crowds of tens of thousands in front of the official residence of the Prime Minister, and which received widespread media attention. Sometimes, citizens are spontaneously joining these demonstrations. Whether we can have hope of countering the dominance of neoliberal globalism and the emergence of new nationalism may, indeed, depend on the resilience of such bottom-up resistance and movements, as well as more modest, but steady, grassroots efforts to engage in cross-cultural exchanges.

Although this essay has focused on the case of Japan, the problem of non-regular employment is increasingly becoming a global phenomenon. It is said, for instance, that China and South Korea have also witnessed the rapid rise in the number of non-regular workers who are facing similar problems of low wages, job insecurity, poor physical and mental health, etc.[21] However, in China and Korea, as well as in Japan, workers are not merely passively accepting their fate; they are organizing, and seeking co-operation with others, to improve their working conditions. What is more remarkable is that there has been "a tendency for similar forms of contesta-tion" to emerge in these countries.[22]

For example, in all three countries, there has been a rise of "social move-ment unionism." It is a varied, less centralized form of workers resistance, in which official unions are either replaced by, or joining hands with, other community-based activists. In fact, "social movement unionism" has the possibility of obtaining wider public support by "connecting labour issues with broader, community problems;" for instance, by linking the issue of work hours with the problem of childrearing.[23] The fact that more and more people are placed in similar working situations means that more peo-ple are now facing similar issues, from which the possibility of solidarity arises—even solidarity across borders. Considering the trend towards simi-lar forms of workers contestations in East Asia, and also the prior success of the Transnationals Information Exchange (TIE), which managed to unite factory workers in Europe with farmers in Latin America and Asia, David Layfield argues that, there may be a development of "labour solidarity" in this region in the future.[24]

While it may take some time for genuine labor solidarity to develop across national borders, when it does, it would not only help improve the conditions of workers, but would also promote cross-cultural understand-ing of situations in each other's country. In fact, various citizens associ-ations have long been engaging in cross-national exchange of ideas and people. Some Japanese labor unions, for example, have been sending their staff to South Korea to learn about the country's democratic process and the ways in which Koreans are dealing with the pressing problem of rising non-regular workers.[25] Also, an association of students, the Japan-China Student Conference, has been continuing the exchange of students for nearly twenty years, even during the period after the worsening of the Sino-Japanese relations in 2012. The students from both countries have visited each other's country and have held productive discussions, even on the thorny topics of politics and history.[26] Such relentless efforts to maintain dialogue among young people will certainly play an important role in fos-tering friendship between two countries.

In this age of growing globalization, when more and more wealth is skewed to a smaller minority in society, and an atmosphere of exclusion is emerging, it would be ever more essential than before for ordinary people to continue raising their voices, seeking solidarity, and maintaining a tireless dialogue across national and ethnic boundaries.

* Unless otherwise noted, all quotations from the Japanese language sources in the text are translated by the author.

Questions for Critical Reflection

1. To what extent in your community, state, or country (as the author observes), has globalization "forced [people] to choose between two rather undesirable alternatives of either being unemployed or taking on unstable work in temporary jobs"?

2. In what particular ways have neoliberal economic policies reshaped the sense of identity that Japanese workers have long had?

3. In what way does being "made redundant more easily" typify current employment conditions in your state or country? Are these working conditions generally viewed by working citizens as typical hallmarks of globalization? How do media characterize (or frame) the practice of making workers "redundant"?

4. The author observes that non-regular workers (*hi-seiki*) began replacing many regular workers (*seiki*) in the early 2000s, which seems to reflect common beliefs about the central tenets of neoliberal economic policy: suppress wages, reduce job security, and decrease the living standards of the lower classes. To what extent do these sorts of practices, from your observation or experience, appear in your community or state?

5. The author points out that globalization has lead the, "drive among employers to look for cheap and flexible labor." What other kinds of language do political and/or business leaders use to impress upon the working class the purported need to have cheap and flexible labor available?

6. To what extent have you seen in your country nationalistic political rhetoric emerging in the midst of the outsourcing of jobs to foreign labor markets?

References

[1] Shōdō Mizuki. *Kōgakureki Wākingu Pua: "Frītā Seisan Kōjō" to shite no Daigakuin.* [The Working Poor with High Academic Qualifications: Postgraduate Schools as the "Part-Timer Producing Factory."] (Tokyo: Kōbunsha, 2007), 21-22.

[2] Kazumichi Goka. "Hiseiki Koyō, Koyō no Rekka no Genkyō to Seisaku Kadai." [Policy Issues Relating to the Current State of Non-Regular Employment and the Deterioration of Work.] *Josei Roudou Kenkyu* 57 (2013): 11.

[3] Goka, "Hiseiki Kōyō," 9-10.

[4] *Ibid.*, 9.

[5] Ministry of Internal Affairs and Communication of Japan. Statistics Bureau. "Heisi 25nen Rōdōryoku Chōsa Nenpō, Heikin Kekka no Gaiyō, I Kihon Shūkei." [Annual Report on the Labor Force Survey, Summary of Average Results for 2013, I Basic Tabulation.] http://www.stat.go.jp/data/roudou/report/2013/pdf/summary1.pdf (accessed October 21, 2014).

[6] Ministry of Internal Affairs. "Labor Force Survey, 2013 Yearly Average Results." http://www.stat.go.jp/english/data/roudou/results/annual/ft/index.htm (accessed October 21, 2014).

[7] *The Ryukyu Shimpo*. "Kyūjin no Nanawari Hiseiki" [70% of Job Vacancies are Non-Regular], September 11, 2014.

[8] Cabinet Public Relations Office, Cabinet Secretariat of Japan. "Nihon Saikō Senryaku." [Japan Revitalization Strategy: Japan is Back], 94. http://www.kantei.go.jp/jp/singi/keizaisaisei/pdf/saikou_jpn.pdf (accessed October 18, 2014); for a discussion of the Japanese government's proposed labor reforms, see, e.g., Scott North, "Limited Regular Employment and the Reform of Japan's Division of Labor." *The Asia-Pacific Journal* 12(15), no. 1 (2014). http://www.japanfocus.org/-Scott-North/ 4106 (accessed October 14, 2014).

[9] Goka, "Hiseiki Koyo," 7-22; Momoyo Kamo. *Hiseiki Rōdō no Mukau Saki.* [The Direction of Non-Regular Employment.] (Tokyo: Iwanami Shoten, 2007).

[10] Mami Nakano. "Hiseiki Koyō o Meguru Hōseido no Kadai to Tenbō. [Issues and Outlook in Legislation on Non-Regular Employment.] *Josei Roudou Kenkyu* 57 (2013): 25.

[11] See Adam Harmes. "The Rise of Neoliberal Nationalism." *Review of International Political Economy* 19, no. 1 (February 2012): 59-86.

[12] Cabinet Public Relations Office, "Nihon Saikō," 37.

[13] *Ibid.*, 18.

[14] *Ibid.*, 42-43.

[15] *Ibid.*, 4.

[16] Tatsuru Uchida. "Kowareyuku Nihon to Iu Kuni" [The Collapsing State, Japan], *Asahi Shimbun*, May 8, 2013.

[17] Uchida, "Kowareyuku."

[18] *Ibid.*

[19] Kōichi Nakano. "Kokumin Kokka no Sōshiki o Dare ga Dasunoka" [Who Will Be Holding a Funeral for the National State?], in *Machiba no Yūkoku Kaigi: Nihon wa Korekara Dōnarunoka* [A Conference in Town on the Worrying Future of the Country: What Will Happen to Japan?], ed. Tatsuru Uchida (Tokyo: Shōbunsha, 2014), 197.

[20] Colin Crouch, quoted in Kōichi Nakano, "Kokumin Kokka," 190.

[21] David Layfield. "Liberalised Labour Markets in China, Japan and South Korea: An Opportunity for Regional Labour Solidarity?" (paper presented at Chinese Labour in the Global Economy sponsored by the Economic and Social Research Council, China Policy Research Institute, University of Nottingham, UK, September 11-12, 2014).

[22] Layfield, "Liberalised Labour," 16.

[23] *Ibid.*, 11.

[24] *Ibid.*, 13.

[25] Kamo, Hiseiki Rōdō, 4.

[26] *The Ryukyu Shimpo*. "Kiro no Kenpō, Hyōryū Suru Kokka 6" [With the Constitution at a Crossroads, the Pacifist State Starts Drifting 6], May 10, 2014.

CHAPTER SIX

LOOKS MAY BE DECEIVING: INVISIBLE GENDER CUES IN ADVERTISING AND HOW THEY CREATE TROUBLE IN THE LADIES ROOM

Kristin Comeforo

Introduction

As I pulled off the highway into the service area to use the restroom, I removed my tie. You see, I am a woman; a woman who wears ties. A woman who confuses others because my looks are deceiving—they don't match up with my sex. I am what you would call "gender non-conforming." The tie, short haircut, among other stylistic cues: never a skirt or dress, never heels, never a purse or pocketbook, and I am deemed "male." While my biological sex organs demand my inclusion, I find myself causing trouble in the ladies room time and time again.

Goffman calls this "institutional reflexivity"[1]—when biological sex differences are extended into the rituals and displays of institutional cultures in ways, which have nothing to do with sex. There is nothing natural about gender, which instead indicates the socially constructed roles, behaviors, and appearances that have come to distinguish between male and female. Gender, thus, resides in our *expectations* that men wear ties and women carry pocketbooks. If not from biological difference then, how and from where, do these gender expectations come?

This essay takes a communication approach, emphasizing gender as performance[2] and produced through the social interaction of displays and ritual.[3] Working with the Frankfurt School's and British cultural studies' applications of Antonio Gramsci's theory of hegemony, it will be argued that advertising provides a site for the hegemonic struggle over gender ideals. Despite counter-hegemonic representations and expressions, the hegemony of gender conformity (when one's gender matches the expectations set by their sex) is maintained, as it must be, to serve the corporate interests that underpin our contemporary, capitalist, society.

The Gender "Construct"—Our Primary Identifier

While gender can be envisioned as purely reflective of biological sex differences, many contemporary gender studies theorists have come to think of gender, most radically, as a social construct divorced from the underlying biological sex categorization; or, more conservatively, as part of a complex circuit in which sex and gender serve to *reproduce* each other, through social interaction.

Goffman,[4] for instance, goes so far as to claim that there is no gender identity at all, only highly choreographed practices between the sexes that create a portrait of the male/female relationship. Butler,[5] on the other hand, while arguing for a "radical splitting" of gender from sex, considers gender as the "discursive/cultural means by which 'sexed nature' or a 'natural sex' is produced" and made hegemonic.[6] This "discursive means" emphasizes the binary structure of man/masculine versus woman/feminine and builds constraint "into what language constitutes as the imaginable domain of gender."[7] Biological differences are "exaggerated and extended"[8] while similarities, which may be more plentiful, are downplayed or ignored, thus presenting masculine *or* feminine as both mutually exclusive and, our only options.

What is presented to us as human nature, it is argued, consists of nothing more than a "capacity to learn" and a "willingness to adhere to" this binary language, or socially expected gestures of gender.[9] Gender displays "provide evidence of the actor's alignment in the situation,"[10] or, don't, causing "gender trouble" not necessarily for the actor, but for others as they struggle to categorize the non-conforming individual. Gender displays are important, however, only insofar as their alignments are—that is, to the extent in which the situation demands an aligned gendered display, such as in the ladies room. In these instances, and others, how we look is perhaps the most prominent cue for gender definition and social reaction/interaction.[11]

While there are many perspectives on sex and gender, and debate over how the two are related, one thing that is largely agreed upon is how fundamental gender is to the existing social order,[12] and making us "socially recognizable individuals."[13] Gender, thus, is one of the most important factors through which we define ourselves, and our relationships to others. Even though representations of gender are all around us, there is seldom a need to describe what "woman" looks like, or what "man" looks like because not only do we already know, but we all *agree upon* certain physical and behavioral *truths* that distinguish male from female. That is hegemony.

Hegemony—The Struggle for Dominance

In 1926, the leader of the Italian Communist Party—Antonio Gramsci—was thrown in jail by the fascist regime of Benito Mussolini. During his imprisonment he wrote a staggering three thousand pages, across thirty notebooks, in which he addressed "general questions of revolutionary theory and strategy in the modern world."[14] Through his consideration of how, and why, Fascism defeated the Proletariat in Italy, Gramsci worked out his most influential concept, that of hegemony.

Hegemony can be defined as "an equilibrium between 'leadership' or 'direction' based on *consent,* and 'domination' based on *coercion*." (emphasis added)[15] The state brings its force, or coercion to the ruling equation, while civil society contributes its consent. The failure of the socialist movement, according to Gramsci, was that it focused on "extinguishing the state" (the holder of *coercion*) rather than building consensus through civil society. Consensus becomes an optimal mode of power, for it places ideas rather than people at the locus of control. This allows for the *appearance of change* as regimes are voted in, or out, while the status quo or dominant ideology that defines society and culture, is solidly maintained.

For Gramsci, it was the "intellectuals" (or, organizers) who acted out hegemony as they brought competing discourses into the "marketplace of ideas," which is civil society.[16] Frankfurt School theorists Theodor Adorno and Max Horkheimer extended Gramsci's thinking with their claim that hegemony operates, and consensus is generated, through mass-mediated cultural artifacts. Adorno and Horkheimer coined the term "culture industries" to "signify the process of the industrialization of mass-produced culture and the commercial imperatives which drove the system."[17] Along with the Frankfurt School, British cultural studies began using the concept of hegemony in the 1960s and 1970s in its study of the media product and its effects.

The two schools converged in regards to viewing culture as both a source of "ideological reproduction and hegemony" and also a "potential form of resistance,"[18] yet diverged in their views of the mass audience. Where the Frankfurt School saw defeated masses totally dominated by the media culture product, British cultural studies saw a force of progressive social change that could be "mobilized and organized to struggle against the inequalities of the existing capitalist societies."[19] Cultural studies, thus, aimed to analyze the forces of domination as exerted by the culture industries, and sought counterhegemonic forces of resistance, and struggle, within audiences. With the postmodern turn in the 1980's, cultural studies began to emphasize media culture as producing "material for identities, pleasure, and empowerment,"[20] thus bringing to life the vision of an active audience that *uses* media on their own terms and for their own purposes, rather than just *receiving* the mediated message. The concept of hegemony, however, places the authenticity of an active audience in question, given that it operates to naturalize the dominant ideology, and place it in the everyday lives of people, as if it were their own.

Given that the working class—according to both the Frankfurt School & British cultural studies—is integrated into capitalist society through the products of the culture industries,[21] it is understandable that advertising would play a primary role in that integration—completing the transformation from worker to consumer. Seeing oneself as a consumer is both encoded through production of the advertising message by an advertiser, but also called upon during the production of the audience, as they decode and make meaning of the ad. As consumers we expect to see ourselves as *the target* of advertisers[22] and come to the understanding that *they* make products for *us* based on who we are. It is in this way that we accept the advertising image as a "mirror" of ourselves—with the unity we cannot perceive organically being provided by proxy, through consumption of a product or service.[23] The next section considers more specifically advertising as an agent of hegemony.

Invisible Cues—Advertising as an
Agent of Gender Hegemony

By the 21st century, advertising has well established itself as one of the most powerful cultural tools. Its ubiquity insures that it reaches audiences with such great frequency that it itself becomes an almost invisible backdrop of our natural environment. Its form and function operates on two levels: one, the "primary" or sales message related to goods and services; the other the "secondary" or ideological message—the invisible cues—that speak to us about society and culture.[24] While audiences focus on the surface sales message, which is the primary goal of advertising, they become more vulnerable to the secondary messages, which have been designed to *represent reality* and are at once made invisible and omnipotent in suggesting how we should look, how we should behave, and what we should value as individuals. In this way, the "primary" goals of advertising may not be primary at all, but rather secondary to the ideological goals, which sell us not so much individual products but rather a culture of consumption. By representing us as inadequate or lacking, ads suggest that consumption is the only way to make us whole. Suggestions of what, and how to consume, vary based on gender, and strictly adhere to gender conforming norms and standards. Thus, ads themselves are "gendered texts"[25] which, through their imagery, "rigorously complete" "what biology" and social selection facilitate.[26] To achieve this "completion" or, for an ad to *resonate*, "advertisers have to draw their materials from the social knowledge of the audience."[27] Audiences interpret messages by accessing systems that are both within the ad (the copy and images, and their relation to one another) and external to the ad (existing knowledge, preconceived notions, worldview). To achieve the desired meaning, advertisers must encode their messages based on the systems or codes that audiences already understand, accept, and expect. For this reason, ads rely largely on stereotypes to convey their messages.

Gender stereotypes in advertising include trait descriptors (men as achieving and women as nurturing), physical characteristics (hair length), role behaviors (such as cooking/serving the meal versus being served the meal), and occupation (executive versus secretary).[28] In ads, women tend to smile more, be attractive in appearance, are vulnerable and sexually available; they are most often portrayed in domestic roles or others in which they are subservient to men.[29] Men are portrayed as husbands or business men at work[30] who are physically bigger, taller, and, generally, wield more girth.[31]

These stereotypes provide much needed shortcuts to advertisers who must increasingly communicate complex messages in the fewer, more fleeting seconds of a TV commercial, or in a moment before a reader turns a magazine page. Jhally points out nicely, why gender is the social resource that is used most by advertisers: "what better place to draw upon than an area of social behaviour that can be communicated almost instantly and which reaches into the very core of our definition of human beings?"[32] Similarly, advertising, like film, operates as both a "screen" and "mirror," allowing us to either objectify, or identity with, the "other" in the ad.[33] This allows for multiple readings, usually along gendered lines,[34] which is attractive to advertisers looking to appeal to both male and female market segments with the same ad.

As a result, both women and men are presented as "gender conforming," meeting our expectations of the shorter haired, more muscular, pants wearing man versus the longer haired, more delicate, skirt wearing woman. The sheer volume of these representations—as part of the background or secondary message—has a large impact on the unspoken consensus of what constitutes male versus what constitutes female.

Dominance & Resistance—Conclusions & Thoughts for the Future

While some gender theorists emphasize the role of biological sex as essential to gender, many others embrace gender as a social construct with a reciprocal relationship to sex—something we *do* rather than something we *are*.[35] In much the same way, hegemony can be thought of as a circuit wherein neither the mediated message, nor the individual's reading of that message is absolute. Instead there is a constant struggle for dominance and a series of slippages, where dominance and resistance are constantly at play. Hegemony, thus, is not something you *have* it is something you *do*.

In *doing* hegemony, advertising monopolizes the cultural world through the sheer volume and pervasiveness of its messages, leaving no space for alternative values to be articulated.[36] In the case of gender, advertising articulates very specific expressions and roles, which are fundamental to the operation of a capitalist society. That is, women must look like women so that corporations can sell, for profit, the products that facilitate those appearances; while women must also behave like women, so that men can be free to dedicate their time and labor to the maintenance of the capitalist system itself—as workers or managers. This argument is born out by the vibrant beauty and personal care industry, which includes products such as skin creams, deodorants, hair dyes, shampoo and mascara, among others, and whose sales are projected to reach nearly $71 billion by 2014 in the United States alone.[37] British cultural studies reminds us that with hegemony comes counter hegemonic struggle, as the less powerful seek to advance alternatives to the dominant ideals. The multiplicity and openness of postmodernity allows for alternatives, but only as surface difference while the deep structures of hegemonic ideals are maintained. "Possibilities" and "gender blurring" perceived at the turn of the century,[38] for instance, were limited to specific industries, such as fashion, and specific markets, such as younger consumers. That both Barnes & Nobles and Borders ordered the magazine *Dossier* to wrap its cover in opaque plastic in 2011 for fear that *some* shoppers might mistake the shirtless, androgynous *male* model for a woman, suggests that mainstream brands, like the women in the ladies room, struggle with gender non-conformity.[39]

As a result, general market and widely reaching advertising is almost perfectly gender-conforming. When non-conforming gender representations are included, they are typically included as plot-twist or punchline, and in their "unusualness" serve to reinforce the "usual" images of the hegemonic ideal.[40] In this way, hegemony *needs* counter-hegemonic struggle to add authenticity to a system that is far from authentic, but rather manufactured to serve the interests of the ruling class. In a true postmodern sense, everything is different, yet there is no difference.

Since civil society holds the means to achieve consensus, and hegemony needs counterhegemony to maintain its legitimacy, spaces for resisting gender conforming representations open up to us, if we have the courage to introduce non-conforming expressions of gender into our everyday lives. Trouble is indeed "inevitable" and the task—as Judith Butler suggests—is "how best to make it, what best way to be in it."[41] The best ways to make it are for gender non-conforming individuals to continue to be visible, to cause trouble in the ladies room and force the broader swaths of conforming society to interrogate the binaries we have already blurred, if not completely wiped away, because in truth they should mean little, if anything in terms of how we relate to one another, or function in this world.

Questions for Critical Reflection

1. How do women tend to appear and act in advertisements, compared to men?

2. Why must women look like women in advertisements?

3. Reflect on any unspoken, but implicitly enforced, gender expectations at work in your community and defend or challenge the author's observation in the introduction that, "There is nothing natural about gender...."

4. The author bridges the gap between hegemony and the common unquestioned social constructions and representations of gender (how men and women should look and behave). If hegemony refers to the economic, cultural, or political dominance of one state over another, then extend the author's point regarding hegemony over cultural definitions and understandings of gender. In your community or country, how is this hegemony maintained or challenged?

5. The author points out that, "advertising articulates very specific expressions and roles, which are fundamental to the operation of a capitalist society." If neoliberalism sees the operation of the market as an ethic in itself, capable of acting as a guide for all human action and substituting for all previously existing ethical beliefs,"[42] then how do marketers act to guide thought and action in ways that seek conformity to long-established social norms regarding gender differences?

6. Discuss and defend (or dispute) the following thesis: Gender roles directly serve the corporate interests that underpin our capitalist society.

References

[1] Goffman, E. (1977). "The arrangement between the sexes." In C. Lemert & A. Branaman (Eds.) *The Goffman Reader* (201-208) Boston, MA: Blackwell Publishers Ltd.

[2] Butler, J. (1990). *Gender trouble: Feminism and the subversion of identity.* NY: Routledge.

[3] Goffman, E. (1976). *Gender advertisements.* NY: Harper & Row. Goffman, E. (1977). "The arrangement between the sexes." In C. Lemert & A. Branaman (Eds.) *The Goffman Reader* (201-208) MA: Blackwell Publishers Ltd.

[4] Goffman, E. (1976). *Gender advertisements.* NY: Harper & Row.

[5] *Op cit.,* Butler.

[6] *Ibid.,* Butler, 7.

[7] *Ibid.,* Butler, 9.

[8] Eckert, P. & McConnell-Ginet, S. (2013). *Language & gender,* 2nd Edition. NY: Cambridge University Press. Retrieved from http://web.stanford.edu/~eckert/PDF/Chap1.pdf

[9] *Op cit.,* Goffman, 1976.

[10] *Ibid.,* Goffman, 209.

[11] Kacen, J.J. (2000). "Girrrl power and boyyy nature: The past, present, and paradisal future of consumer gender identity." *Marketing Intelligence & Planning,* 18(6/7), 345-355.

[12] Van Zoonen, L. (1994). *Feminist media studies.* Thousand Oaks: Sage Publications.

[13] Jhally, S. (1990). *The codes of advertising: Fetishism and the political economy of meaning in the consumer society.* NY: Routledge, 137.

[14] Lawner, L. (1973). *Letters from prison—Antonio Gramsci.* NY: Harper & Row.

[15] *Ibid.,* Lawner, 42.

[16] Bates, T. R. (1975). "Gramsci and the theory of hegemony." *Journal of the History of Ideas,* 36(2), 351-366.

[17] Kellner, D. (nd). "The Frankfurt School and British Cultural Studies: The missed articulation." Retrieved from http://pages.gseis.ucla.edu/faculty/kellner/Illumina%20Folder/kell16.htm

[18] Kellner, D. (2005). "Cultural Marxism and British cultural studies." In G. Ritzer (Ed.), *Encyclopedia of social theory.* Thousand Oaks, CA: SAGE Publications, Inc. Retrieved from http://pages.gseis.ucla.edu/faculty/kellner/essays/culturalmarxism.pdf

[19] *Ibid.,* Kellner.

[20] *Ibid.,* 38.

[21] *Op cit.,* Kellner, nd.

[22] Johnson, G.D. & Grier, S.A. (2011). "Targeting without alienating: Multicultural advertising and the subtleties of targeted advertising." *International Journal of Advertising,* 30(2), 233-258.

[23] Williamson, J. (1982). *Decoding advertisements: Ideology and meaning in advertising.* NY: Marion Boyars.

[24] Frith, K.T. (1997). *Undressing the ad: Reading culture in advertising.* NY: Peter Lang; and O'Barr, W.M. (1994). *Culture and the ad: Exploring otherness in the world of advertising.* Boulder: Westview Press.

[25] Stern, B.B. (1993). "Feminist literary criticism and the deconstruction of ads: A postmodern view of advertising and consumer responses." *Journal of Consumer Research*, 19, 556-566.

[26] *Op cit.*, Goffman, 28.

[27] Jhally, S. (1989). "Advertising, gender and sex: What's wrong with a little objectification?" *Working Papers and Proceedings of the Center for Psychosocial Studies* (edited by Richard Parmentier and Greg Urban) No. 29, 1989, 127.

[28] Knoll, S., Eisend, M., & Steinhagen, J. (2011). "Gender roles in advertising: Measuring and comparing gender stereotyping on public and private TV channels in Germany." *International Journal of Advertising*, 30(5), 867-888.

[29] Kacen, J.J. (2000). "Girrrl power and boyyy nature: The past, present, and paradisal future of consumer gender identity." *Marketing Intelligence & Planning*, 18(6/7), 345-355. and Goffman, E. (1976). *Gender advertisements.* NY: Harper & Row.

[30] *Ibid.*, Kacen.

[31] *Ibid.*, Goffman.

[32] Jhally, S. (1990). *The codes of advertising: Fetishism and the political economy of meaning in the consumer society.* NY: Routledge, 136.

[33] Mulvey, L. (1999). "Visual pleasure and narrative cinema." In L. Braudy & M. Cohen (Eds.), *Film theory and criticism: Introductory readings* (833-844). New York: Oxford UP.

[34] Stern, B.B. (1993). "Feminist literary criticism and the deconstruction of ads: A postmodern view of advertising and consumer responses." *Journal of Consumer Research*, 19, 556-566.

[35] *Op cit.*, Butler 1990, Goffman 1976, and Jhally 1989.

[36] McLaren, C. (1999). On advertising: Sut Jhally vs. James Twitchell. Stay Free! Retrieved from https://mediasrv.oit.umass.edu/~sutj/twitchell.pdf

[37] Burton, T.M. (2014, 7 Mar). "Corporate news: Cosmetics industry takes heat from FDA." *The Wall Street Journal.* Eastern Edition. B.4.

[38] *Op cit.*, Kacen.

[39] Abraham, T. (2011, May 18). "Barnes & Noble and Borders censor image of androgynous male model Andrej Pejic 'in case customers think he is a woman." *The Daily Mail.* Retrieved from http://www.dailymail.co.uk/femail/article-1387792/Barnes--Noble-Borders-censor-image-androgynous-male-model-Andrej-Pejic-case-customers-think-woman.html#ixzz3DhnBtlbh.

[40] O'Barr, W.M. (1994). *Culture and the ad: Exploring otherness in the world of advertising.* Boulder: Westview Press.

[41] *Op cit.*, Butler 1990, vii.

[42] For elaborated definitions of neo-liberalism, visit: http://web.inter.nl.net/users/Paul.Treanor/neoliberalism.html

CHAPTER SEVEN

BEAUTY AT ALL COST: THE TYRANNY OF APPEARANCE IN GLOBAL FOOD PRODUCTION[1]

Reisa Klein & Michèle Martin

Introduction

For avid farmer's market enthusiasts like us, fruits and vegetables evoke images from 'farm to table' and have become synonymous with words such as 'local' and 'fresh'. However, in Canada, the season of fresh produce from the farm is short, so that stores specialising in fruits and vegetables and supermarkets soon become the most accessible options. We have noticed that these stores often employ various marketing techniques to manufacture images of farm freshness in produce, even though fruits and vegetables often take days or even weeks to arrive from other countries such as the US, Mexico, and China. Such techniques include spraying mist on display cases to suggest that fruits and vegetables have just been picked, or using wax on produce to accentuate their bright and shiny aspects.

These techniques, essential in increasing global flows of food production and consumption, create standardised visual aspects of fruits and vegetables which we call a 'global beauty'—universal standards where appearance stands in for taste, blurring the distinction between the two senses. Our day-to-day observations showed that these global beauty standards and practices influence our purchasing and consumption practices: consumers are obviously trying to find the perfect product! Yet, we believe that this global beauty operates as a two-way flow where developing countries have to adapt their practices of production to meet global standards in order to make their produce more palatable to importing countries. We were therefore intrigued by what seems to be the importance of beauty in the global food and agriculture industries.

Given the trend towards rationality in communication and food consumption studies, the role of beauty[2] is often minimized, such as in studies on food distribution, especially those on fruits and vegetables where the notion of beauty could shed an interesting light on several points. In politico-economic terms, the existing works in these fields concentrate on the mechanisms used to make profit in a sector where losses are sometimes enormous. From a sociocultural perspective, they address the needs and desires of consumers. But none, to our knowledge, include beauty in its criteria for analysis. There is a definite omission in the way beauty takes a role as a global means of communication in various food industries.

In our study, the concept of beauty is not conceived in essentialist terms, but rather as an attribute associated with the appearance of an "actor"[3] and socially constructed according to standards set by the beauty industry (fashion, cosmetics, etc.). The beauty of fruits and vegetables, for its part, entails a certain familiarity, symmetry, colour and other characteristics set by the food and agriculture industries and being able to reach a final stage seen as perfection. It creates a 'population' of food that involves specific power relations—which we will discuss below—in which beauty operates as a means of visual communication that raises tensions and even paradoxes. We offer a critical approach that will help explore the complexity of integrating beauty, even perfection, in the analysis of production, distribution and food consumption processes, particularly in regard to fruits and vegetables. We choose to examine fruits and vegetables because of their unique qualities: they are perishable; their appearance, such as shape, colour and freshness, or simply put their beauty, is very important; and they are generally not identified in terms of 'branding,' at least not in the manner usually adopted by the producers. Nonetheless, before we critically analyse the concept of beauty, we will briefly discuss the role of political economy and communication in the global food and agriculture industries.

The Political Economy of Food Production and Consumption

We mean by food and agriculture industries the network of companies and consumers located in given geographical areas and attached to a global system. These companies operating within the global system are part of the flow of goods and services related to consumers' food supply and their driving force is the pursuit of profits.

According to Silvia Gorenstein, the dynamic of this system causes tensions between the strategies used by the food and agriculture industries on one hand, and local producers on the other hand, tensions that are exacerbated by the international race for beautiful and even perfect produce.[4] These tensions gave rise to new forms of production and consumption, which advocate ecological and biological values that support ideas of the product's appearance in contrast with the hegemonic notion of beauty that tends to link product quality and configuration. According to Valceschini, the product quality would be associated with two concepts: premium quality that comes from local and niche producers; and quality of origin related to its guarantee as a local product.[5] In particular, fruits and vegetables must meet very rigid standards, which results in a significant part of the production being rejected as soon as it shows signs of aging, thereby decreasing the potential for profit. For instance, Canadians waste more than 2.5 billion dollars in fruit and vegetable produce each year.[6]

This system of global food industry is based on a huge market that involves local, regional and national production and consumption, but also international exportation and importation of large quantities of fresh food. As an example, in 2012, the global import/export market for vegetables only, amounted to almost $84 billion. Canada, a relatively small actor in that system, still exported over one billion dollars of vegetables, and imported over two billion dollars.[7] These vegetables were coming from, and going to, more than 25 different countries that have to adapt to and adopt the beauty standards required by Agri-Food Canada[8] standards of near perfection that will satisfy the consumers. To reach that level of perfection, many strategies and techniques have to be adopted through the different stages of the food market. Communication is at the heart of this complex dynamic organisation.

Essential Means of Communication in
Food and Agriculture Distribution

Valérie Borde argues that communication is essential to the food market.[9] We therefore ground our analysis in a political economic approach to communication as the central point of all industrial production in which the pursuit of profit and capital accumulation—to this end, branding and marketing strategies—are essential to establish a link between distributors and consumers of goods. Branding and marketing are social as well as economic constructs designed to promote the name of a company and its products.[10] According to Selon Chrysochou, consumers would choose their food according to its brand, which connotes quality and health (no additives or preservatives, organic, etc., such as McDonald's and its healthy salad!).[11] Would production and distribution of fruits and vegetables be an exception? We do not think so, but their branding was not associated with a producer (except for example for Chiquita bananas), but rather with the products themselves and the message they convey: 'beauty' and 'health'. The more beautiful they are, the more healthful they seem.

Beauty: A Relationship between Woman and Food

Beauty has been widely discussed in the field of communication by feminist scholars who argue that the standards and practices of beauty are socially constructed in relation to patriarchal and capitalist interests, and work to keep women in positions of subordination. Their findings stem from research on media that reproduce unrealistic beauty ideals that 'tyrannize' the average woman unable to meet these standards.

John Berger[12] states that, in this demanding world: "men look at women, women watch themselves being looked at."[13] He explains that women exist to satisfy the appetite of men, the former having no appetite of their own. This kind of terminology constitutes a link between the discourse of beauty and the food women consume. In this radical feminist approach, which we will further elaborate, women—like food—become commodities that must look attractive to be devoured. In this context, the media develop strategies whereby women are fragmented (e.g. mouth, legs, buttocks), becoming pieces to consume.[14] In the same vein, Heather Brook argues that beauty and food intersect in the marketing techniques of women's magazines in at least three cases: (1) food as cosmetics; (2) cosmetics as food; (3) women as objects of consumption. She therefore concludes that food and women are consumed interchangeably: We can taste them, we can devour them.[15] This interchangeability can be generalised in Western societies, and more and more globally, with the expansion of the Internet and social media. For instance, the relationship between women and food has been explored by the media, which has been extended to the concept of 'food porn'.

Beauty and 'Food Porn'

Milton defines pornography as, "any media basically construed as intended to entertain or arouse erotic desire."[16]It is a visual or written expression of fantasies that provides sexual pleasure to the user. One characteristic of porn images is that the content is "realistically unattainable."[17] Applying a similar concept to food, Alexander Cockburn used the term 'gastro-porn' in 1977 for the type of food that increased, "the sense of the unattainable by proffering coloured photographs of various completed recipes."[18] Two years later, Barthes described the food shown in the magazine *Elle* in similar ways, namely as, "ornamental cookery...meant for the eye alone...."[19] The same year, Michael Jacobson, co-founder of the Center of Science in the Public Interest, coined the expression 'food porn' to connote, "a food that was so sensationally out of bounds of what a food should be that it deserved to be considered pornography."[20]

Nowadays, the term food-porn has emerged, adopting a popular and sensual, rather than sexual, connotation describing mouth-watering images of food [see Image 1] seen in different types of media,[21] including posters hanging in diverse types of markets and showing fruits and vegetables that are of an impossible perfection and hide practices of production that might be unpalatable to the consumers. All these definitions, although diversified in many ways, imply an unattainable sense of beauty; yet, they affect the diverse groups committed to the production, distribution and consumption of fruits and vegetables.[22] This section of our paper explores the complexity of the relationship between beauty and food, the potential contradictions that it involves and the impact that it has globally.

Image 1

The role of beauty in the food and agriculture industries is not subjected to a traditional hierarchy. Consequently, we adopt an Actor Network Theory (ANT) approach developed by Michel Callon.[23] As it is generally believed that beauty sells products, we have designated the beauty of fruits and vegetables as the main "actor"[24] of the food organisation because, as a quality required by many consumers, it tyrannizes producers as well as distributors. In this sense, it constitutes the obligatory passage point (OPP) of the system, and therefore an essential element of capital accumulation. In fact, all actors—fruits and vegetables, producers, distributors—equally face similar problems related to the appearance of the produce: for the fruits and vegetables, it is to deteriorate rapidly; for the producer, it is the lack of cooperation by environmental factors; for the distributor, it is the length of shelf time. Each of these actors must develop strategies that will help at least minimize, if not eliminate, these problems [see Chart 1].

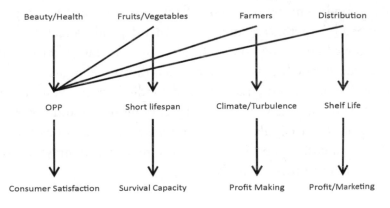

The Tyranny of Beauty in Food and Agricultural Industries:
Challenges to Overcome

Chart 1

In the large food industry, the fragility and short life of fresh produce com-plicate the role of beauty and require, as a first technique, a well-regulated communication between producers and distributors, especially in light of the global market. This type of communication not only shortens the re-sponse time between each step, but also helps establish the nature, quan-tity and quality requirements of the commodities requested. This step is essential because produce that shows 'wrinkles' causes a direct loss of profit for distributors. Communication is also essential between distributors and consumers where it takes a more complex form. Strictly speaking, there is no marketing for fruits and vegetables, but their presentation in the stores is based on a display—not unlike that used by the garment industry—which is increasingly more 'artistic', sensual, even close to techniques used in food porn, and requires experts to create it. For example, common strat-egies include well-appointed colours and regular watering, which make the produce appear more tantalising by giving the impression of freshness. Similarly, the presentation of certain vegetables in their natural form such as carrots with their stems or in a sandbox, establishes a direct link between production and consumption. All these techniques convey characteris-tics that represent healthiness, in the same way that the cosmetic industry seeks to convince women that they will look younger, more beautiful, and healthier by using their products.

However, only 73% of fruits and vegetables produced by farmers are

sold to industrial food chains,[25] the rest being sold by the farmers themselves either to restaurants or on the farm where it is possible to sell less perfect products at lower prices.[26] We thus see that the organisation supporting
the sale of food commodities such as fruits and vegetables is complex. The
practices of all the actors are imbricated. They depend on each other but, as
there is no well-established hierarchy, they have a vital need to communicate to be coordinated. This situation entails diverse elements: politico-economic, sociocultural and environmental conditions; the tyrannical role of
beauty in food; and the way this beauty communicates and functions as a
technique of power (similar to techniques we see in discourses on beauty
regarding women). To do justice to this complexity, we draw on the concept of bio-power proposed by Foucault.

A Critical Theory of Beauty in the Food and
Agriculture Industries

According to Michel Foucault,[27] biopower is a productive form of regulation of individuals that involves body control and the wellbeing of the
population. In our view, the beauty of fruits and vegetables communicates
health, freshness and wellbeing, and as such constitutes a form of biopower
that guides the behaviour of producers, distributors and consumers. This
aspect of production also guides government regulations on food and agriculture industries. Yet, its first and foremost objective is economic.

To stimulate the interest of consumers, display techniques are often
used in the fruit and vegetable industry: for instance, the inclusion of images of ripe fruits presented in a sensual way; and of active and healthy
individuals suggesting that if they eat this beautiful produce, its nutritional
value will keep them healthy. These fruits and vegetables thus become actors who have the power to feed people and take care of their wellbeing,
thereby forcing producers at the international level to adjust their practices
in order to encourage distributors to offer them. Indeed, as we have seen
above, these commodities are produced in various countries and are often
imported or exported. As such, they are submitted to international rules
and regulations that control their qualities closely related to the appearance
of the produce.[28]

Actors' Resistance

The concept of bio-power also includes a notion of resistance. In our case, fruits and vegetables, just like women, do not always cooperate with the other actors. They can resist by refusing perfection, displaying an ugly and imperfect form, bruises, strange colours or unusual shapes. At the same time, when they collaborate, their beauty and perfection does not necessarily guarantee that consumers will buy them, with some opting for imperfect fruits and vegetables—too ripe, even bruised—in the same way that some people resist giving in to the ideals of standard beauty. Increasingly some distributors are offering imperfect produce at lower prices to consumers who are becoming more willing to forego the perfect items.[29]

In this imperfect situation, organic produce also breaks rank. We can see in bold in Chart 2[30] the contrast between standard (shown in Chart 1) and organic commodities:

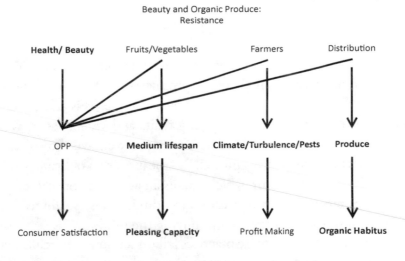

Chart 2

Consumers who, as a rule, enjoy organic produce constitute a habitus in the sense used by Pierre Bourdieu,[31] as they form a group whose predispositions are acquired by its members through socialization and confirmed by practices. In our case, this habitus is a rather elitist form of resistance, insofar as organic commodities are often expensive and not readily accessible to small incomes. Organic produce entails two forms of distribution: the products offered by specialty stores; and those sold in supermarkets, whose role is either to accommodate customers aware of their health without being dogmatic, or to showcase the beauty of other products. In fact, whether they are sold in supermarkets or specialty stores, organic produce always seem less beautiful, and even less fresh than their non-organic counterparts. In addition, their shape and colour are often less regular, which convey healthiness because they are flawed! Could this be a branding technique? Beauty and perfection are no longer needed here, in fact if the produce is too perfect, it becomes suspicious as it suggests the use of chemicals.

Resistance can also take shape when farmers and consumers are opposed to the practices of industrial food production, by adopting behaviours consistent with their own cultural values. When consumers buy locally and/or choose organic produce, they put pressure on the global food practices and on farmers. Again, ugliness, imperfection, bruising become features that may attract some consumers.

Conclusion

We have seen that beauty in food and agriculture production practices likewise regulates the relationship between producers/farmers, distributors and consumers who are all subjected to its tyrannical role. This affects not only people involved in the system supplying fruits and vegetables in Western societies, but has an international impact since we have shown that the import/export market is alive and well. So, beauty as an obligatory passage point (OPP) is a global actor, which entails all aspects of the capitalist system, efficient means of communication to minimize losses, and techniques of persuasion to woo consumers into buying the produce.

As we discussed earlier, these practices fall under non-hierarchical power relationships between actors whatever their roles are in the encompassing food and agriculture system. Nevertheless, they are asymmetric in the sense that they are subjected to various constraints and create tensions, if not paradoxes, among the actors of this system, making communication essential to their resolution. It is in this context that the beauty of fruits and vegetables becomes essential in food production and distribution as it may either help accumulate profit, or decrease it if nature does not cooperate. So beauty can become a form of resistance, in Callon's meaning;[32]

for instance, in the habitus of organic consumers, it can sometimes mean declining to buy the produce.

In addition, our critical analysis sheds light on a double concept of consumption—that of women and that of produce—which correlates in the concept of beauty. More precisely, women are both objects of beauty and actors associated with consumption, and so are fruits and vegetables. These actors participate in practices and techniques in the food and agriculture industries, and as we have seen, are sometimes associated with objectification techniques, which may converge into food porn. Still, for fruits and vegetables as well as for women, the concepts of health and beauty merge and are interchangeable, and as such correspond to the Foucauldian notion of bio-power.

Our theoretical approach provides an understanding of the global role of beauty—that of women and that of produce—in the politico-economic, socio-cultural and environmental context of the food and agriculture industries. By examining the ways beauty operates as a practice of communication in an international system of food supply, we can identify certain types of power and resistance. Like women, fruits and vegetables are not always in a submissive role, and sometimes (effectively) refuse to cooperate. We therefore believe that our approach may be useful for other studies in global communication.

Questions for Critical Reflection

1. The authors cite the content in Image 1 as one example, among countless others, that typify the pervasiveness of 'food porn' today in the marketplace. If the image qualifies as 'food porn' in advertising, discuss what its content is "selling" to consumers.

2. Discuss the relationship between 'food porn' in advertising and higher profits. Does the former necessarily imply the latter?

3. The authors make a persuasive case that women are often cast unfairly as "objects of consumption," especially as regards the marketing technique of 'fragmenting.' Can a similar case be made for the 'fragmenting' of men in advertising as an effort to sell something? If so, what products depict men in similar fashion?

4. What does the appearance (existence) of 'food porn' in contemporary culture and its relative appeal to us as consumers exemplify about us as people?

5. Throughout the essay, the authors draw parallels between the visual beauty of women and the manufactured beauty of produce. Which particular words (or expressions) serve to establish these connections? How do these connections illustrate the kind of 'global beauty' we might seek as consumers?

References

[1] This essay can also be found in the original French: Klein, R. et Martin, M. (2013). « La tyrannie de la beauté en production alimentaire », dans OÙ [EN] EST LA CRITIQUE EN COMMUNICATION ? Actes du colloque international Dans le cadre du 80ème congrès de l'Association francophone pour le savoir (Acfas), Palais des congrès de Montréal, 7 au 11 mai 2012 (OÙ [EN] EST LA CRITIQUE EN COMMUNICATION ? Colloque international Dans le cadre du 80ème congrès de l'Association francophone pour le savoir (Acfas), Montréal, Québec, Canada, 7 au 11 mai 2012), sous la dir. de Kane, Oumar; George, Éric et Naoufal, Nayla. Montréal, Québec, Canada, Centre de recherche GRICIS, 226-238.

[2] Beauty here is not understood in its aesthetic meaning, so it differs from studies on aesthetics that considers the latter as non-rational yet meaningful attributes of cultural expression (Lithgow 2012, 281). We consider that beauty in food and agriculture industries is a rational element in the political economic aspects of food production and consumption.

[3] Actor is understood here in the sense developed in the Actor Network Theory (ANT), which we will discuss in detail later.

[4] Gorenstein, S. (2003). Nouveaux territoires du systeme agroalimentaire de la Pampa. Etudes rurales, 165 (6), 147-170.

[5] Valceschini, E. (1996). Elements the oriques et empiriques pour une analyse e conomique de la qualite dans l'agroalimentaire. *Fruits*, 51 (5), 289-297.

[6] *The Vancouver Sun* 16.07.2013 Internet Version. The *Globe and Mail* specifies that Canada wastes up to 25 millions pounds in fruits and vegetables every year. "Ugly. Misshapen. Beautiful. How an award-winning European Campaign is changing the way customers—grocers— think about fruit." August 1st, 2014, p. B5.

[7] Government of Canada, *Quality in our Nature*. Market analysis and statistical overview of Canadian agriculture industry. Report by Agriculture and Agri-Food Canada, November 2013.

[8] A label not condoned by all consumers. For more see, the *Ottawa Citizen's* article "'Agri-Food' in name confuses consumers." 14.07.2014, p. A9.

[9] Borde, V. (1996). Saint-Hyacinthe : une technopole en plein essor. Biofutur, 158.

[10] Forman, J., Halford, J. C., Summe, H., MacDougall, M. et Keller, K.L. (2009). "Food branding influences ad libitum intake differently in children depending on weight status. Results of a pilot study." *Appetite*, 53, 76-83.

[11] Chrysochou, P. (2010). "Food health branding : the role of marketing mix elements and public discourse in conveying a healthy brand image." *Journal of Marketing Communications*, 16 (1-2), 69-85.

[12] Despite the fact that Berger's statement was made 40 years ago, we believe it is still relevant, as some feminist studies show, e.g. Bordo 2003, Harlow 2008, Tinknell 2011.

[13] Berger, J. *Ways of Seeing*, (New York: Penguin Books), 1972, 42.

[14] Kilbourne, J. *Deadly Persuasion: Why Women and Girls Must Fight the Addictive Power of Advertising*, (New York: Free Press), 1999. and Langton, Rae. *Sexual Solipsism: Philosophical Essays on Pornography and Objectification*, (Oxford: Oxford University Press), 2009.

[15] Brook, H. (2008). "Feed your Face." *Continuum*, 22(1), 141-157.

[16] Milton, D. "Pornography, public acceptance and sex related crime: A review." *International Journal of Law and Psychiatry* 32(2009): 304-314.

[17] *Ibid.*

[18] In McBride, A. "Forum: Food Porn." *The Journal of Food and Culture*. 10, no.1(2010): 38-46, 38.

[19] Barthes, R. *Mythologies*. (New York: Hill & Wang), 1979, p. 78.

[20] Quoted in McBride, *Op. cit.*, 38.

[21] Not all scholars agree with this new definition of food porn, but it is not the aim of this paper to discuss these discrepancies.

[22] For more on the impact of cosmetic food defects and their effects on consumers, see Thompson, G.D. & J. Kidwell. "Explaining the choice of organic produce: Cosmetic defects, prices and consumer preferences." *American Journal of Agriculture Economy* 80, no. May (1998): 277-187. We believe that the arguments in that paper still apply to organic and particularly inorganic food.

[23] Callon, M. 1986. "Some Elements of a Sociology of Translation: Domestication of the Scallops and the Fishermen of St. Brieuc Bay." In *Power, Action, and Belief: A New Sociology of Knowledge?* edited by J. Law. London: Routledge & Kegan Paul.

[24] The main actor in ANT is the element of analysis that is essential in the sense that all other actors in the relationship depend on it.

[25] For more on this issue, see Dimitri, C. and C. Green. "Recent growth patterns in the U.S. foods market. *Agriculture Information Bulletin No. AIB777*. United States Department of Agriculture, Economic Research Service, Washington, D.C. , 2003, http://www.ers.usda.gov/Publications/AIB777/.

[26] In this system, there exist various grades identifying different qualities of produce: e.g. grades A, B, C etc.

[27] Foucoult, M. "Society must be defended," Lectures at the Collège de France, 1975-76 accessed at http://rebels-library.org/files/foucault_society_must_be_defended.pdf

[28] We acknowledge that the beautiful appearance of these commodities often hides the use of chemical products that are also regulated inter-nationally. However, with the decrease in the number of inspectors acting as gatekeepers at the borders, there is an increased possibility for undetected faulty products to pass through.

[29] For more information see the video produced by the French supermarket *Intermarché*, https://www.youtube.com?watch?v=p2nSECWq_PE#t=43

[30] In terms of climate limitations, farms in countries with bad weather such as, lately, flooding and hail in South Africa, Ghana and Kenya, could leave crops with blemishes and imperfections. *Globe and Mail*, August 1st, 2014, p. B5.

[31] Bourdieu, P. *Distinctions. A Social Critique of the Judgment of Taste. Conclusion. 1984*, translated by Richard Nice, (Cambridge: Harvard University Press), 1984, pp. 466-484.

[32] In his article, Callon examines noncooperation as a tool of resistance.

CHAPTER EIGHT

HERITAGE LANGUAGE LOSS IN THE NAME OF GLOBALIZATION: PREVENTION AND REVITALIZATION

Hinako Takahashi

Introduction

Today, the widespread belief is that globalization is an economic reality from which we cannot escape, that it is an unavoidable and necessary sort of inoculation administered by the elite, for our benefit, from the travails of some new world order. Globalization purports to be the saving grace of our economic ills, a rational antidote to the volatile free market developed by and handed down from the owners and managers at top of the social pyramid. Surely, with the massive success that the mainstream media have had in squashing the Occupy Movements throughout America and Europe, resistance against the globalization vaccine certainly seems to be futile as well as potentially hazardous to the public health. Perhaps nowhere more evident are these realities than in the language that is used to reinforce the supposed benefits of this new system. The present success of the global elite in modifying common perceptions can be understood, in part, through the very language that people use and associate with cultural capital the world over.

When I share with others my experiences of growing up in Spain as a child and then living in the U.S., I often hear something like, "Wow, you are such a 'global' person!"—often with some extra stress on 'such.' Yes, I have experienced much living outside of Japan for many years and have learned the Spanish language and culture as well as English and American culture. My first and native language is Japanese, and my second is Spanish. While I was living as a teenager with my parents in Spain, they encouraged me to transfer to an international school from a local Spanish school before I was to start high school. They felt that knowing English would be more beneficial for my future.

As I reflect on those years, it's clear to me that they were correct. Knowing English got me into a good Japanese university when I finally returned to Japan, and English also helped me acquire a good job after graduation. I was also able to succeed in the U.S. when I decided to go back to school for postgraduate and doctoral studies. With higher English language skills, I became a so-called "global" person granted with the access to participate in the great "globalizing" experiment.

To "globalize" means to involve or affect the entire world, according to Merriam-Webster's dictionary. My parents and I had bought into the idea that English is the language that holds a kind of global power. I had been globalized, yet I still hold onto my identity as Japanese even though I missed a sustained immersion in Japanese culture and tradition being educated outside of Japan. When I began thinking more consciously about the whole process of being "globalized," I had already entered parenthood. While my American husband and I had our daughter in New Mexico, I began to feel a strong sense of responsibility to teach my daughter Japanese language and culture.

As the only source of Japanese to my daughter, I discovered that exposure to the culture and language was, in fact, a much more challenging prospect than I had imagined. After she began her schooling at the age of five, she began resisting my efforts to communicate with her in Japanese. By then, she no longer felt some sense of pride in being Japanese. As a result, I felt ashamed that my parents could not communicate with their only granddaughter in Japanese. I failed to teach my daughter what was a part of her heritage and identity. Failures such as this are the prizes we win in the race toward being "global." Indeed, the loss of heritage language and culture has been widespread in a multicultural society such as the U.S.

where the majority language overpowers other minority languages generation after generation.

Globalization and Heritage Language

As the "globalization" movement infects the entire world, the phenomenon of "heritage language loss" is also globalized. With the privilege of being a "global" person there also comes the responsibility of making an effort to make the "globalization" process an egalitarian process wherein the great variety of cultures, languages, and, therefore, people hold the same value without inequalities. We can learn much, in fact, about these sorts of growing inequalities from careful observations of what is happening to minority languages and cultures as well as what efforts are now being made to maintain or revitalize these languages and cultures in the U.S., where English holds the power of the majority.

The survival of heritage languages depends on the transferring of language knowledge from one generation to the next within communities and families.[1] As regards the maintenance of heritage languages for immigrants, newcomers to a new country can import with them their own language resources so as to refresh and preserve heritage communities. Unfortunately, in the case of indigenous languages that are overpowered (so to speak) by the conqueror's language, the survival of heritage languages depends solely on the process of intergenerational transmission.[2] With regards to Hispanic immigrant families in the U.S., for example, by the third generation, they totally lose their Spanish, with seven out of ten children of immigrant parents using English, almost exclusively.[3] Among immigrant language minorities, a characteristic pattern has been that the first generation acquired some English while remaining stronger in the native tongue while the second generation usually becomes bilingual with more developed literacy skills in English because English is the language of instruction. The third generation has a tendency to become English speaking with little or no capability in the language of their grandparents.[4]

Children from minority language families require sufficient and continual linguistic exchange with family members and peers over the crucial periods of natural language learning. Anything short of sufficient and meaningful interactions will result in incomplete development of language, which can lead to language loss.[5]

Furthermore, it is not just the language that is lost—most of the culture is embedded in the language and expressed through the language that is lost. Culture could not be expressed or handed down in any other way. When you lose your culture, "you are losing all those things that essentially are the way of life, the way of thought, the way of valuing, and the human reality that you are talking about."[6] What's more, "the destruction of a language is the destruction of a rooted identity"[7] for both communities as well as individuals. The loss of a heritage language can destroy a sense of self-worth, limiting human potential and compelling efforts to solve other problems, such as poverty, family breakdown, school-failure, and substance abuse.[8]

In the case of indigenous languages, there are approximately 210 indigenous languages spoken in the U.S. and Canada. Among them, 35 are being spoken by parent generations and older; 84 are being spoken by only a handful of speakers who are most likely of the oldest generations.[9] The existence of weak heritage languages is part and parcel of an inevitable pattern in a country under such dominant English-only ideological and social conditions. For most of U.S. history, the English hegemony seemed self-evident: English has always been the mainstream language in all social functions as well as in the imposition of English-only social movements and school policies, all of which have played powerful roles in keeping English at the top of the power structure.[10]

Learning the Heritage Language in School

In the state of New Mexico where I lived for many years and undertook graduate studies, as much as 48% of the state population (as of 2012) was of Hispanic descent. Many citizens spoke only English, predominantly, with the knowledge of some vernacular Spanish used in their homes or communities. New Mexicans followed the same trend as the rest of the U.S. in losing their Spanish by the third generation under the strong English-only ideology. This pattern is closely tied to the widely held belief that speaking English leads to better jobs and, therefore, to a better life.

As immigrant children learn English in school, the patterns of language use change in their homes, and the younger the children are when they learn English, the greater the effect of losing their heritage language. To address the needs of the Hispanic students who no longer speak Spanish, the universities and high schools in New Mexico have offered Spanish as heritage language classes.

Beyond these efforts, though, the instructional agenda used in teaching heritage language learners needs to be about more than simply teaching a language as a second or foreign language. More attention can also be given to validating cultural identity, determining linguistic needs, and adjusting curricular goals and instructional approaches in accord with students' sociolinguistic and family background.[11] When I spoke to my New Mexican Hispanic friends in Spanish, they often told me that they felt embarrassed because their Spanish was not good. They indicated that they felt proud to be New Mexican Hispanic, yet not being able to speak Spanish was a lingering shame. Fortunately, there are now some signs of improvement. While the practice of heritage language teaching in elementary schools is decreasing, the number of Dual Language Immersion Programs is increasing.

Heritage Language Learning in a Dual Language Immersion Program

During the days of my graduate research, I had the opportunity to study how the children of an elementary school were learning both Spanish and English in the Spanish/English Dual Language Immersion program (DLIP). DLIP is an innovative method of providing educational opportunities for both language minority and language majority students. The programs focus on linguistic minority students in their studies of English while they interact with their native English-speaking peers, and for native English-speaking students to learn their second language while interacting with native speakers of that language. The key features of a DLIP include: 1) the program involves some form of dual language instruction where the non-English language is used for a significant portion of the instructional day; 2) the program involves periods of instruction during which only one language is used; 3) both native English speakers and native speakers of the second language (preferably in balanced numbers) are participating; and 4) the students are integrated for most of the content instruction.[12]

Depending on the target community, DLIPs vary considerably in terms of the languages used (most common programs are of Spanish and English in the U.S., but there are programs with Korean, French, Cantonese, Navajo and others), how (by time of day, by day, by week, by month, by subject, by teacher, etc), and how much (50/50, 90/10) the two languages are allocated, and how students are integrated.

The elementary school with a Spanish/English Dual Language Immersion program where many Hispanic children are learning Spanish as their heritage language was situated in a neighborhood in an old Hispanic community near the downtown area of a large city in New Mexico. The community was first established in 1662 and has since been a significantly important region for Hispanic people. In the late 1800s with the establishment of the railroad, the community flourished and attracted a great many people. Around this time, the community transformed from a quiet, rural, trade community into a busy, urban, commercial center. The language of the community was largely Spanish, even after its incorporation in 1912 to official statehood.

After World War II, railroad activity decreased, but when the main highway passed through the heart of the community, economic survival then shifted to automobile and service-oriented businesses. In the 1970s, the community slipped into an economic depression when the two main crossroads were closed down, and the new interstate freeway system bypassed the community. During this time of depression, many businesses and buildings were shut down and boarded up. In the early 1990s, efforts to revive the neighborhood were continually put forward by the community members. Today, it stands as an historic neighborhood with both old historic sites and newly built sites, such as The National Hispanic Cultural Center, which attracts visitors from outside of the area.

For over 300 years, the neighborhood had maintained itself as a largely Nuevomexicano[13] community where people lived for many generations. The demographics began changing noticeably during the economic depression when a number of immigrants from Mexico and other Latin American countries began to settle in the community in the 1980s. Until then, the student population of the neighborhood schools consisted mostly of bilingual speakers with English as the official language and Spanish as the vernacular home language. The school, therefore, used Spanish in oral form, whereas most of the academic and literacy language was English.[14]

Valle del Sur Elementary School was and has always been a Spanish/ English bilingual school. Before it moved to its current location, the predecessor of this school was known for being the first bilingual public school in the state. The principal of fifteen years at this school then regarded the school as "very important from the perspective that people have been together all along. We have very few transfers, very few people leave. A few retire but we don't have turnover of teachers at this school." Spanish language was very much a part of this historically bilingual school.

The principal passionately explained the role of Spanish in her school: "For our school, Spanish means as much as English does. It means that it's a language of communication, it's a language of academics, it's a language of reading and writing, language of pride and cultural heritage." The commitment of school staff and of parents to be a truly bilingual school is apparent when one enters the school grounds. Both languages are heard from the students, teachers, office staff, and visiting parents at the school. The bulletin boards are covered with notices in both languages, and the walls feature displays of many students' work in both languages.

The mission statement of the school states that the institution is 'committed to providing an effective bilingual education program that allows *all* students to successfully demonstrate appropriate grade level skills in all academic disciplines while becoming bilingual/biliterate.' As a response to the change in demographics in the community, the school began the Spanish/English DLIP in the early 1990s in order to serve the children of the community. The principal explained: "At that point the demographics had begun to change with more immigrant families coming in and many of those students were coming in with Spanish as their only language. So, for those children, the little bit of Spanish they were getting to support their heritage, their first language, was not sufficient. And we knew that. And we knew that if they were going to excel academically, they had to be taught in their home language. And could we do that in a bilingual program that devotes maybe an hour of Spanish a day? No. We couldn't do that. So, that is how the concept of Dual Language Immersion Program originated."

The team of teachers and principal also wanted to explore the needs of the neighborhood students. They were noticing that the grandparents in this neighborhood tended to speak Spanish, but the parents did not speak enough Spanish to teach their children. Reviving Spanish for these children became another focus of the DLIP. The loss of Spanish as the heritage language was a part of this community's history. In order to change the course of heritage language loss in the community, something, obviously, had to change. The introduction of a DLIP in this local elementary school was this change. The neighborhood children had the opportunity to learn their heritage language in school while learning the necessary subject matters. Fundamental changes began developing because of a few dedicated and conscientious teachers and supportive administrators and parents.

The program encourages children of recent immigrant families, mostly from Mexico, to learn English while maintaining their Spanish, and English speaking Nuevomexicano children to learn Spanish as their heritage language and also to maintain their English. For the bilingual children, the program maintains and develops their bilingual abilities. The program further reinforced the school's commitment to its central mission. A conscious effort is made in this school to demonstrate equal validation of both languages, by assigning them equal time and separation for use in delivering classroom instruction—therefore the program is called the Dual Language Immersion Program. The DLIP in this school developed as a result of the school's unflagging commitment to bilingualism for all students and community members.

In this DLIP, immigrant children from Mexico and other Latin American countries as well as local Nuevomexicano children learn together in both Spanish and English. New Spanish speaking students could learn best in this program where subject areas—Language Arts, Math, Social studies, Science—are taught in Spanish. They also become excellent language models during Spanish time for English speaking students. The Nuevomexicano 'neighborhood' students who are English speakers at the beginning of their school life learn to be truly bilingual in this program. According to the principal, "the major accomplishment or reward is to see neighborhood children who are English speakers do just as well in Spanish academically." The school consistently achieves high scores in the state's mandated standardized tests in both English and Spanish. The principal attributes this outstanding accomplishment to the school's well-implemented DLIP: "It proves that the program works. It proves that if the children have qualified teachers, excellent teaching, outstanding attention to detail and how, again how children are taught which content, what percentage of the day, who delivers the instruction, how is instruction delivered, you are going to have results."

In learning Spanish as their heritage language in this DLIP, these children feel that they have benefited on both the personal and social levels. The children report that they are able to communicate with their grandparents in Spanish, and also feel good about making their parents proud of being able to not only speak Spanish, but also read and write in Spanish. They also feel good that they have been able to help their Spanish-speaking classmates and community members if they needed help with English. Some of the parents had expressed a hope that their children would be helpful toward the Spanish-speaking newcomers who might be recent immigrants from Mexico in the neighborhood.

Anthony

One of the children attending this DLIP as a heritage language learner was Anthony. He was more comfortable in English than in Spanish, but showed the same eagerness to speak both languages. He sometimes faced teasing from his Spanish-speaking classmates for his uses of Spanish words, but he did not let the periodic teasing dissuade him from learning. He wrote in his journal that he felt discrimination from his Mexican classmates in the past because he was not a native Spanish speaker. Not understanding Spanish was also a source of embarrassment for him through the years. He had started his education in pre-school as an English speaker. Anthony's father was a Mexican American who spoke Spanish growing up and his mother was a Nuevomexicana who did not speak Spanish growing up. Anthony grew up speaking only English as his mother only spoke English at home.

Anthony's family was extremely proud of him becoming bilingual. The primary reason why he had wanted to learn Spanish in the DLIP was to communicate with his Spanish-speaking friends in the school and neighborhood. His father had also wanted Anthony to learn Spanish, so he could communicate with the people in the neighborhood who were speakers of Spanish. His mother's reasons for wanting her children to learn Spanish were more personal. She did not want her children to endure the same experiences as she had suffered—not knowing their heritage language. Anthony's mother revealed some resentment for not having learned her heritage language at home: "When I was young, I didn't have the opportunity to speak Spanish, learn Spanish. My parents didn't teach me. Well, they said they didn't want me to learn. I don't know what it was back then. It was a 'no no,' I guess."

She nursed a fairly strong resentment toward the fact that what her parents did from out of their best intentions actually lead to the loss of her heritage language. She mentioned how proud she was of Anthony for having developed so many compositions in Spanish. She added with sadness, even though she could not read them herself. When she was asked to identify herself with a term, she identified herself as an American first. And then, she said, "If I were fluent in Spanish, I would be (qualified to call myself) Hispanic."

Conclusion

DLIP created opportunities for these Nuevomexicano children to directly interact with recent immigrant Mexican children as their classmates, friends, and community members. These children were learning their heritage language with the help of their elementary school's DLIP and the beliefs of the parents in the importance of learning their heritage language, therefore their culture and identity. The parents and educators stopped being the observers of the forces of mainstream language and culture dominate their heritage language and culture. They realized that they could maintain their heritage and still succeed in the society and took action for a change through education of their children.

Maintaining a heritage language is not an easy task. The widespread trend of losing their heritage languages in the U.S. is a powerful force for minority language speakers. In her book about the Northern New Mexican Hispanic community, Roberts explains the continuing decline in traditional New Mexican Spanish language use and facility in the community:

> ...blame for the loss of language goes around and comes around. Students and teacher blame the parents for not reinforcing Spanish at home; parents first blame their own teacher for punishing them for speaking Spanish, and then their children's teachers for not instilling the language in the young; former teachers blame the state for forcing them to comply with the English-only law; and finally, the state department of education blames current teachers for not immersing children in Spanish.[15]

Recognizing the trend of heritage languages declining in the usage and fluidity as the generations grow in the global environment of English being the dominant language, bilingual education programs such as a DLIP could be a tool to change the course of globalization to create a multicultural society—moving towards an egalitarian society where no majority culture or language dominates others. "Bilingual education programs of the 21st century will have new dreams and new keywords that reflect the new and more powerful dreams of a diverse nation: biliteracy, enrichment, two-way program, language for global understanding, and heritage language preservation"[16]

In this day and age, with the powerful homogenizing forces of globalization sweeping our world, educators, community leaders, and parents all have to be aware of their responsibility to protect the invaluable knowledge traditions and culture preserved in diverse languages that still manage to survive today.

Questions for Critical Reflection

1. If you were forced to choose between being "global" or preserving your heritage, language and culture for yourself and/or your children, what would you do and why?

2. Discuss the extent to which concepts of, or business practices in, globalization in your community, or country, have driven people to abandon their native language.

3. Anthony's mother expressed regret for not having developed language skills in Spanish. She identified herself as American first, but she also pointed out that if she had Spanish as well, she would be Hispanic. To what extent do you feel that a language is an expression of a national identity?

4. How many languages are spoken in your country? How many are indigenous, and how many are imported from other regions of the world? Which are varieties are granted the label "language," and which are handed the label "dialect?"

5. Discuss possible objections that linguistic imperialists, or language purists, in your country might have as regards the kind of dual language immersion program (DLIP) discussed by the author. If globalization is so important, in what ways does bilingualism, or multi-lingualism, benefit people? What counter-arguments can be given to those who hastily criticize the kind of program discussed here?

References

[1] Joshua Fishman, *Language Loyalty in the United States* (The Hague: Mouton, 1966).
[2] Russell N. Campbell & Donna Christian, "Directions in research: Intergenerational transmission of heritage languages," in *Heritage Language Journal* (Spring 2003), 1.
[3] Calvin Veltman, "The Future of the Spanish Language in the United States," (NYC and Washington DC: Hispanic Policy Development Project, 1988).
[4] Veltman, *Ibid.*
[5] Eduardo Hernandez-Chavez, "Native Language Loss and its Impli-cations for Revitalization of Spanish in Chicano Communities," In *Language and Culture in Learning: Teaching Spanish to Native Speakers of Spanish,* eds. B.J. Merino, H.T. Trueba & F.A. Somaniego (Washington, DC: Falmer Press, 1993).
[6] Fishman, *Op. cit.* 81.
[7] *Ibid,* 4.
[8] James Crawford, *At War with Diversity: US Language Policy in an Age of Anxiety* (Clevedon, UK: Multilingual Matters Ltd, 2000).
[9] Christine Sims, "Native American Heritage Languages," In *Heritage Language Journal. v.1* (Spring 2003).
[10] Crawford, *Op. cit.*
[11] Maria Carreira, "Seeking Explanatory Adequacy: A Dual Approach to Understanding the Term 'Heritage Language Learner,'" in *Heritage Language Journal. v. 2* (Fall 2004).
[12] Kathryn J. Lindholm, "Bilingual Immersion Education: Criteria for Program Development," in *Bilingual Education: Issues and Strategies,* eds. H. Fairchild & C. Valadez (Newbury Park, CA: Sage, 1990), 91-105.
[13] The term Nuevomexicano addresses the ethnically Hispanic people who are natives of New Mexico, distinguishing them from Hispanic people who are native of Mexico, and the Hispanic/Latino population from other parts of the country. The unique history of New Mexico—being isolated from influences of other cultures especially in rural areas of the state—maintained unique Nuevomexicano culture (Gonzales-Berry & Maciel, 2000).
[14] Leroy Ortiz & Guillermina Engelbrecht, "Partners in Biliteracy: The School and the Community," *Language Arts* (1986).
[15] Shelley Roberts, *Remaining and Becoming: Cultural Crosscurrents in an Hispano School.* (Mahwah, NJ: Lawrence Erlbaum Associates, 2001), 50.
[16] Josue Gonzalez, "Editor's Introduction: Bilingual Education and the Federal Role, if any…" *Bilingual Research Journal. v. 26-2* (2002), v-ix.

CHAPTER NINE

FRIENDING FACEBOOK, EMBRACING YOUTUBE, AND TRUSTING TWITTER: THE INTERCULTURAL INFLUENCE OF SOCIAL MEDIA IN INDIA'S NETWORKED PUBLIC SPHERE

Debashis 'Deb' Aikat

Reading the morning newspaper is the realist's morning prayer.
One orients one's attitude toward the world either by God or
by what the world is. The former gives as much security
as the latter, in that one knows how one stands.
—Georg Wilhelm Friedrich Hegel[1]

Introduction

German philosopher Georg Wilhelm Friedrich Hegel's aphorism in the above epigraph aptly describes India's contemporary media consumption. India is among a few nations in the world where newspapers still thrive. More people read a newspaper in India every day compared to people in the United States, Europe and other parts of the developed world, where newspaper circulation has declined.[2]

In striking contrast to the sharp decline in newspaper readership worldwide, India's print media remain buoyant and have, arguably, been experiencing their most successful run in terms of journalism, profits, circulation, and growth. In India, "reading a print newspaper is a prestigious activity, instead of a throwback to a bygone era, in much the same way that it was for immigrants in the United States in the late 19th and early 20th centuries, when papers were aimed explicitly at European immigrants," according to the 2011 State of the News Media report.[3]

With sparse competition from the fledgling Internet media, India's newspaper market is the largest in the world. India's print media revenue and profits have soared and continues to grow by over 5.5% each year, according to 2013-2014 data compiled by India's Ministry of Information and Broadcasting.[4]

The significance and status of India's news media have been further enhanced by the rise of social media.[5] As the seventh-largest country by area and the second-most populous country after China, India is home to social media entities that complement a thriving traditional media that serve people from diverse social, ethnic, religious, and cultural origins.

India's news media represent a media milieu characterized by a booming readership of 94,067 registered print publications, more than 120 million Facebook subscribers interacting with friends and family, 80 million users trusting Twitter's microblog news messages, and more than 70 million viewers embracing YouTube.

India's proliferating news media inform, educate, empower and entertain a surging population of 1.3 billion, which is roughly one-sixth of the world's people. As one of the world's most ancient surviving civilizations, India's pre-historic origins date back to 70,000-50,000 BCE, when humans first migrated to India. With greater diversity than the continent of Europe, 21st century India is still one country fostered by a rich legacy in art, culture and learning that has endured with unbroken continuity to modern times.[6] In the post-modern digital age, social media are now playing an important new role in transforming Indian democracy.

Theoretical Preamble and Research Method

In a vibrant democracy such as India's, news content curation significantly contributes to the role of news as the "first rough draft of history," which is a theoretical concept that originated from the journalistic act of recording important events and disseminating information, at short notice and under quick deadlines.

India's media meticulously curate news content. In both scope and definition, curating news content refers to the act of discovering, gathering, and presenting news content typically using professional or expert knowledge. India's news content curators comprise journalists, bloggers, common citizens, and some amateurs engaged in identifying, selecting, collating and sharing relevant news content to target, and sometimes generate, audience interest.

In a world where news consumers are overwhelmed by a deluge of news information, in both digital and traditional forms, curating news content is an important journalistic mission. Besides filtering the news for easy consumption, curating news content facilitates a reliable and accessible record of news events as the "first rough draft of history" in India's democratic public sphere.

By situating the role of India's news media within a larger context of communication and challenges to globalization, this chapter reports on research that synthesizes multidisciplinary perspectives on how thriving newspapers, the rise of social media, and the forces of globalization have transformed lives, communities, and environments in India's democratic society. Based upon the results of an extensive case study, this chapter presents research that theorizes the role and significance of India's newspaper boom and the rise of social media. Drawing upon news as the "first draft of history" theoretical framework, this chapter concludes with analysis of the role of India's contemporary news media landscape in the democratic public sphere.

As a vast and highly complex nation, India provides intriguing insights into the role that news media play in the world's largest democratic society. Five methodological steps constituted the case study research to systematically analyze India's contemporary news media. As outlined by Eisenhardt, the case study research paradigm enables researchers to build theories.[7] The case study method was also selected because of its power to intrinsically effectuate a coherent contribution to theoretical developments.[8] Leading research methodologists, such as Creswell, Maxwell, and Merriam, have emphasized that case studies should incorporate the theoretical and philosophical underpinnings of the research paradigm.[9]

The theoretical concept of news as the "first rough draft of history" has engendered aspirations among journalists across the world to objectively report news events and accurate information within deadline pressures. Since such ethically responsible practices are specific to news media, we designed research analyses of multiple cases that were intricately merged with diverse theoretical issues in media research.[10] Runyan observed that a common criticism of the case study method was that, "many of them are based on conceptual confusions."[11] Other scholars have warned against "the risks of misjudging a single event and exaggerating available data."[12] The research reported in this chapter reduced these risks in methodology by increasing the number of cases in India's news media landscape for comparative analysis. We also enhanced the case study research method by drawing upon the methodology of related studies.[13] The case study method has been well established in studies of information systems[14] and media issues.[15] For instance, Lee analyzed in 2014 the introduction of NASDAQ by gathering news articles from six publications.[16] George and Pratt examined in 2012 socio-cultural issues associated with crisis communication from international perspectives.[17] Jaeger studied in 2005 the conceptual foundations of electronic government in a deliberative democracy.[18] The case study reported in this chapter also incorporated a comparative method by melding qualitative and quantitative strategies.[19]

India's Thriving Newspapers

Social media comprise a central role in the nation's political, socioeconomic, and cultural life where newspapers continue to thrive as a distinctive part of the India's rich cultural heritage. Mahatma Gandhi, the architect of India's freedom from British rule, played a prominent role as editor of three newspapers, *Young India*, *Harijan* (meaning "child of God," coined as a euphemism for Untouchables by Gandhi in 1931) and *Navajivan* ("new life"), which galvanized the demure people of India to fight against the seemingly invincible British ruler. After India won independence from Britain in 1947, newspapers gained increasing prominence as the democratic watchdogs for the nation, especially after the state-imposed press censorship of the mid-1970s.[20] India's social media have since reinforced Gandhi's vision of freedom in a democratic society.

Unaffected by the 2009 economic recession that dwindled advertising revenues and newspaper circulation worldwide, India emerged as the world's largest newspaper market by superseding China.[21] Six Asian nations dominated the world's top 100 paid newspapers by circulation in 2013. They were China (with 28 dailies), India (24), Japan (17), South

Korea (6), Thailand (3), and Indonesia (1), according to 2013 data from the International Federation of Audit Bureaux of Circulations.[22] In these Asian nations, rising incomes, population growth, burgeoning advertising revenues, escalating news readership, and surging literacy have contributed to a rapid rise in newspapers.

In sharp contrast to the rise of Asia in the world's top 100 paid newspapers by circulation, newspaper markets in the U.S. and Europe are reeling under vanishing revenues, job cuts, and the widespread belief that print media are now past their prime. The number of the world's top newspapers in European countries are down to single digits with the United Kingdom (9 dailies), Germany (1), and France (1). Only four U.S. newspapers, *The Wall Street Journal*, *The New York Times*, *USA Today*, and the *Los Angeles Times,* feature in the world's top 100 paid newspapers by circulation.[23] India, China, and Japan accounted for more than 60 percent of the world's newspaper sales, with United States comprising 14 percent, according to the World Association of Newspapers and News Publishers (WAN-IFRA).[24]

India's Internet penetration is low (15 %) and ranks 159 among 228 nations, according to 2013 global statistics from the International Telecommunication Union (ITU).219 The nation's low Internet penetration has prompted newspapers to enjoy rising circulation. The Registrar of Newspapers for India confirmed in 2013 that India was home to 94,067 registered print publications, comprising 12,511 newspapers and 81,556 periodicals with a total circulation of nearly 405 million copies every day.[25] This averaged to nearly 32 print media copies per 100 people for India's population of 1.27 billion.[26] Most of India's mainstream print media publish and maintain an active presence online, including social media. India's elite newspapers simultaneously publish color broadsheet editions in several cities and provide breaking news on their web sites for their domestic and international readers.

India may be among the few countries experiencing minimal effects of digital disruption because Internet penetration is still nascent and migration to the Internet is, at best, modest. In addition, few people in India have access to computers and this low digital penetration has enabled newspapers in India to summarily subdue the influence of the Internet era. This trend may change in the future, when Internet penetration rises.

The Dominant Reach of India's Broadcast Media

With a legacy of nearly a century, India's radio broadcasting represents a rich tradition that began with the Radio Club of Bombay's historic broadcast in 1923. Two private transmitters in Bombay and Calcutta began regular radio services in 1927. The Indian Government took over the transmitters in 1930 under the aegis of Indian Broadcasting Service, renamed All India Radio in 1936 and Akashvani (meaning "voice from the sky") after 1957. India's radio industry has grown rapidly with government reforms in 2005.

India's television landscape comprises a complex mix of cable television of over 686 active television channels featuring news and entertainment programs in English and 22 national languages. Of the 247 million television households, nearly 61% (150 million homes) are served by cable TV systems, direct-to-home (DTH) services, Internet Protocol television (IPTV) services, according to the Telecom Regulatory Authority of India (TRAI), the official body.[27]

India's state-run terrestrial TV network, Doordarshan (meaning "view from afar") reaches more than 92% of India's population through 1415 terrestrial transmitters and is one of the largest terrestrial television networks in the world. Faced with competition from private channels, Doordarshan has reconfigured its programs with sports, news and entertainment content and introduced a satellite television service with no subscription fees. Doordarshan's direct-to-home television service reaches nearly all (93%) of India's population through 35 channels beamed from 67 studio centers and a network of 1,415 terrestrial transmitters. While a significant part of Doordarshan's television content is entertainment, its news channel reaches nearly half (49.4%) of the Indian population, according to Doordarshan data. Doordarshan remains the most widely available network, especially in rural areas, where a majority of the population lives.

In addition to the traditional broadcast fare, India globally ranks among the top five YouTube content countries. YouTube had set up an India edition in May 2008; however, until 2011, India's YouTube content primarily constituted mainstream production houses and broadcast companies. Since 2012, native creators embraced YouTube by posting videos and hosting channels to reach new audience segments across genres.

International News Firms Launch Editions in India

To better understand the development of digital media in India, we should first trace the evolution of online news media worldwide. With the advent of a fully commercialized Internet in the 1990s came the digital transformation of the print, video, news, entertainment, and advertising industries. The disruptions to traditional media globally were significant and lasting. Even the mainstays of traditional media in America had to move with the new demands of a changing digital landscape. Long-established newspapers published online versions such as *The New York Times on the Web*, which went online on January 19, 1996, while *The Wall Street Journal Interactive Edition* was launched April 29, 1996. These developments marked a historic shift in the global media industry as the news consumer began reading news online and circulation of paper publications declined.

The first decade of the 21st century saw the appearance of "born on the World Wide Web" news entities such as Huffington Post (founded May 2005 in New York City), Buzzfeed (founded 2006 in New York City), and Mashable (founded May 2005 in Scotland). They were called "born on the World Wide Web" to distinguish them from the online versions of traditional newspapers. Additionally, the rise of social media in 2004 (when the social media giant Facebook was founded) initiated a dominant engagement of news content on social networks and on mobile devices. As multiple news platforms emerged, news media companies quickly evolved to provide rigorous and accessible journalism that targeted millions of people as their global audience.

Since Internet content can be accessed anywhere (by anyone with a connection), these global news media companies have reached out to India's surging population of English-speaking, web-savvy audience members who were eager to read a wide array of content comprising news, information, and entertainment. This has prompted multinational media firms and international entrepreneurs to invest in India's print media. Such investments began in 2002 when the Indian government eased a 1955 ban on foreign investment in the nation's magazines and newspapers among other media entities.

In the 21st century, India's high mobile phone penetration and a growing population of consumers have catalyzed renowned digital media companies to establish Indian editions. Since 2013, prominent digital news brands such as Gizmodo, Huffington Post, Quartz, Business Insider,

BuzzFeed, and Mashable have launched editions in India to offer localized content and garner advertising revenue. Digital ad spending in India is estimated to be around $900 million in 2015, compared to over $55 billion in the U.S. Many of these online media companies set up operations through media partnerships with prominent news organizations in India.

The News Narrative on India's Social and Mobile Platforms

India's low Internet penetration also highlights a striking contrast that reflects the urban-rural divide. Indians with "always on" Internet access are predominantly young, urban, web-savvy and influential. Indians without Internet access typically represent populations segments that are either senior citizens, rural, low income, neo-Luddites, or laggards in technology adoption. This has resulted in a noticeable digital divide in India. As Facebook Chief Executive Mark Zuckerberg announced in February 2015, "...we have to connect India. More than a billion people in India don't have access to the Internet. That means they can't enjoy the same opportunities many of us take for granted, and the entire world is robbed of their ideas and creativity."[28]

On February 9, 2015, Zuckerberg facilitated Facebook's India launch of the Internet.org initiative, which provides affordable mobile access to 38 websites for news, music, education, weather, and health facts. Internet.org seeks to accelerate Internet penetration in India and open new socio-economic opportunities for education, information and commerce. Such initiatives underscore the significance of Internet access in India, which was the sixth Internet.org nation with Zambia, Tanzania, Kenya, Colombia, and Ghana.

Even as India seems to lack widespread Internet access for the under-privileged population, India's digitally savvy segment revels in the large-scale use of technology, connects to open-access Internet platforms, and engages in online interactions that generate ideas, mobilize opinion, and engender citizen action.

Elections are always important news events, and the 2014 Indian elections were dubbed India's first "social media election" due to the significant online participation of citizens and politicians.[29] Social media platforms, which have opposed government censorship since 2011, became vital political campaign tools and a digital agora for free political expression and electioneering. As Cadel observed, "the 814 million eligible voters" and "a record 66% turnout" indicated that elections dominated the media agenda, and a significant segment of India's electorate "turned to Facebook and Twitter to talk politics."[30]

It was bigger news when India's elected officials effectively used social media. Since his May 26, 2014, election victory, India's Prime Minister Narendra Modi has featured in the elite group of global politicians active on social media. With more than 23 million Facebook fans and 7 million Twitter followers, Narendra Modi ranked second only to the US President Barack Obama. Such developments are significant because not everyone in India is an Internet consumer, let alone a social media innovator.

India's news media leaders closely monitor mobile connection trends because this kind of connectivity is driving India's digital growth. A majority of India's new users exclusively access the Internet through mobile devices. More than 70 percent of Internet page views in India originate from mobile devices, while 87 percent of all Facebook users access the net through mobile platforms. Nearly 94 percent of India's 300 million Internet subscriptions are mobile. But three-quarters of those mobile Internet users—over 210 million—use an excruciatingly slow 2G or Edge connection, instead of the latest version of mobile access. By 2016, India is likely to emerge as among the world's largest smartphone market with the United States. India's smartphone base, now at 135 million, is estimated to grow two to three times as fast as its overall mobile base (about 920 million subscriptions) or satellite and cable TV (145 million set-top boxes), which transcends the number of television sets with DVD or other media players attached to them.

News coverage of India's consumer rants on social media has increased. Thanks to burgeoning online access, consumers are increasingly complaining about various brands on Facebook, Twitter, and online consumer fora. India's online consumers follow discussions of popular brands on social media and vent their grievances online before seeking redress of complaints in India's time-consuming courts of law.

In India's emerging crowd-sourced communities, consumers also submit online reviews that evaluate their experience about a brand's services or products. Market studies indicate that more than two-thirds of consumers, who are online, read reviews before making their purchase decisions. Better information has led to a simple and obvious trend. Satisfied customers be come brand evangelists spreading praise about their products and services, whereas unhappy customers vilify the brand in their social circles.

As India's media function in a global 24/7 media environment, social media have emerged as an important source for companies to promote, to target and, more importantly, to connect with their consumers. Influential multinational firms and local companies are learning to appreciate the social media's power of making friends and influencing public opinion. Several Business to Consumer (B2C) companies are strategically developing Customer Relationship Management (CRM) programs to immediately resolve problems and avoid the possibility of a negative buzz vibrating across social media, which also attracts reports in traditional news entities.

With the growing number of smartphone and Internet users, India has emerged as a key market for social media activity with B2C companies engaged in CRM programs. According to the results of a February 2015 study on India's social media marketing carried out by Ernst & Young, major brands across India's industries are continuing to increase their participation in the new social media landscape. "Nearly 81 percent of the brands surveyed considered Facebook to be the most important platform. Almost 48 percent of surveyed brands think that Twitter is the second-most important platform to be on, closely followed by YouTube (43 percent surveyed brands considered it to be the third–most important channel)," the Ernst & Young study concluded.[31]

India's News Media as First Rough Draft of History

The theoretical evolution of news as "the first rough draft of history" may date back to the pre-historic development of journalism, but its conceptual origins can be traced to the 20th century. Significant theorizing of news as "the first draft of history" dates back to 1905 when a newspaper article in *The State* (Columbia, South Carolina) observed that, "The newspapers are making morning after morning the rough draft of history." The insightful article entitled, "The Educational Value of News," persuasively accentuated the importance of newspapers for daily readers, historians—and students in "modern" classrooms."[32] Some researchers attribute the news as "draft of history" aphorism to the *Washington Post* editorial writer Alan Barth who in a 1943 *New Republic* book review observed, "News is only the first rough draft of history."[33] Several contemporary writers attribute, "the first draft of history" dictum to Phil Graham (1915-1963), the *Washington Post's* late publisher and co-owner. His wife, Katharine Graham, who led the *Post* to prominence, stated in her 1997 autobiography, *Personal History*, that Phil Graham's statement about "first rough draft of history" has been "quoted to this day."[34]

News historians have successfully used computer-based linguistic and statistical tools to study events (such as strikes, demonstrations, and other types of collective conflict).[35] Several studies in the 1980s analyzed collective action using data from newspapers to focus on the occurrence, timing and sequencing of events such as regime changes, riots, revolutions, protests, and the founding of social movement organizations.[36] These and other studies highlight the theoretical value of news in reinvigorating media content as the "first rough draft of history."

As the first rough draft of history, newspapers have chronicled life and times in India since the 19th century with an intense emphasis on reporting politics, corruption, crime, fashion, business, scientific advances, investigative journalism, and human-interest events. Using newspapers as sources of cultural data, sociologist Roberto Franzosi has shown how news reports help researchers explore the rise of Italian fascism (1919-22)[37] and lynching in the U.S. state of Georgia (1875-1930) as narrated in over 1,200 newspaper articles from over 200 national, regional and local newspapers.[38] Franzosi explored issues of language and the measurement of text and narrative[39] and proposed that, "set theory provides the basic tools (namely, the cardinal number) necessary to go "from words to numbers" and this basic transformation has enabled researchers to quantitatively analyze qualitative data such as words.[40] Digital archives of India's news media have also facilitated research into how India's media have served society as an independent watchdog and contributed, invaluably, to efforts in maintaining a broader democratic exchange of ideas.

News researchers posit that the theoretical application of news as "the first rough draft of history" contributes significantly to the public memory of a nation. "It has become clichéd to assert that journalists write the first draft of history. Far less attention has been paid to who does the rewrites. Frequently, second drafts of history are also written by journalists," observed Edy, who studied in 2006 the journalistic uses of collective memory to propose a typology of how journalists used public past for collective memory in the news media.[41]

Any theoretical discussion of India's news media as the "first rough draft of history" is incomplete without assessing the veracity of news media as research resources. A growing number of researchers use digital technologies, such as online news archives, to analyze yesterday's newspapers and archived social media content. Such research has also prompted caution about the methodological attributes of validity and reliability while analyzing the text-based, digital archives of newspapers.[42] News reports may be subject to validity and reliability problems because they are influenced by journalistic news values and the vagaries of cultural reproduction.[43] Some studies have concluded that newspapers report "hard news" of protest events in a "relatively accurate" way, although news reporting is affected by selection bias, which suggests that the select subset of events covered and description biases may affect the veracity of coverage.[44]

India's news media have often been criticized for being shallow, inaccurate, and sometimes flagrantly biased. David Stoker warned about media bias in these words: "Of course, any reasonably sophisticated reader knows that all newspapers are at times inaccurate or else select, interpret and, at times, distort the events they report. Indeed, some newspapers will print what amounts to little more than barefaced lies. They must, therefore, be used with care, yet this must apply to any historical source."[45] The accuracy of news archives, in their digital form, has been another vital element. A 2013 study in the *Newspaper Research Journal* identified disparities between *The New York Times* database search results and the microfilm of its print edition raising concerns about the accuracy of the database content.[46] Despite such advantages and limitations, India's news media continue to be valued as the "first rough draft of history" and have emerged as a dependable source to analyze people, places, and viewpoints from various theoretical perspectives.[47]

Conclusion

In both theory and practice, India's news media, comprising the emerging online media and traditional entities, have thrived on a long-established tradition of creating the "first rough draft of history" from the nation's early days of newspaper journalism during British rule. Online media extend that cherished journalistic tradition of interpreting and enunciating news events with boundless possibilities such as in verbal and visual content and near-real-time coverage of news events as they occur.

Nearly 85 percent of all of our news originates in the work of newspapers (whether they produce it in print or online), posited author Alex Jones in his 2009 book on the future of the news and democracy.[48] The case study results that inform this chapter indicate that the prosperous times for India's news media may be attributed to six factors: (1) a rising literacy rate and a sustained culture of newspaper readership; (2) a vibrant economy that has reinvigorated India with increased advertising revenues, growing income levels with related surge in consumer spending, increased purchasing power of the middle class and rise in consumerism; (3) low Internet penetration that limits news choices to a media fare devoid of free content online; (4) widespread use of newspapers as primary sources of news consumption; (5) most of India's media entities are not affected by the profit motives of the stock market. For instance, most newspapers in India are owned and operated over succeeding generations by family entrepreneurs who have maintained decades-long ties with their community; and, (6) India's ongoing economic liberalization from 1991 led to rising international investment that has spurred growth of media. That growth has continued into the 21st century.

With up-to-the minute news disseminated in Twitter messages, YouTube videos, and Facebook newsfeeds, India's news media have strengthened their democratic duties of documenting the nation's general knowledge and public opinion. Such news media fare has enriched the interplay between old and new media. For instance, journalists monitor social media posts to compile insightful analyses of public opinion and, on the other hand, bloggers constantly crosslink to news articles online to ratify their considered reflections and opinions on a topic.

Based upon the theory and practice of news as the "first rough draft of history," this chapter has elucidated perspectives on India's news media, which clarify the extent to which India's intercultural communications have been transformed by the nation's globalized media paradigm. Research presented in this chapter reveals how India's news media have strengthened democracy by informing, educating, connecting, and entertaining people from diverse social, ethnic, religious, and cultural origins. India's multifaceted news platforms have raised the ante in democratic redress and thereby enriched the public mind in the nation's cherished democratic society. India's news media are, thus, not merely mediated sources of information for people to consume, but they have emerged as vitally important news sources open to anyone eager to understand, analyze, participate, and interpret the collective psyche of the nation. This model of intrinsic respect for democracy, peculiar to contemporary India, may well be the ideal antidote to the spread of neoliberal globalization—an infection plaguing democracies in many regions of the world.

Questions for Critical Reflection

1. The news media present wide range of representative views from people whose lives, communities, and environments have been reshaped, devalued, or erased by the forces of globalization. In what ways are emerging media revising or deviating from established norms by conceiving, perceiving, or disregarding intercultural boundaries?

2. In the ever-expanding globalization of the 21st century, do you find any apparent biases, stereotypes, or other problems in the news content of traditional media (such as newspapers, radio, and television) and emerging media (such as social media, mobile apps) as they refer and represent the cultures across the globe?

3. How do emerging media transgress traditional media? List and discuss some ways in which new media have wrested power and control from the global elite.

4. What are some of the ways in which media manipulate language and conceal or obscure the harsher realities of globalization?

5. What are some social, political, and economic behaviors that signify the rise of social media use in your community or society?

6. Various constitutive activities of social media lead to alternative modes of exchange and production (such as user-generated content), low cost distribution (such as email, web pages) and widespread consumption (such as YouTube videos, music sharing), and other forms of communication (such as Twitter messages, selfie images). What are some of the ethical and legal challenges to those who engage with these media?

7. What norms, values, and social hierarchies do social media promote or disrupt in relation to race, gender, and sexual identity?

Acknowledgments

The author gratefully acknowledges the work of Dr. Daniel Broudy, Dr. Jeffery Klaehn, and Dr. James Winter for leading this book project and offers thanks to five anonymous reviewers for their critiques to earlier versions of this research project. The author also thanks Ms. Divya Aikat and Mr. Vikram Aikat for research help and Dr. Jay Aikat for research feedback and ideas to enhance this study.

References

[1] Hegel wrote this and other aphorisms between 1803 and 1806 when he was an academician at University of Jena in Germany. For more details, see Georg Wilhelm Friedrich Hegel, *Miscellaneous Writings of G. W.F. Hegel*, ed., Jon Stewart. (Evanston, IL: Northwestern University Press, 2002), 247.

[2] See World Association of Newspapers and News Publishers (WAN-IFRA) "2009 and 2010 World Press Trends Database." accessed March 11, 2015, http://www.wptdatabase.org/

[3] Laura Houston Santhanam and Tom Rosenstiel, "Why U.S. Newspapers Suffer More than Others," *State of the Media 2011*, accessed March 11, 2015, http://stateofthemedia.org/2011/mobile-survey/international-newspaper-economics/.

[4] Government of India, *Ministry of Information & Broadcasting Annual Report 2013-14*, August 28, 2014, accessed March 11, 2015, http://mib.nic.in/linksthird.aspx.

[5] The term "social media" is used as plural in this chapter in accordance with the Chicago Manual of Style guidelines. It is worth noting that some other publications designate social media with initial capital letters, such as "Social Media."

[6] Monier Williams, *Indian Wisdom or Examples of the Religious, Philosophical, and Ethical Doctrines of the Hindūs: With a Brief History of the Chief Departments of Sanskrit Literature, and Some Account of the Past and Present Condition of India, Moral and Intellectual*. (London, UK: W.H. Allen & Company, 1875), accessed March 11, 2015, http://babel.hathitrust.org/cgi/pt?id=mdp.39015047654432;view=1up;seq=7

[7] Kathleen M. Eisenhardt, "Building Theories from Case Study Research," *Academy of Management Review* 14, no. 4 (1989): 532-550.

[8] Khairul Baharein Mohd Noor, "Case Study: A Strategic Research Methodology," *American Journal of Applied Sciences* 5, no. 11 (2008): 1602-1604; Robert K. Yin, *Applications of Case Study Research* (Los Angeles: Sage, 2012).

[9] Joseph A. Maxwell, *Qualitative Research Design: An Interactive Approach* (Thousand Oaks, Calif.: Sage Publications, 2013); Sharan B. Merriam, *Qualitative Research: A Guide to Design and Implementation* (San Francisco: Jossey-Bass, 2009).

[10] Robert E. Stake, *The Art of Case Study Research* (Thousand Oaks, Calif.: Sage, 1995).

[11] Charles C. Ragin, *The Comparative Method: Moving Beyond Qualitative and Quantitative Strategies.* (Berkeley, Calif.: University of California Press, 1987).

[12] Chris Voss, Nikos Tsikriktsis, and Mark Frohlich, "Case Research in Operations Management," *International Journal of Operations & Productions Management,* 22 (2), (2002): 202.

[13] See Amiso M. George and Cornelius B. Pratt, *Case Studies in Crisis Communication: International Perspectives on Hits and Misses* (New York: Routledge, 2012); Micky Lee, "What Can Political Economists Learn from Economic Sociologists? A Case Study of NASDAQ," Communication, Culture & Critique, 7 (June 2014), 246–263, doi: 10.1111/cccr.12043.

[14] Izak Benbasat, David K. Goldstein, and Melissa Mead, "The Case Research Strategy in Studies of Information Systems," *MIS Quarterly* 11, issue 3, (Sept. 1987): 369-386.

[15] Randall S. Sumpter, "Daily Newspaper Editors' Audience Construction Routines: A Case Study," *Critical Studies in Media Communication* 17, no. 3 (2000): 334-346.

[16] Micky Lee, "What Can Political Economists Learn from Economic Sociologists? A Case Study of NASDAQ," *Communication, Culture & Critique,* 7 (June 2014), 246–263, doi: 10.1111/cccr.12043.

[17] Amiso M. George and Cornelius B. Pratt, *Case Studies in Crisis Communication: International Perspectives on Hits and Misses,* (New York: Routledge, 2012).

[18] Paul T. Jaeger, "Deliberative Democracy and the Conceptual Foundations of Electronic Government," *Government Information Quarterly,* 22 (2005): 702–719.

[19] Charles C. Ragin, *The Comparative Method: Moving Beyond Qualitative and Quantitative Strategies.* (Berkeley, Calif.: University of California Press, 1987).

[20] Jyotika Ramaprasad, "Pre-, During and Post-Censorship Coverage of India by the *New York Times*," *Newspaper Research Journal* 9, no. 1 (fall 1987): 19-29.

[21] See World Association of Newspapers and News Publishers (WAN-IFRA) 2009 and 2010 World Press Trends Database. Accessed Sept. 6, 2014. http://www.wptdatabase. org/

[22] The International Federation of Audit Bureaux of Circulations, http://www.ifabc.org/ resources/data-reports%2065/country-specific-circulation-data.

[23] Based on data compiled from the Alliance for Audited Media, Media Intelligence Center, http://www.auditedmedia.com/data/media-intelligence-center.aspx.

[24] The World Association of Newspapers and News Publishers, or WAN-IFRA, accessed March 11, 2015, http://www.wan-ifra.org/microsites/publications.

[25] See ITU, "International Telecommunication Union Report on Percentage of individuals using the Internet." accessed March 11, 2015, http://www.itu.int/en/ITU-D/ Statistics/Pages/stat/default.aspx; ITU, "2014 Information and Communication Technologies Figures," news release of May 5, 2014, accessed March 11, 2015, http:// www.itu.int/net/pressoffice/press_releases/2014/23.aspx#.VCM9MxY1N8E; Also, Government of India, *Ministry of Information & Broadcasting Annual Report 2013-14*, August 28, 2014, accessed March 11, 2015, http://mib.nic.in/linksthird.aspx .Government of India, *Ministry of Information & Broadcasting Annual Report 2013-14*, August 28, 2014, accessed March 11, 2015, http://mib.nic.in/linksthird.aspx.

[26] Registrar of Newspapers for India, *Ministry of Information & Broadcasting: Press in India: 2012-13 Annual Report of the Office of the Registrar of Newspapers for India*, December 28, 2013, accessed March 11, 2015, http://rni.nic.in/.

[27] Census of India, "Population Enumeration Data (Final Population)," August 24, 2014, accessed March 11, 2015, http://www.censusindia.gov.in/Ad_Campaign/Referance_material.html.

[28] See Telecom Regulatory Authority of India (TRAI), "Highlights on Telecom Subscription Data as on 30th June 2014," TRAI press release of September 10, 2014, accessed March 11, 2015, http://www.trai.gov.in/WriteReadData/PressRealease/Document/PR-TSD-July,%2014.pdf

[29] Mark Zuckerberg, "We just launched Internet.org in India," last modified February 9, 2015, https://www.facebook.com/zuck/posts/10101899223817041:0.

[30] Press Trust of India. "Facebook, Twitter, Google change face of Indian elections." *The Times of India*. May 6, 2014, accessed March 11, 2015, http://timesofindia.indiatimes.com/home/lok-sabha-elections-2014/news/Facebook-Twitter-Google-change-face-of-Indian-elections/articleshow/34721829.cms. See also Raheel Khursheed, May 15, 2014 (3:41 p.m.), India's 2014 #TwitterElection, Twitter India Blog, accessed March 11, 2015, https://blog.twitter.com/2014/indias-2014-twitterelection.

[31] Emily Cadel, "Biggest winner in Indian election: American social media," USAToday.com, May 17, 2014, accessed March 11, 2015, http://www.usatoday.com/story/news/world/2014/05/17/ozy-india-election-social-media/9200069/.

[32] Ernst & Young. "Ernst & Young Social Media Marketing: India Trends Study: Insights from social media-savvy brands in India," last accessed February 19, 2015, http://www.ey.com/IN/en/Services/Advisory/EY-social-media-marketing-india-trends-study-2014

[33] See "The Educational Value of News" in *The State* (Columbia, South Carolina), December 5, 1905, Page 4, Column 4, accessed March 11, 2015, http://www.readex.com/blog/newspapers-rough-draft-history.

[34] Jack Shafer, "On The Trail of the Question, Who First Said (or Wrote) That Journalism is the 'First Rough Draft of History'?" *Slate*, Aug. 30 2010, accessed March 11, 2015, http://www.slate.com/articles/news_and_politics/press_box/2010/08/who_said_it_first.html.

[35] Katharine Graham, *Personal History*, 1st ed. (New York: A.A. Knopf, 1997), 324.

[36] Roberto Franzosi, "Narrative as Data: Linguistic and Statistical Tools for the Quantitative Study of Historical Events," *International Review of Social History* 43, no. S6 (1998): 81-104.

[37] Susan Olzak, "Analysis of Events in the Study of Collective Action," *Annual Review of Sociology* (1989): 119-141.

[38] See Roberto Franzosi, "Mobilization and Counter-Mobilization Processes: From the 'Red Years' (1919–20) to the 'Black Years' (1921–22) in Italy," *Theory and Society* 26, no. 2-3 (April 1997): 275-304; Roberto Franzosi and John W. Mohr, "New Directions in Formalization and Historical Analysis," *Theory and Society* 26, no. 2-3 (April 1997): 133-160; Roberto Franzosi, "The Return of the Actor. Interaction Networks among Social Actors during Periods of High Mobilization (Italy, 1919-1922)," *Mobilization: An International Quarterly* 4, no. 2 (Fall 1999): 131-149.

[39] Roberto Franzosi, Gianluca De Fazio, and Stefania Vicari, "Ways of Measuring Agency an Application of Quantitative Narrative Analysis to Lynchings in Georgia (1875–1930)," *Sociological Methodology* 42, no. 1 (August 2012): 1-42.

[40] See Roberto Franzosi, *From Words to Numbers: Narrative, Data, and Social Science*.

(Cambridge, UK: Cambridge University Press, 2004); Roberto Franzosi, *Content Analysis* (Los Angeles: Sage, 2008); and Roberto Franzosi, *Quantitative Narrative Analysis* (Thousand Oaks, Calif.: Sage, 2010).

[41] Roberto Franzosi, "From Words to Numbers: A Set Theory Framework for the Collection, Organization and Analysis of Narrative Data," *Socio-logical Methodology* 24 (1994): 105-136.

[42] Jill A. Edy, "Journalistic Uses of Collective Memory," *Journal of Communication* 49, no. 2 (1999): 71-85.

[43] David Deacon, "Yesterday's Papers and Today's Technology Digital Newspaper Archives and 'Push Button' Content Analysis," *European Journal of Communication* 22, no. 1 (2007): 5-25.

[44] Jose Barranco and Dominique Wisler, "Validity and Systematicity of Newspaper Data in Event Analysis." *European Sociological Review* 15, no. 3 (1999): 301-322.

[45] Jennifer Earl, Andrew Martin, John D. McCarthy, and Sarah A. Soule, "The Use of Newspaper Data in the Study of Collective Action," *Annual Review of Sociology* (2004): 65-80.

[46] David Stoker, "Should Newspaper Preservation Be a Lottery?" *Journal of Librarianship and Information Science* 31, no. 3 (1999): 133.

[47] Norman E. Youngblood, Barbara A. Bishop, and Debra L. Worthington, "Database Search Results Can Differ from Newspaper Microfilm," *Newspaper Research Journal* 34, no. 1, (winter 2013), 36-49.

[48] Glenn A. Bowen, "Document Analysis as a Qualitative Research Method," *Qualitative Research Journal* 9, no. 2 (2009): 27-40.

[49] Alex Jones, *Losing the News: The Future of the News that Feeds Democracy* (New York: Oxford University Press, 2009), 4.

Part III

Mass Communication, Media, and Manipulation

CHAPTER TEN

JOURNALISM: ROYAL, PROPHETIC, APOCALYPTIC

Robert Jensen

Introduction

I have spent my entire adult life working as either a journalist or a university professor, developing a love/hate relationship with both professions but learning one clear lesson: No matter how much we may try to avoid facing the question, intellectuals in every field have choices about how to position ourselves in relationship to power and privilege. That is especially true for journalists, despite the fact that they tend to reject the label of "intellectual" (thinking it sounds a bit haughty) and that many critics of journalism label the profession anti-intellectual (thinking that practitioners are not rigorous enough).

So, first, a definition of "intellectual work," which should not be used just as a synonym for "thinking," given that every day everyone thinks about things. Intellectual work suggests a systematic effort to (1) collect relevant information and (2) analyze that information to discern patterns that help us deepen our understanding of how the world works, (3) all in the service of helping people make judgments about how we want to shape the world. The key is "systematic effort," which requires intention and discipline. Defined that way, it's clear that lots of different kinds of people do this kind of intellectual work—not just professors, but students, organizers, political activists, journalists, and writers and researchers of various kinds. They engage in that systematic effort in search of the answers to questions about the natural world, technology, human behavior, and societies. Some focus on fairly small questions while others look more broadly.[1]

Societies subsidize intellectual work, allowing certain people the freedom to engage in those systematic efforts while others do the work of producing food, building shelter, providing services. This arrangement comes with some built-in tensions, since most intellectuals are subsidized by the institutions of the dominant culture. The people who run those institutions generally expect a return on the investment, which often leads them to want to put restrictions on the work of those subsidized intellectuals. At the same time, intellectual work requires creative and critical thinking, which argues for letting intellectuals operate with minimal control. These institutions prefer that research, writing, and teaching support the existing power system, and most intellectuals conform to that implicit expectation—either because they honestly believe in the system of power or because they want to avoid trouble.[2] But tensions arise when intellectuals follow paths that lead them to challenge the pre-ordained conclusions that the powerful prefer.

To explore those choices and tensions, I focus here on journalism, though these observations are relevant more generally. Journalism is a good place to look more closely because it is the intellectual arena where illusions of neutrality are most institutionalized, and because in a mass-mediated world it is a crucial institution in the shaping of public perceptions about almost everything.

Back to definitions: What is journalism? Ideally, journalists offer the public, in a timely fashion, a critical, independent source of information, analysis, and the varied opinions need-ed by citizens who want to play a meaningful role in the formation of public policy. The key terms are "critical" and "independent"—to fulfill the promise of a free press, journalists must be willing to critique not only specific people and policies, but the systems out of which they emerge, and they must be as free as possible from constraining influences, both overt and subtle. Included in that definition is an understanding of democracy—"a meaningful role in the formation of public policy"—as more than just lining up to vote in elections that offer competing sets of elites who represent roughly similar programs.

Mainstream Journalism

This discussion will focus on what is typically called mainstream journalism, the corporate-commercial news media. These are the journalists who work for daily newspapers, broadcast and cable television, and the rapidly expanding platforms on the Internet and other digital devices. Although there are many types of independent and alternative journalism of varying quality, the vast majority of Americans receive the vast majority of their news from these mainstream sources, which are almost always organized as large corporations and funded primarily by advertising.

Right-wing politicians and commentators sometimes refer to the mainstream media as the "lamestream," implying that journalists are comically incompetent and incapable of providing an accurate account of the world, likely due to a lack of understanding of conservatives. While many journalists—especially those at larger media outlets with more elite status—may be dismissive of the cultural values of conservatives, this critique from the right ignores the key questions about journalism's relationship to power. Focusing on the cultural politics of individual reporters and editors—pointing out that they tend to be less religious and more supportive of gay and women's rights than the general public, for example—diverts attention from more crucial questions about how the institutional politics of corporate owners and managers shapes the news and keeps mainstream journalism safely within a centrist/right conventional wisdom.

The managers of commercial news organizations in the United States typically reject that claim by citing the unbreachable "firewall" between the journalistic and the business sides of the operation, which is supposed to allow journalists to pursue any story without interference from the corporate front office. This exchange I had with a newspaper editor captures the ideology: After listening to my summary of this critique of the commercial news media system in the United States, this editor (let's call him Joe) told me proudly: "No one from corporate headquarters has ever called me to tell me what to run in my paper." I asked Joe if it were possible that he simply had internalized the value system of the folks who run the corporation (and, by extension, the folks who run the world), and therefore they never needed to give him direct instructions. He rejected that, reasserting his independence from any force outside his newsroom.

I countered: "Let's say, for the purposes of discussion, that you and I were equally capable journalists in terms of professional skills, that we were both reasonable candidates for the job of editor-in-chief that you hold. If we had both applied for the job, do you think your corporate bosses would have ever considered me for the position, given my politics? Would I, for even a second, have been seen by them to be a viable candidate for the job?"

Joe's politics are pretty conventional, well within the range of mainstream Republicans and Democrats—he supports big business and U.S. supremacy in global politics and economics. In other words, he's a capitalist and imperialist. On some political issues, Joe and I would agree, but we diverge sharply on the core questions of the nature of the economy and foreign policy.

Joe pondered my question and conceded that I was right, that his bosses would never hire someone with my politics, no matter how qualified, to run one of their newspapers. The conversation trailed off, and we parted ways without resolving our differences. I would like to think my critique at least got Joe to question his platitudes, but I never saw any evidence of that. In his subsequent writing and public comments that I read and heard, Joe continued to assert that a news media system dominated by for-profit corporations was the best way to produce the critical, independent journalism that citizens in a democracy needed. Because he was in a position of some privilege and status, nothing compelled Joe to respond to my challenge.

Partly as a result of many such conversations, I continue to search for new ways to present a critique of mainstream journalism that might break through that ideological wall. Here I will try theological terms, invoking the royal, prophetic, and apocalyptic traditions. Though journalism is a secular institution, the struggles that intellectuals have had with power are also a part of religious traditions, which provides a helpful vocabulary. The use of these terms is not meant to imply support for any particular religious tradition, or for religion more generally, but only to recognize that the fundamental struggles of human history play out in both religious and secular settings, and we can learn from all of that history. These categories are particularly helpful because of the multiple, cascading ecological crises we now face.

Ecological Sustainability

There is a growing realization that modern humans have disrupted planetary forces in ways we cannot control and do not fully understand. If we remain on our current trajectory there likely will come a point—not in some future millennium but possibly, perhaps likely, in this century—when the ecosphere cannot sustain human life as we know it. We cannot predict the specific times and places where dramatic breakdowns will occur, but we can know that the living system on which we depend is breaking down. When people ask James Howard Kunstler about the time frame for the "long emergency" (his phrase for our moment in history), he tells them that, "we've entered the zone."[3] As Bill McKibben puts it, "The world hasn't ended, but the world as we know it has—even if we don't quite know it yet."[4]

Look at any crucial measure of the health of the ecosphere in which we live—groundwater depletion, topsoil loss, chemical contamination, increased toxicity in our own bodies, the number and size of "dead zones" in the oceans, accelerating extinction of species and reduction of bio-diversity—and ask a simple question: Where we are heading? Remember also that we live in an oil-based world that is rapidly depleting the cheap and easily accessible oil,[5] which means we face a huge reconfiguration of the infrastructure that undergirds our lives.[6] Meanwhile, the desperation to avoid that reconfiguration has brought us to the era of "extreme energy" using even more dangerous and destructive technologies (hydrofracturing, deep-water drilling, mountain-top removal, tar sands extraction).[7] And, of course, there is the undeniable trajectory of climate disruption.[8]

Scientists these days are talking about tipping points[9] and planetary boundaries,[10] about how human activity is pushing the planet beyond its limits. Paleoecologist Anthony Barnosky of the University of California-Berkeley and 21 of his colleagues warn that human activity is likely forcing a planetary-scale critical transition, "with the potential to transform Earth rapidly and irreversibly into a state unknown in human experience."[11] This means that, "the biological resources we take for granted at present may be subject to rapid and unpredictable transformations within a few human generations."

This also means we are in trouble. The authors conclude with a simple set of recommendations:

> [A]verting a planetary-scale critical transition demands global cooperation to stem current global-scale anthropogenic forcings. This will require reducing world population growth and per-capita resource use; rapidly

increasing the proportion of the world's energy budget that is supplied by sources other than fossil fuels while also becoming more efficient in using fossil fuels when they provide the only option; increasing the efficiency of existing means of food production and distribution instead of converting new areas or relying on wild species to feed people; and enhancing efforts to manage as reservoirs of biodiversity and ecosystem services, both in the terrestrial and marine realms, the parts of Earth's surface that are not already dominated by humans.

McKibben, the first popular writer to alert the world to the threat of climate change, argues that humans have so dramatically changed the planet's ecosystems that we should rename the Earth, call it Eaarth:

> The planet on which our civilization evolved no longer exists. The stability that produced that civilization has vanished; epic changes have begun. We may, with commitment and luck, yet be able to maintain a planet that will sustain some kind of civilization, but it won't be the same planet, and hence it won't be the same civilization. The earth that we knew—the only earth that we ever knew—is gone.[12]

If McKibben is accurate—and I think the evidence clearly supports his assessment—then we can't pretend all that's needed is tinkering with existing systems to fix a few environmental problems; massive changes in how we live are required, what McKibben characterizes as a new kind of civilization.[13] No matter where any one of us sits in the social and economic hierarchies, there is no escape from the dislocations that will come with such changes. Money and power might insulate some from the most wrenching consequences of these shifts, but there is no escape. We do not live in stable societies and no longer live on a stable planet. We may feel safe and secure in specific places at specific times, but it's hard to believe in any safety and security in a collective sense.

These warnings are not new. In 1992, about 1,700 of the world's leading scientists issued a warning, which began:

Human beings and the natural world are on a collision course. Human activities inflict harsh and often irreversible damage on the environment and on critical resources. If not checked, many of our current practices put at serious risk the future that we wish for human society and the plant and animal kingdoms, and may so alter the living world that it will be unable to sustain life in the manner that we know. Fundamental changes are urgent if we are to avoid the collision our present course will bring about.[14]

Two decades later, warnings continue to be ignored. Pick a metaphor. Are we a car running out of gas? A train about to derail? A raft going over the waterfall? Whatever the choice, it's not a pretty picture.[15] Again, this kind of realization is not confined to "radical environmentalists" or "leftist revolutionaries." Consider the judgment of James Wolfensohn near the end of his term as president of the World Bank:

It is time to take a cold, hard look at the future. Our planet is not balanced. Too few control too much, and many have too little to hope for. Too much turmoil, too many wars, too much suffering. The demographics of the future speak to a growing imbalance of people, resources, and the environment. If we act together now, we can change the world for the better. If we do not, we shall leave greater and more intractable problems for our children.[16]

Royal Journalism

Most of today's mainstream corporate-commercial journalism is royal journalism, using the term "royal" not to describe a specific form of executive power but as a critique of a system that concentrates authority and marginalizes the needs of ordinary people. The royal tradition, in this context, describes ancient Israel, the Roman empire, European monarchs, or contemporary America—societies in which those holding concentrated wealth and power can ignore the needs of the bulk of the population, societies where the wealthy and powerful offer pious platitudes about their beneficence as they pursue policies to enrich themselves.

Theologian Walter Brueggemann identifies this royal consciousness in ancient Israel after it sank into disarray, when Solomon overturned Moses—affluence, oppressive social policy, and static religion replaced a God of liberation with one used to serve an empire. This dangerous royal consciousness develops not only in top leaders, but also throughout the privileged sectors, often filtering down to a wider public that accepts royal power. Brueggemann labels this a false consciousness: "The royal consciousness leads people to numbness, especially to numbness about death."[17]

The inclusion of the United States in a list of royalist societies may seem odd, given the democratic traditions of the country, but consider a nation that has been at war for more than a decade, in which economic inequality and the resulting suffering has dramatically deepened for the past four decades, in which the level of climate change denial has increased as the evidence of the threat becomes undeniable. Brueggemann describes such a culture as one that is "competent to implement almost anything and to imagine almost nothing."[18]

Nearly all of mainstream corporate-commercial journalism is, in this sense, royal journalism. It is journalism without the imagination needed to move outside the framework created by existing systems of power. CNN, MSNBC, and FOX News all practice royal journalism. *The New York Times* is ground zero for royal journalism. Marking these institutions as royalist doesn't mean no good journalism ever emerges from them, or that they employ no journalists who are capable of challenging the royal arrangements. Instead, the term recognizes that these institutions lack the imagination necessary to step outside of the royal consciousness on a regular basis.

Over time, they add to the numbness rather than jolt people out of it.

The royal consciousness of our day is defined by unchallengeable commitments to an industrial worldview, within a hierarchical economy, run by an imperial nation-state. These technological, economic, and national fundamentalisms produce a certain kind of story about us, a dominant narrative that Brueggemann describes as "therapeutic, technological, consumerist militarism." The dominant culture encourages the belief that we can have anything we want without obligations to anyone within a system that fosters "competitive productivity, motivated by pervasive anxiety about having enough, or being enough, or being in control." All of this bolsters notions of "US exceptionalism that gives warrant to the usurpa tious pursuit of commodities in the name of freedom, at the expense of the neighbor."[19]

If one believes royal arrangements are just and sustainable, then royal journalism could be defended. If the royal tradition requires deep critique, then a different journalism is necessary.

Prophetic Journalism

Given the failure of existing systems and the multiple crises those systems have generated, the ideals of journalism call for a prophetic journalism.[20] The first step in defending that claim is to remember what real prophets are not: They are not people who predict the future or demand that others follow them in lockstep.

In the Hebrew Bible and Christian tradition, prophets are the figures who remind the people of the best of the tradition and point out how the people have strayed. In those traditions, using our prophetic imagination and speaking in a prophetic voice requires no special status in society, and no sense of being special. Claiming the prophetic tradition requires only honesty and courage.

When we strip away supernatural claims and delusions of grandeur, we can understand the prophetic as the calling out of injustice, the willingness not only to confront the abuses of the powerful but also to acknowledge our own complicity. To speak prophetically requires us first to see honestly—both how our world is structured by systems that create unjust and unsustainable conditions, and how we who live in the privileged parts of the world are implicated in those systems. To speak prophetically is to refuse to shrink from what we discover or from our own place in these systems. We must confront the powers that be, and ourselves.

The Hebrew Bible offers us many models. Amos and Hosea, Jeremiah and Isaiah—all rejected the pursuit of wealth or power and argued for the centrality of kindness and justice. The prophets condemned corrupt leaders but also called out all those privileged people in society who had turned from the demands of justice, which the faith makes central to human life. In his analysis of these prophets, the scholar and activist Rabbi Abraham Joshua Heschel concluded:

Above all, the prophets remind us of the moral state of a people: Few are guilty, but all are responsible. If we admit that the individual is in some measure conditioned or affected by the spirit of society, an individual's crime discloses society's corruption. In a community not indifferent to suffering, uncompromisingly impatient with cruelty and falsehood, continually concerned for God and every man, crime would be infrequent rather than common.[21]

Following Brueggemann's critique of royal consciousness, the task of those speaking prophetically is to "penetrate the numbness in order to face the body of death in which we are caught" and "penetrate despair so that new futures can be believed in and embraced by us."[22]

Brueggemann encourages preachers to think of themselves as "handler[s] of the prophetic tradition," a job description that also applies to other intellectual professions, including journalism. Brueggemann argues that this isn't about intellectuals imposing their views and values on others, but about being willing to "connect the dots":

Prophetic preaching does not put people in crisis. Rather it names and makes palpable the crisis already pulsing among us. When the dots are connected, it will require naming the defining sins among us of environmental abuse, neighborly disregard, long-term racism, self-indulgent consumerism, all the staples from those ancient truthtellers translated into our time and place.[23]

None of this requires journalists to advocate for specific politicians, parties, or political programs; we don't need journalists to become propagandists. Journalists should strive for real independence, but not confuse that with an illusory neutrality that mainstream journalists invoke to stay safely within the boundaries defined by the powerful. Again, real independence means the ability to critique not just the worst abuses by the powerful within the systems, but to critique the systems themselves.

Apocalyptic Journalism

Invoking the prophetic in the face of royal consciousness does not promise quick change and a carefree future, but it implies that a disastrous course can be corrected. But what if the justification for such hope evaporates? When prophetic warnings have not been heeded, what comes next? This is the time when an apocalyptic sensibility is needed.

Again, to be clear: "Apocalypse" in this context does not mean lakes of fire, rivers of blood, or bodies lifted up. The shift from the prophetic to the apocalyptic can instead mark the point when hope in existing systems is no longer possible and we must think in dramatically new ways. Invoking the apocalyptic recognizes the end of something. It's not about rapture but a rupture severe enough to change the nature of the whole game.

So, while the prophetic imagination helps us analyze and strategize about the historical moment we're in, it is based on a faith that the systems in which we live can be reshaped to stop the worst consequences of the royal consciousness, to shake off that numbness of death in time. What if that is no longer possible? Then it is time to think about what's on the other side. Because no one can predict the future, these two approaches are not mutually exclusive; people should not be afraid to think prophetically and apocalyptically at the same time. We can simultaneously explore immediate changes in the existing systems and think about new systems.

Fred Guterl, the executive editor of *Scientific American*, models that spirit when he describes himself on the "techno-optimistic side of the spectrum" but does not shy away from a blunt discussion of the challenges humans face:

> There's no going back on our reliance on computers and high-tech medicine, agriculture, power generation, and so forth without causing vast human suffering—unless you want to contemplate reducing the world population by many billions of people. We have climbed out on a technological limb, and turning back is a disturbing option. We are dependent on our technology, yet our technology now presents the seeds of our own destruction. It's a dilemma. I don't pretend to have a way out. We should start by being aware of the problem.[24]

137

I don't share Guterl's techno-optimism, but it strikes me as different from the routine technological fundamentalism of the culture. He doesn't deny the magnitude of the problems and recognizes the real possibility, perhaps even the inevitability, of massive social dislocation. Though he ends up with a different sense of where hope lies, he doesn't avoid reality:

> [W]e're going to need the spirit with which these ideas were hatched to solve the problems we have created. Tossing aside technological optimism is not a realistic option. This doesn't mean technology is going to save us. We may still be doomed. But without it, we are surely doomed.[25]

A bit closer to my own assessment is James Lovelock, a Fellow of the Royal Society whose work led to the detection of the widespread presence of CFCs in the atmosphere. Most famous for his "Gaia hypothesis" that understands both the living and non-living parts of the earth as a complex system that can be thought of as a single organism, he suggests that we face these stark realities immediately:

> The great party of the twentieth century is coming to an end, and unless we now start preparing our survival kit we will soon be just another species eking out an existence in the few remaining habitable regions....We should be the heart and mind of the Earth, not its malady. So let us be brave and cease thinking of human needs and rights alone and see that we have harmed the living Earth and need to make our peace with Gaia.[26]

In a culture that encourages, even demands, optimism no matter what the facts, it is important to consider alternative endings. As Barbara Ehrenreich points out, this obsession with so-called positive thinking undermines critical thinking and produces anxiety of its own.[27] Anything that blocks us from looking honestly at reality, no matter how harsh the reality, must be rejected. To borrow from James Baldwin, "Not everything that is faced can be changed; but nothing can be changed until it is faced." That line is from an essay titled "As Much Truth as One Can Bear,"[28] about the struggles of artists to help a society, such as white-supremacist America, face the depth of its pathology. Baldwin, writing with a focus on relationships between humans, suggested that a great writer attempts "to tell as much of the truth as one can bear, and then a little more." If we think of Baldwin as sounding a prophetic call, an apocalyptic invocation would be "to tell as much of the truth as one can bear, and then all the rest of the truth, whether we can bear it or not."

That task is difficult enough when people are relatively free to pursue the truth without constraints. Are the dominant corporate-commercial/advertising-supported media outlets likely to encourage journalists to pursue the projects that might lead to such questions? If not, the apocalyptic journalism we need is more likely to emerge from the margins, where people are not trapped by illusions of neutrality or concerned about professional status.

The apocalyptic tradition reminds us that the absence of hope does not have to leave us completely hopeless, that life is always at the same time about death, and then rejuvenation. While all the other creatures of this world will experience death, we will not only experience death, but will also have to ponder it. When the evidence of our failure is final and all hope is gone, can we retain our ability to imagine beyond the failure? Earth is over, but we can start to imagine what we can salvage on Eaarth.

Questions for Critical Reflection

1. The author observes that, "tensions [in society] arise when intellectuals follow paths that lead them to challenge the preordained conclusions that the powerful prefer." Nicolaus Copernicus famously followed his assumptions, overturned the preordained belief that Earth was the center of the universe, and consequently received widespread castigation from the centers of social power during his time. Discuss a more recent example of someone following his or her scientific, or moral instincts, only to be marginalized, vilified, or imprisoned.

2. The author observes that the, "owners and managers" of mass media "shape the news and keep mainstream journalism safely within a centrist/right conventional wisdom." Cite and discuss a recent example that supports this view and an example that challenges it.

3. If large agenda-setting media organizations are constrained by their corporate charters to serve the interests of profit, discuss one way in which the public might acquire unbiased news free from the management and influence of corporate power.

4. The author refers to our current tendencies to avoid the massive "re-configuration" of our comfortable lives and cites the latest explorations of "extreme energy" as examples of that pervasive avoidance. Discuss any details you already understand about the examples of "extreme energy" given in the essay. How do media inform the public about their dangers to the environment and to society? What other examples of "extreme energy" can be discussed?

5. Discuss any contemporary journalist (or concerned citizen) who in the "prophetic" tradition the author describes has "condemned corrupt leaders" and "called out all those privileged people in society who had turned from the demands of justice."

6. Suppose the author is donning the hat of a journalist here. Does he strike a "royal," "prophetic," or "apocalyptic" tone? What words or expressions does the author use which lend support to this view?

References

[1] For a more extensive discussion, see Robert Jensen, *Arguing for Our Lives* (San Francisco: City Lights, 2013).

[2] For a foundational discussion of this in the context of the United States, see Noam Chomsky, "The Responsibility of Intellectuals," *New York Review of Books*, February 23, 1967.

[3] James Howard Kunstler, *Too Much Magic: Wishful Thinking, Technology, and the Fate of the Nation* (New York: Atlantic Monthly Press, 2012), p. 2.

[4] Bill McKibben, *Eaarth: Making Life on a Tough New Planet* (New York: Times Books/Henry Holt, 2010), p. 2.

[4] Bill McKibben, *Eaarth: Making Life on a Tough New Planet* (New York: Times Books/ Henry Holt, 2010), p. 2.

[5] One leading experts sums up this "inescapable conclusion": "[T]he major oil finds of the postwar era—those mammoth discoveries whose prolific output sustained rising global energy needs for nearly half a century—are no longer capable of satisfying the world's requirements." Michael T. Klare, *The Race for What's Left: The Global Scramble for the World's Last Resources* (New York: Metropolitan, 2012), p. 31.

[6] For an accessible review of the data and a blunt evaluation of options, see James Howard Kunstler, *The Long Emergency: Surviving the End of Oil, Climate Change, and Other Converging Catastrophes of the Twenty-First Century* (New York: Grove, 2006).

[7] Naomi Klein, "Addicted to Risk," TED, December 2010. http://www.ted.com/talks/naomi_klein_addicted_to_risk.html

[8] Naomi Klein, "Capitalism vs. the Climate," *The Nation*, November 28, 2011. http://www.thenation.com/article/164497/capitalism-vs-climate/; "Naomi Klein Warns Global Warming Could Be Exploited by Capitalism and Militarism," Democracy Now! March 9, 2011.

[9] See the June 7, 2012, issue of *Nature*. http://www.nature.com/nature/journal/v486/n7401/index.html

[10] See the September 23, 2009, issue of *Nature*. http://www.nature.com/news/specials/planetaryboundaries/index.html

[11] Anthony Barnosky, et al, "Approaching a state shift in Earth's biosphere," *Nature*, June 7, 2012. http://www.nature.com/nature/journal/v486/n7401/full/nature11018.html

[12] McKibben, *Eaarth*, p. 25.

[13] See Naomi Klein's book, *This Changes Everything: Capitalism vs. The Climate* (Toronto: Alfred Knopf, 2014), for latest elaboration.

[14] Henry Kendall, a Nobel Prize physicist and former chair of the Union of Concerned Scientists' board of directors, was the primary author of the "World Scientists' Warning to Humanity." http://www.ucsusa.org/ucs/about/1992-world-scientists-warning-to-humanity.html

[15] For a review of the threats, see Fred Guterl, *The Fate of the Species: Why the Human Race May Cause Its Own Extinction and How We Can Stop It* (New York: Bloomsbury, 2012).

[16] James D. Wolfensohn, address to the Board of Governors of the World Bank Group, September 23, 2003. http://siteresources.worldbank.org/NEWS/Resources/jdwsp-092303.pdf

[17] Walter Brueggemann, *The Prophetic Imagination*, 2nd ed. (Minneapolis: Fortress Press, 2001), p. 41.

[18] *Ibid.*, p. 40.

[19] Walter Brueggemann, *The Practice of Prophetic Imagination* (Minneapolis: Fortress Press, 2012), p. 4.

[20] I use this term to describe an ideal that all journalists should aspire to achieve. One former journalist and journalism professor uses the term in a slightly different and more limited way, to describe a segment of the existing industry. He defines "prophetic journalism" as "a journalism of passion, polemic, and moral opinion that has come to exist alongside the modern ethic of objectivity and the commercial elements of profit making that dictate so much of what journalism constitutes today." Doug Underwood, *From Yahweh to Yahoo! The Religious Roots of the Secular Press* (Urbana: University of Illinois Press, 2002), p. 21.

[21] Abraham J. Heschel, *The Prophets* (New York: HarperCollins, 1962/2001), p. 19.

[22] Brueggemann, *The Prophetic Imagination*, p. 117.

[23] Brueggemann, *The Practice of Prophetic Imagination*, p. 69.

[24] Guterl, *The Fate of the Species*, p. 5.

[25] *Ibid.*, p. 170.

[26] James Lovelock, *The Revenge of Gaia: Earth's Climate Crisis and the Fate of Humanity* (New York: Basic, 2006), p. xiv.

[27] Barbara Ehrenreich, *Bright-sided: How Positive Thinking Is Undermining America* (New York: Picador, 2010).

[28] James Baldwin, "As Much Truth As One Can Bear," in Randall Kenan, ed., *The Cross of Redemption: Uncollected Writings* (New York: Pantheon, 2010), pp. 28-34.

CHAPTER ELEVEN

THE RELEVANCE OF THE HERMAN-CHOMSKY PROPAGANDA MODEL IN THE 21ST CENTURY MEDIA ENVIRONMENT

Florian Zollmann

Introduction

In their classic work *Manufacturing Consent: The Political Economy of the Mass Media*, Edward S. Herman and Noam Chomsky set forth a propaganda model (henceforth PM) of news media performance.[1] The PM proceeds on the assumption that corporate-capitalist interests are situated in opposition to societal interests. Accordingly, Herman and Chomsky argue that it is the media's

> ...function to amuse, entertain, and inform, and to inculcate individuals with the values, beliefs, and codes of behaviour that will integrate them into the institutional structures of the larger society. In a world of concentrated wealth and major conflicts of class interest, to fulfil this role requires systematic propaganda.[2]

The PM is based on industrial organization analysis. Building on the so called Gatekeeper research published in the 1970s and 1980s and applying a political economy framework, PM's analytical categories identify the institutional composition and market environment of the news media as a state-corporate power structure that impacts on media performance.[3] More specifically, the PM situates the news media in a market system guided by a set of five interacting and reinforcing news "filters": (1) The size and ownership of the media, (2) advertising funding, (3) use of official sources, (4) anti-communism, fear, and ideology, and (5) the pressure that powerful groups exercise on news organizations also referred to as "flak."[4] These operating principles lead the Western news media to operate as a propaganda system on behalf of dominant state-corporate elite interests.

The PM provides a structural model based on the assumption of a rather homogenous and powerful media system that facilitates ideological media discourses. This perspective has been marginalized in contemporary academic curricula and debates. I had this experience when studying for a Media and Communication degree at a major university in Germany. Herman and Chomsky's work was not included in the curriculum. The same, arguably, applies for universities in the USA, UK, and Canada where the PM has been marginalized.[5]

It has to be expected that with the emergence of the new digital media environment, critical perspectives such as the PM's are further challenged. Scholars and media pundits celebrate the deliberative potential of the new media environment. In fact, the Internet has emerged as the major media platform in the early 21st century impacting on how news is produced, distributed, and consumed.[6] Consequently, scholars such as Andrew Hoskins and Ben O'Loughlin see, "a new media ecology" in "the emergence of networked, diffuse communication and participatory media."[7] New technologies, Hoskins and O'Loughlin suggest, enable multi-dimensional and interactive communication flows. This, it is further argued, has led to a diversification of communication channels opening up the public sphere. As a consequence, models such as the PM that emphasize linear and homogenous media performance appear to be redundant.[8]

In this essay, I argue that contrary to these postulations, there is strong evidence that the PM is still relevant today. Cracks in the system have, at times, allowed for more open coverage, as predicted. Grassroots interventions, facilitated by online media, have been able to alter the dominant discourse on issues. However, on a macro-level, the elite grip over news media as postulated by the PM's "filters" is still decisive. This will be elaborated in the following discussion that updates the PM's filters to account for changes in the new media environment. I will mostly draw from studies about the media systems of the USA and UK.[9] However, it is plausible and supported by academic research that other state-corporate-capitalist media systems such as the Canadian operate in a similar fashion.[10] Indeed, under neoliberal "globalization," the corporate sector has consolidated its power over states situated in the northern hemisphere. As William K. Carroll mapped out in an empirical study:

> The global corporate network is overwhelmingly a Euro-North American configuration. This shows the enduring influence of a North Atlantic ruling class, which has long been at the centre of global corporate power.[11]

The US, UK, and Canadian media are integrated into the corporate power structure that overlaps these three core states of the world capitalist system.[12] Hence, as will be discussed in the following sections, multileveled corporate influences on news choices are to be expected.

Corporate-Market Pressures: Ownership, Size, and Advertising Dependency

In its initial formulation, the PM's first and second news "filters" describe the media's concentration in size/ownership as well as dependencies on and links with other elite institutions particularly the advertising industry. While media organizations constitute independent entities, they are integrated into the corporate market system and rely on advertising revenues for their economic survival. This has several structural implications: corporations are legally obliged to prioritize profits over other—such as journalistic—imperatives. Markets further pressure media to operate cost effectively. These institutional constraints encourage media concentration and the recycling of information at the expense of investigations. As a further consequence, media corporations are integrated into conglomerates that share interests in various business sectors.

The advertising industry comprises similar corporate conglomerates that aim to place advertisements in a business supportive environment. Hence, media have to produce content worthy to be funded by corporate shareholders and advertisers in order to maintain operations. As a result, media can reflect audience interests only in so far as their messages do not violate the core interests of the corporate sector. Moreover, a bias towards the interests of wealthier audiences who are targeted by advertisers is to be expected. [13] Within media organizations, owners and managers, who are themselves part of the business community via interlocking boards and social circles, guide journalistic behavior through the selection and appointment of personnel as well as rewards and reprimands. Journalists adjust to such pressures via internalization of dominant values and self-censorship. Because of the identified market, corporate funding, and the internal constraints that the PM assumes, as Herman argues, formally autonomous media entities operate on the basis of "common outlooks."[14]

In contrast to the PM's perspective, scholars have pointed out that the economic structure of the news media has changed as a result of technological advances and the Internet. For instance, Robert G. Picard sees a transformation of the classic business model of news media organizations that rested on media power and the domination of audience and advertising markets diversifying the norms and practices of journalism thus potentially bringing down media conglomerations.[15] It could be asked then whether the Internet has disabled the PM's first and second filters. We can answer this question by assessing the degree to which the Internet has impacted on (1) the proliferation and concentration of news media organizations and markets and (2) advertising dependency. As will be shown below, both issues are interrelated.

(1) Digital Internet technology has removed spectrum scarcity entry barriers thus allowing for the establishment of a substantial amount of so-called "online-only" news providers.[16] These organizations add to the mix as they publish news from the international to the hyper-local level. If online-only providers operate outside traditional media conglomerates and are able to produce independent journalistic content, this might weaken the significance of the PM's first filter. However, there are several caveats in regard to this assumption. Although there are no technological barriers, the market actually functions as an entry barrier for online-only operations. While it is technically easy to establish news-based web-offerings or individual weblogs, it is costly to produce editorial content on the scale of a traditional newspaper publication or news broadcaster. Thus, the amount of online-only providers that actually comprise journalistic editorials is small in comparison to offshoots of traditional news media organizations. In fact, most online news is provided by traditional media operations.[17]

Additionally, the majority of online-only operations that produce independent journalistic content tend to provide lifestyle, entertainment, and sports information rather than factual news of social importance.[18] The market also incentivizes online-only providers to use aggregated news and PR material in order to remain cost-effective.[19] Moreover, online-only operations must appeal to the advertising industry as personalized and other advertisements are still the major revenue source in the online realm.[20] Investigative news offerings that do not rely on advertising funding such as *The Intercept*—which is an exception—have to cope with ownership pressures as they rely on wealthy donors.[21]

The insignificance of online-only operations is also reflected in terms of audience reach. If online visits are considered, in 2010/11, the world's top ten sites included only one online-only operation.[22] According to a Pew survey, in 2010, 80 percent of online traffic to news and information sites was concentrated on 7 percent of sites. 67 percent of these top sites were under control of traditional news organisations, 13 percent were content gathering sites, and only 14 percent were online-only operations.[23] In the US, there was only one online-only operation in the top ten of the most used sites whereas in Britain the top ten included only television and newspaper offshoots as well as content aggregators.[24] James Curran consequently argues that the Internet "has not undermined leading news organisations" but "enabled them to extend their hegemony across technology."[25]

Online audience concentration is related to search engine biases and network effects. Matthew Hindman studied the number of hyperlinks pointing to political information websites because linkage correlates with a site's search engine ranking and visits. According to the study, link distribution "approximates a power law, where a small set of hypersuccessful sites receives most of the links."[26] Hindman's study provides "little support" to the argument that the Internet enables "an epochal shift from broadcasting to narrowcasting" because the prospect of establishing a political website "is usually equivalent to hosting a talk show on public access television at 3:30 in the morning."[27] Moreover, Hindman provides evidence that "online audience concentration equals or exceeds that found in most traditional media."[28]

In effect, the multileveled economic constraints outlined above facilitate economic and journalistic media concentration and point to the fact that PM's first filter is highly relevant for the online realm.[29]

(2) An argument could be made that the power of the advertising filter

has decreased because the adindustry has shifted investment away from traditional news media to Internet advertising, thus decreasing the leeway that the advertising industry has over news production.[30] However, such an argument misses a crucial point: the traditional news media has largely been unable to compensate for its advertising losses via alternative revenue streams. Curran speaks of "devastating consequences" as the "loss of advertising has led to closure and contraction" in the news media industries of the US and UK.[31]

Thus, by implication, the advertising filter remains in place for that part of the news media, which has been able to sustain advertising funding. In fact, it could be argued that as ad competition increases, commercial news media operations have to act even more sensitively towards the interests of the remaining advertising sponsors. This is so because, as yet, advertising losses can hardly be recuperated via alternative revenue streams.[32] As a further consequence, those segments of the news media that had been unable to sustain sufficient advertising funding have either ceased to exist or had to downsize newsroom capacities. This has led to closures of news operations, shrinkages of staff, and further reliance on recycled information that is used at the expense of original journalistic content.[33]

It can thus plausibly be argued that, at this point in time, the Internet has indirectly strengthened the power of advertising vis-à-vis the news media industry. Moreover, losses in advertising funding have encouraged media concentration thereby increasing the relative size of media conglomerations. The news media's losses in advertising revenue have not only contributed to strengthening PM's second news filter but also the first one.

In conclusion, far from breaking up media monopolies, the new media environment has facilitated conglomeration and the power of sponsors. As Robert W. McChesney states: "The Internet has proven to be more effective at centralizing corporate control than it has been at enhancing decentralisation, at least in news media."[34]

Sources

PM's third filter stresses the media's reliance on elite sources related to the government as well as to other powerful institutions. These ties are established in order to maintain a stable and "reliable flow of the raw material of news."[35] The third filter implies that as a result of organizational and professional/ideological imperatives heavy inclusion of official sources at the expense of societal perspectives is to be expected. Additionally, the PM theorizes the market component behind the media's sourcing strategies. Herman and Chomsky argue that economic constraints force media personnel to concentrate on a narrow range of news beats, which guarantee the daily demand for fresh news and information. Elite sources tend to be seen as more credible due to their "status and prestige" in society.

Furthermore, elite sources can sanction media organizations with access denials in cases of unfavorable coverage. Following other, less credible sources enhances the costs of research and fact-checking, in particular if media organizations anticipate "criticism of bias and the threat of libel suits."[36] Herman and Chomsky also point to the ability of the corporate community and state institutions to produce massive PR campaigns which, by far, exceed the resources that can be spent by the cumulative effort of non-governmental or grassroots organizations and are often used by the media for their cost effectiveness.[37] In sum:

> [...] the large bureaucracies of the powerful *subsidise* the mass media, and gain special access by their contribution to reducing the media's costs of acquiring the raw materials of, and producing, news [emphasis in the original].[38] The PM expects the news media to be drawn towards official elite circles when acquiring news sources and story angles. With the emergence of the new media environment the pool of available news queues has potentially increased. Technological devices such as the Internet and mobile phones might facilitate the media's use of alternative sources.[39] Thus, Aleks Krotoski writes in the British liberal newspaper *The Observer* that reporters "find a multiplicity of perspectives and a library of available knowledge that provides the context for stories" online and "increasingly, the stories are coming from the web."[40] If that were the case, then the impact of the PM's third filter would have been mitigated to the degree that journalists rely on non-official news sources and angles drawn from the new media environment. But have journalists actually altered their working routines in a substantive way?

It is theoretically implausible to assume significant changes in journalistic behavior. As discussion of the PM's first and second filters has revealed, commercial bottom-line pressures have increased in the new media environment. It is, thus, to be expected that the news media will be drawn towards officials in order to operate cost effectively—precisely as theorized by the PM. As Curran writes:

> [...] fewer journalists are expected to produce more content, as a consequence of newsroom redundancies, the integration of online and offline news production, and the need to update stories in a 24-hour news cycle. This is encouraging journalists to rely more on tried-and-tested, mainstream news sources as a way of boosting output.[41]

This observation gains support from a study by Justin Lewis, Andrew Williams, and Bob Franklin who examined major British news media (*Guardian, Independent, The Times, Daily Telegraph, Daily Mail*, BBC and ITV) in order to understand domestic newsroom reliance on pre-packaged news material.[42] The research found evidence for overwhelming newsroom reliance on PR subsidies:

> Overall then, the study verified that at least 41 per cent of press articles and 52 per cent of broadcast news items contain PR materials which play an agenda-setting role or where PR material makes up the bulk of the story [...] [emphasis in the original].[43]

Considering the origins, a significant amount of PR emerged from powerful sectors: 38 percent originated from the business /corporate sector, 23 percent from public bodies, and 21 percent from the government. In contrast, only 11 percent were sourced from NGOs/charities, 5 percent from professional associations and 2 percent from citizens.[44] These findings support the PM's assumption that due to their economic might and perceived credibility, powerful organizations are better positioned to subsidize news than are grassroots and civil society organizations. Moreover, if Lewis, Williams and Franklin's study mirrors the performance of the best part of the liberal news media in Britain, it is unlikely that other news media sectors differ for the better.

Empirical evidence also suggests that the news media have favored official sources when covering a range of important issues. For instance, major studies on UK and US news media coverage of the 2003 Iraq War and the subsequent military occupation point to the news media's heavy inclusion of official viewpoints at the expense of other societal perspectives in accordance with the traditional gate-keeping pattern.[45]

We can also assess striking cases that potentially allowed for open coverage because they constituted so-called uncontrolled events. For example, the Abu Ghraib torture scandal of 2004 had the potential to draw critical and diverse news coverage because of the existence of photographic material that could have easily been spread via technological devices. In fact, such material was available and facilitated in news media channels. However, as W. Lance Bennett, Regina G. Lawrence, and Steven Livingston argue, the Bush administration was able to impose its frames on the US news media, which portrayed Abu Ghraib as an isolated story of abuse despite the existence of extensive evidence indicating "a possible policy of torture laid bare."[46] This case study suggests that the media rarely steps outside of the discourse parameters provided by official elites. Bennett, Lawrence, and Livingstone consequently argue, in line with PM predictions, that news reporting on foreign policy "is seriously constrained by mainstream news organizations' deference to political power."[47]

There are, of course, examples when news media have been able to break away from official perspectives. For instance, the US news media provided a more independent picture in its coverage of the aftermath of Hurricane Katrina.[48] Critical coverage was possible because the Katrina case was largely devoid of official news management activities. Absence of an official government response allowed reporters on the scene to file and publish an independent picture of the event.[49] However, as such events occur only rarely, Bennett, Lawrence, and Livingston describe Katrina coverage as "the exception that proves the rule of the press being largely dependent on the government to filter, define, and accent the news."[50]

In conclusion, the third filter remains highly relevant in the new media environment particularly when media covers issues that affect elite interests. Open coverage in terms of sources and perspectives only occurs under rare circumstances, when uncontrolled events and elite disengagement with media activities convene.

When observing news media performance on a macro level, it becomes evident that the constraints of the corporate market system facilitate traditional journalistic practices that tend to marginalise the vast range of possible story angles and sources that the new media environment potentially provides. To quote again from Bennett, Lawrence, and Livingstone:

> Despite all the jostling and scooping, the explosion of the Internet and the blogosphere, and the persistence of hard-nosed independent journals of opinion, the bulk of the nation's news media still ends up with much the same daily result across the vast number of papers and programs.[51]

Flak

PM incorporates *flak* as the fourth filter. Flak campaigns can generally be described as a "negative response to a media statement or program."[52] Flak puts pressure on media organizations to abide by or follow a specific agenda. The impact of flak is usually related to the power of the originator. Due to their economic might, governments, corporations and state-corporate sponsored think tanks are the dominant producers of flak.[53]

The technological structure of the Internet potentially allows for a free flow of information. Sheldon Rampton thus argues that flak may only be relevant for the offline realm.[54] However, it could be expected that flak is actually used to undermine dissenting voices which make use of the deliberative aspects of the new technology. Furthermore, considering the striking inequality in Western democracies and the monetary power of state and corporate agencies, it seems plausible to assume that flak campaigns unfold in accord with the pattern described by the PM.[55] It is difficult to establish a representative picture of flak campaigns that are presently instituted because they often occur in secret. In the following, I will discuss a range of contemporary campaigns and techniques that can be regarded as flak.

The major flak campaign of the day currently unfolds in the online realm against the platform WikiLeaks and its lead editor Julian Assange. WikiLeaks has been releasing classified government, intelligence and military information provided by whistleblowers.[56] Reports released in 2010—such as *Collateral Murder, The War Logs,* and *Cablegate*—shed light on government and military abuses. US government agencies responded to the publications with criminal investigations into Assange and other WikiLeaks affiliates. A Grand Jury to investigate possible charges under the Espionage Act of 1917 was established.[57] The US government also pressured online providers, public bodies, and commercial companies to abstain from publishing material circulated by WikiLeaks or otherwise support the organization.[58] Institutions such as VISA, Master Card, PayPal, and Bank of America ceased providing financial services to WikiLeaks.[58] These actions were accompanied by a public smear campaign against Assange and WikiLeaks that was echoed in major mainstream media channels.

A second major flak campaign has been orchestrated against Edward Snowden and the journalists who published his revelations of classified documents that led to the NSA Scandal. This included public smear campaigns against Snowden and the investigative journalist Glenn Greenwald who broke the Snowden case for the British national newspaper *The Guardian* and who is, at the time of this writing, employed by *The Intercept*.[60]

It should be further noted that the extensive surveillance apparatus revealed by the Snowden revelations can be regarded as an important element of flak in the online realm.[61] Surveillance potentially targets news media organizations, journalists and their sources, political activists as well as whistleblowers. Knowing about surveillance puts pressure on actors and organizations to toe the official line. As Christian Fuchs argues:

> Surveillance by nation states and corporations aims at controlling the behavior of individuals and groups, i.e., they should be forced to behave or not behave in certain ways because they know that their appearance, movements, location, or ideas are or could be watched by surveillance systems.[62]

Overall, WikiLeaks and the Snowden case constitute only the tip of the iceberg. Western governments have tightened pressures on potential whistleblowers and journalists who might publish their material. For instance, the Obama administration's Department of Justice has arguably engaged in an unprecedented attack against whistleblowers, which includes retroactive spying on prominent journalists to obtain the identity of their sources.[63] The Obama administration has charged several whistleblowers because they leaked classified information. As Jamie Tarabay writes on Al Jazeera America: "President Barack Obama campaigned on a pledge of expanded government transparency, yet his administration has charged more Americans with violating the Espionage Act by leaking classified information than all previous administrations combined."[64] Similarly, in its first-ever published report on the USA, the Committee to Protect Journalists commented: "The [Obama] administration's war on leaks and other efforts to control information are the most aggressive [...] since the Nixon administration."[65]

The outlined activities add to a range of flak measures that are currently exercised: pressures by powerful lobby groups, government restrictions on journalists' movements (censorship, press pools, embedding, escorts), and violent acts against media personnel.[66]

Ideology

The ideology of "anti-communism," as Herman and Chomsky argue, has been used to mobilize the domestic population against actors and states who threaten US state-corporate interests. For instance, the media has often adopted anti-communist rhetoric in order to gain support in favor of foreign interventions or to weaken domestic working-class organization and legislation.[67] Scholars such as Robert M. Entman argue that the dissolution of the Soviet Union destabilized the ideological Cold War consensus allowing for more nuanced coverage than the PM would predict.[68] Does this then signify the end of ideology?

While after the disintegration of the Soviet Union anti-communism has declined, other ideological devices have been substituting for the PM's fifth filter. For example, a belief in the free market has been reinforcing ideological pressures in the media industries. Herman suggests that political developments in support of markets are assumed to be benevolent whereas "non-market mechanisms are suspect"—and these assumptions are reflected in ideological discourses.[69] Moreover, after the 9/11 terrorist incidents in New York, the "war on terrorism," sometimes accompanied by "a liberal 'humanitarian' discourse," has become a new and powerful notion to frame and understand political events.[70]

Finally, there is an overarching ideological device that has prevailed throughout the Cold War and is applied in manifold ways today. The British historian Mark Curtis terms this concept the idea of "basic benevolence" of Western democracies.[71] This concept is particularly relevant for assessing media reporting on foreign policy issues and conflicts. News media coverage, Curtis argues, endorses or accepts that foreign policy is driven by noble intentions such as to promote "democracy, peace, human rights, and development."[72] Even if media criticism is extensive, Curtis writes, journalists still assume benevolent intent.[73]

Indeed, it is perhaps one of the most consistent findings in research on media representations of foreign policy issues that coverage tends to neglect what is referred to as fundamental criticism—which translates into questioning underlying mo-tives and doctrines of Western policy as well as their devastating outcomes.[74] On the other hand, this ideology is constructed in ways that actions by so-called "enemy" states are easily reprimanded and, at times, inflated to the highest levels of criminality.[75] This leads to a double standard in media reporting as casualties of state-violence are only worthy to be covered if victimisation can be utilized to enforce elite interests.[76]

Conclusion

As Herman and Chomsky stated in 1988, the PM's filters illuminate the "basis and operations of what amount to propaganda campaigns;" they define newsworthy items and set the parameters of discourse.[77] Journalists work under these constraints mostly with integrity and commitment, and formally adhere to professional news values, because "the operation of these filters occurs so naturally [...] that alternative bases of news choices are hardly imaginable."[78]

This discussion clearly evidences the workings and applicability of the PM's news filters in the 21st century new media environment. Of course, as Herman and Chomsky noted the impact of the PM's filters on media performance can vary in different time/space contexts leaving room for variations in coverage. For instance, a country's political, military, and economic investment can impact on the degree of closure in foreign policy reporting.[79] Yet, as a net result of the workings of the PM's filters, the news media systematically serves state-corporate elite interests in important domains. And this process has been encouraged by neoliberal globalization during the course of which corporate power was strengthened.

Moreover, it is clearly visible that the PM emphasizes dynamics in the sense that the dominant state-corporate institutions will counteract openings in the propaganda system that occur as a result of technological progresses or ideological changes. This process is currently unfolding as state-corporate interests close up open spaces in the new media environment via flak and surveillance. Moreover, large corporations have been colonizing the new media environment restricting the diversity of and access to the Internet. But even more significant than these developments are the major institutional flaws of the corporate capitalist media system. As long as news media operate in a profit-driven market system underpinned by advertising funding, propagandistic media performance will be incentivized. And this also applies to the new media environment.

Questions for Critical Reflection

1. If mass media reflect the interests of the "dominant state-corporate power structure," the author suggests that, "Grassroots interventions, facilitated by online media, have been able to alter the dominant discourse on issues." Discuss any examples of these so-called grassroots inventions that have successfully changed the discourse.

2. The author points out that large media organizations rely on advertising revenue and, thus, prioritize profits over journalism. The implication, he observes, is that information is recycled at the expense of investigation. Elaborate on this phenomenon in the corporate news market. Cite evidence of this in your community, state, or country.

3. One criticism of corporate media is that it serves to reinforce the social and economic status quo. What are some possible reasons why Herman and Chomsky's Propaganda Model has seen such a sustained exclusion from media analysis in academia throughout Europe and North America? To what extent can the PM help explain media performance in your community or country?

4. The author cites Julian Assange as a figure whose work in Wikileaks has created a potential threat to established power. Since the publication of *Collateral Murder*, *The War Logs*, and *Cablegate*, among others), how has the corporate media been used by the elite to marginalize and manage the public image of Assange?

5. The author refers to previous pressures that helped shape news stories during the Cold War era, such as anti-communism ideology. He notes that

today these pressures have morphed into an ideology of free market capitalism. Discuss any examples from national media that appear to reinforce the promise of wealth and power preached through the gospel of the free market.

6. If the neoliberal form of globalization, at present, wields the greatest influence over the public discourse and the news, why is it important (or useful) to take a systematic approach, such as the one offered by the PM, to critically analyze news media?

References

[1] Edward S. Herman and Noam Chomsky, *Manufacturing Consent: the Political Economy of the Mass Media* (1988; repr., London: The Bodley Head, 2008).

[2] Herman and Chomsky, 1.

[3] The PM was initially put forward by Edward S. Herman, see "Gatekeeper Versus Propaganda Models: a Critical American Perspective," in *Communicating Politics: Mass Communications and the Political Process*, eds. Peter Golding, Graham Murdock and Philip Schlesinger (New York, NY: Holmes & Meier, 1986), 171-196.

[4] For an overview, see Herman and Chomsky, 2-29.

[5] See also Andy Mullen, "Twenty Years On: the Second-Order Prediction of the Herman-Chomsky Propaganda Model," *Media, Culture & Society* 32, no. 4 (2010): 673-690.

[6] See Robert G. Picard, "Twilight or New Dawn of Journalism? Evidence from the changing news ecosystem," *Journalism Studies* 15, no. 5 (2014): 500-510.

[7] Andrew Hoskins and Ben O'Loughlin, *War and Media: the Emergence of Diffused War* (Cambridge: Polity Press, 2010), 2; 185.

[8] Hoskins and O'Loughlin, 10; 185. For a similar arguments see Manuel Castells, "Communication Power: Mass Communication, Mass Self-Communication, and Power Relationships in the Network Society," in Media and Society, ed. James Curran (London: Bloomsbury Academic, 2010), 12.

[9] The first part of each of the following sections discussing how the PM's filters were originally described by Herman and Chomsky draws from this author's Ph.D. thesis. See Florian Zollmann, "Manufacturing Wars? A Comparative Analysis of US, UK and German Corporate Press Coverage of the US Occupation of Iraq" (Ph.D. diss., University of Lincoln, UK, 2012).

[10] For comparative data see Zollmann. See also Jeffery Klaehn, *Filtering the News: Essays on Herman and Chomsky's Propaganda Model* (Montreal: Black Rose Books, 2005). Anthony DiMaggio, *When Media Goes to War: Hegemonic Discourse, Public Opinion and the Limits of Dissent* (New York: Monthly Review Press, 2009).

[11] William K. Carroll, *The Making of a Transnational Capitalist Class: Corporate Power in the 21st Century* (London: Zed Books, 2010), 224.

[12] For evidence on global media integration see Edward S. Herman and Robert W.

McChesney, *The Global Media: The New Missionaries of Corporate Capitalism* (London: Cassell, 1997). For the world capitalist system see Immanuel Wallerstein, "The Rise and Future Demise of the World Capitalist System: Concepts for Comparative Analysis," *Comparative Studies on Society and History* 16, no. 4 (1974): 387-415.

[13] For the classic work on advertising sponsorship of the news media see Erik Barnouw, *The Sponsor: Notes on Modern Potentates* (1978; repr. 3rd edn., New Brunswick: Transaction Publishers, 2006).

[14] Edward S. Herman, "The Propaganda Model: a Retrospective," *Journalism Studies* 1, no. 1 (2000): 105.

[15] See Picard 504-505, who writes:

> Large, inefficient, slow-moving news organizations are being transforming into smaller, more agile forms and embracing new processes and approaches to news. They are becoming more networked, cooperating with other information providers and producers, and engaging with the public itself. This is producing competing and colliding logics of professional journalism, commerce, and participation, and the tensions between these is forcing negotiations of values, norms, and practices.

[16] Online-only organizations are news operations that are not subsidiaries from traditional print and broadcasting news media. They include professional media organizations, news portals, search engines, user platforms, and weblogs. For this classification of online only providers see Christoph Neuberger, Christian Nuernbergk and Melanie Rischke, "Journalismus—neu vermessen. Die Grundgesamtheit journalistischer Internetangebote—Methode und Ergebnisse," in *Journalismus im Internet: Profession— Partizipation—Technisierung*, eds. Christoph Neuberger, Christian Nuernbergk and Melanie Rischke (Wiesbaden: VS Verlag für Sozialwissneschaften, 2009), 204-206.

[17] For instance, a census study of journalistic online offerings in Germany found that only 8 percent of all offerings were online-only providers with a professional editorial department. The total amount of online-only operations was 22.9 per cent, of which 7.8 percent were portals, 3.6 percent weblogs, 1 percent user platforms, and 2.6 percent news search engines. 77.1 percent of all offerings were offshoots from traditional news media organisations. For the data see Neuberger, Nuernbergk and Rischke, 222.

[18] See Robert W. McChesney, *Digital Disconnect: How Capitalism is Turning the Internet Against Democracy* (New York, NY: The New Press, 2013), 193.

[19] See McChesney, 188-189.

[20] See McChesney, 188.

[21] See Ted Rall, "What Really Went Wrong at First Look Media." *Ted Rall's Rall Blog*, November 4, 2014, http://rall.com/2014/11/04/exclusive-syndicated-column-what-really-went-wrong-at-first-look-media.

[22] See James Curran, "Reinterpreting the Internet," in *Misunderstanding the Internet*, eds. James Curran, Natalie Fenton and Des Freedman (London: Routledge, 2012), 19.

[23] See Curran, 19.

[34] See Curran, 19.

[35] Curran, 19.

[26] Matthew Hindman, *The Myth of Digital Democracy* (Princeton: Princeton University Press, 2009), 40.

[27] Hindman, 56.

[28] Hindman, 17.

[29] See McChesney, 188, who argues that "if anyone can make money doing online journalism, it will almost certainly be as a very large, centralized operation, probably a monopoly or close to it."

[30] For this argumentation see Picard, 507. For data on the decline in advertising revenues see Curran, 20.

[31] Curran, 20.

[32] For instance, in the USA, advertising still accounts for about two thirds of the news industry's overall revenue. New income streams only account for about 7 percent of the revenue and investments from other sources such as venture capital or philanthropy account for about 1 percent of the revenue. For data see Amy Mitchell, "State of the News Media 2014." *Pew Research Journalism Project*, March 26, 2014, http://www.journalism.org/2014/03/26/state-of-the-news-media-2014-overview/.

[33] For evidence see Curran, 20-1. See also McChesney, chapt. 6.

[34] McChesney, 190.

[35] Herman and Chomsky, 17.

[36] Herman and Chomsky, 18.

[37] Herman and Chomsky, 18-21.

[38] Herman and Chomsky, 21.

[39] For an overview of the argument see Steven Livingston and W. Lance Bennett, "Gatekeeping, Indexing, and Live-Event News: Is Technology Altering the Construction of News," *Political Communication* 20, no. 4 (2003): 363-380.

[40] Aleks Krotoski, "What effect has the internet had on journalism? The web is a valuable tool, but old-fashioned press practices can still be the best." *The Observer*, February 20, 2011, http://www.theguardian.com/technology/2011/feb/20/what-effect-internet-on-journalism.

[41] Curran, 20-21.

[42] See Justin Lewis, Andrew Williams, and Bob Franklin, "A Compromised Fourth Estate? UK News Journalism, Public Relations and News Sources," *Journalism Studies* 9, no. 1 (2008): 1-20.

[43] Justin Lewis, Andrew Williams, and Bob Franklin, 10.

[44] Justin Lewis, Andrew Williams, and Bob Franklin, 12.

[45] For studies on UK news media coverage of the Iraq War that demonstrate heavy inclusion of official at the expense of alternative sources and actors see Piers Robinson, Peter Goddard, Katy Parry, and Craig Murray, with Philip M. Taylor, *Pockets of Resistance: British News Media, War and Theory in the 2003 Invasion of Iraq* (Manchester: Manchester University Press, 2010), 78-80. Justin Lewis, Rod Brookes, Nick Mosdell, and Terry Threadgold, *Shoot First and Ask Questions Later: Media Coverage of the 2003 Iraq War* (New York: Peter Lang, 2006). Howard Tumber and Jerry Palmer, *Media at*

War: The Iraq Crisis (London: Sage, 2004). For US news media coverage of the Iraq War see Susan D. Moeller, *Media Coverage of Weapons of Mass Destruction* (Maryland: Center for International Security Studies at Maryland, 2004). John Nichols and Robert W. McChesney, *Tragedy and Farce: How the American Media Sell Wars, Spin Elections, and Destroy Democracy* (New York: New Press, 2005). For US and UK news media coverage of the occupation of Iraq see Zollmann.

[46] W. Lance Bennett, Regina G. Lawrence, and Steven Livingston, *When the Press Fails: Political Power and the News Media from Iraq to Katrina* (Chicago, ILL: University of Chicago Press, 2007), 107.

[47] Bennett, Lawrence and Livingston, 107.

[48] See Bennett, Lawrence and Livingston, 10.

[49] See Bennett, Lawrence and Livingston, 10.

[50] Bennett, Lawrence and Livingston, 10.

[51] Bennett, Lawrence and Livingston, 56.

[52] Herman and Chomsky, 24.

[53] Herman and Chomsky, 24-27.

[54] According to Rampton: "On the internet itself, however, flak is not much of a deterrent to free discourse. Lawsuits are difficult to mount and even more difficult to win, especially given the ease with which people can blog or email anonymously." See "Has the Internet Changes the Propaganda Model?" *The Center for Media and Democracy's PR Watch*, 22 May, 2007, http://www.prwatch.org/news/2007/05/6068/has-internet-changed-propaganda-model.

[55] For data on inequality and corporate monetary power in the USA see William Domhoff, "Wealth, Income and Power." *Power in America*, 2013, http://www2.ucsc.edu/whorulesamerica/power/wealth.html. For data on corporate power in Britain see David Miller and William Dinan, "The Rise of the PR Industry in Britain, 1979-98," *European Journal of Communication* 15, no. 1 (2000): 5-35. For corporate power and coercion see David Miller and William Dinan, *A Century of Spin: How Public Relations Became the Cutting Edge of Corporate Power* (London: Pluto Press, 2008).

[56] The following section on WikiLeaks mainly draws from Julian Assange with Jacob Appelbaum, Andy Müller-Maguhn and Jérémie Zimmermann, *Cypherpunks: Freedom and the Future of the Internet* (New York, NY: OR Books, 2012), 13-19.

[57] Assange et al., 13-14.

[58] Assange et al., 14-15.

[59] Assange et al., 16.

[60] For a discussion of the campaign against Greenwald see Glenn Greenwald, *No Place to Hide: Edward Snowden, the NSA and the Surveillance State* (London: Hamish Hamilton, 2014), chapter 5.

[61] For an overview see "The NSA Files." *The Guardian*, 2014, http://www.theguardian.com/us-news/the-nsa-files.

[62] Christian Fuchs, "Critique of the Political Economy of Web 2.0 Surveillance," in *Internet and Surveillance: The Challenges of Web 2.0 and Social Media*, eds. Christian Fuchs, Kees Boersma, Anders Albrechtslund and Marisol Sandoval (London: Routledge, 2012), 43.

[63] See Greenwald, 214.

[64] Jamie Tarabay, "Obama and leakers: Who are the eight charged under the Espionage Act?" *Aljazeera America*, 5 December, 2013, http://america.aljazeera.com/articles/2013/12/5/obama-and-leakerswhoaretheeightchargedunderespionageact.html.

[65] Cited in Greenwald, 214.

[66] For an overview see Zollmann, chapter 4. See also Florian Zollmann, "Todesopfer als Normalfall: Zur Gesellschaftlichen Bedeutung des Journalismus in Kriegszeiten." *Journalistik Journal*, April 19, http://journalistik-journal.lookingintomedia.com/?p=928. For *flak* by lobby groups see Greg Philo and Mike Berry, *More Bad News From Israel* (London: Pluto Press, 2011). See also Edward S. Herman and David Peterson, "The Kagame-Power Lobby's Dishonest Attack on the BBC's Documentary on Rwanda." *MrZine*, November 1, 2014, http://mrzine.monthlyreview.org/2014/hp011114.html.

[67] Herman and Chomsky, 27-29.

[68] See e.g. Robert M. Entman, *Projections of Power: Framing News, Public Opinion, and U.S. Foreign Policy* (Chicago, Ill: University of Chicago Press, 2004).

[69] Herman, 109.

[70] Piers Robinson, "Researching US Media–State Relations and Twenty-First Century Wars," in *Reporting War: Journalism in Wartime*, eds. Stuart Allan and Barbie Zelizer (London: Routledge, 2004), 96-112.

[71] Mark Curtis, *Web of Deceit: Britain's Real Role in the World* (London: Vintage, 2003), 380.

[72] Curtis, 380.

[73] Curtis, 380.

[74] For the classic elaboration see Daniel C. Hallin, *The Uncensored War: The Media and Vietnam* (Berkeley and Los Angeles, CA: University of California Press, 1989). For an in-depth review of the literature in relation to the marginalization of substantive criticism see Zollmann. For a contemporary treatment of the topic see David Cromwell, *Why are We the Good Guys?* (Winchester, UK: Zero Books, 2012).

[75] For evidence on cases after the Cold War see Edward S. Herman and David Peterson, *The Politics of Genocide* (New York, NY: Monthly Review Press, 2010). See also Edward S. Herman and David Peterson, "The Dismantling of Yugoslavia," *Monthly Review* 59, no. 5 (2007), http://monthlyreview.org/2007/10/01/the-dismantling-of-yugoslavia.

[76] Herman and Chomsky, 31.

[77] Herman and Chomsky, 2.

[78] Herman and Chomsky, 2.

[79] See DiMaggio, 55.

CHAPTER TWELVE

IDEOLOGY AND THE CRISIS IN EUROPE: WHAT CAN A
LOW-COST AIRLINE IN-FLIGHT MAGAZINE ARTICLE TELL
US ABOUT THE RELATIONSHIP BETWEEN IDEOLOGY AND
AUSTERITY?

Thomas Fazi

Introduction

In late 2014, I was invited by a Scandinavian university to give a talk about 'Ideology and the Crisis'—on how in recent years ideology has been employed in Europe to render acceptable policies that would have been politically unthinkable prior to 2008-10 (this being the interregnum between the financial crisis and the so-called 'euro crisis', and as far as Europe is con-cerned between the pre-crisis era and the post-crisis era). I was satisfied with the talk I had prepared, but I was well aware that it was lacking a crucial element: a 'piece of evidence', as in a newspaper or magazine piece that I could use to demonstrate how ideology is embedded—often very subtly so—in almost every news piece written about the crisis.

Fortunately, and ironically, I found precisely what I was looking for in the most unlikely of places: the easyJet in-flight magazine. Nestled between an article on 'business gadgets' and one on 'Speed Networking' ('a king of work-based speed dating', if you're wondering) was a fantastic (in every sense of the word) piece called 'Modern Greek Heroes', about the 'super-powered go-getters who are turning every street corner in Athens into a business opportunity'.[1] The article is a superb example of (a) how seemingly innocent 'arts and culture' news items often reinforce the dominant narrative by implicitly (and unwittingly, in most cases) adopting its ideological framework; in this sense it is also (b) paradigmatic of how ideology—in the Marxist sense of the word, i.e. a mystification of reality which ensures the continual dominance of the ruling class—works, and why in this day and age it is a much more effective tool for shaping the forces of material and mental production than old-fashioned propaganda (though the two are related, as we shall see, the latter being a necessary prerequisite for the former).

Adopting and Reinforcing the Dominant Narrative

Let's begin with point (a). The article focuses on a group of young Greek entrepreneurs: these include Lazaros Mavrakis, editor of *MOTO* magazine, who has hatched the idea of showing tourists around Athens on his Honda Transalp Dual Purpose 600; Vasillis Monastirlis, who runs En Athenais 1928, a 1920s-style retro barbershop; and Nayia Kourti, an architect who has converted a derelict 19th-century shop into the city's first bathhouse in fifty years. According to the author, Adrian Mourby, "[t]hese are just three examples of a new entrepreneurial spirit that has breathed fresh life into the city after years of darkness." Mourby concedes that the country was hit hard by the crisis, with output shrinking by almost 25%, tens of thousands of family-owned businesses and jobs disappearing almost overnight, and the once-vibrant historic centre becoming 'a wasteland of shuttered shops and silent-sprayed buildings'.

But all this is changing, he says: 'Today, however, those shutters are reopening and what's fascinating is what they're revealing inside: exciting new ventures, like bars, boutiques and high-tech enterprises'. Even more fascinating, though, is the fact that, according to the author, all this is happening precisely because 'Greece implemented austerity programmes faster than any other EU country': 'In many ways, the lack of jobs in Greece has actually spurred people into action', he writes. '[I]t's encouraged people to think more creatively about finding work', and it has inspired many

Athenians, 'to follow their dream of opening a shop or starting a retail brand'. As a result, 'Athens, once a place of big business and big government, has seemingly reinvented itself as a hotbed of individual endeavour. And the buzz is back'. As Andria Mitsakos, owner of the Wanderlista Concept Stores, is quoted saying: 'Ingenuity is paramount here—it feels like the land of opportunity'.

All this leads Mourby to conclude—and logically so, given the scenario that he presents—that 'the adjustment was a success', as further proven by the fact that 'the country successfully returned to international capital markets in April [2014] and growth this year is set to become positive again'.

Deploying the Rhetorical Tools of Ideology

What I love so much about this article is that is literally imbued with ideology—both neoliberal ideology in general, as well as its two modern variants, which we shall call the 'ideology of crisis' and the 'ideology of austerity' (the first referring in general to the economic slowdown witnessed in advanced economies since 2008, and more specifically to the global financial crisis that struck that year; the second referring to the political response given to the crisis, most notably in Europe). So, for example, you have the notion of austerity as a 'painful but necessary cure', which in turn is related more generally to the Schumpeterian idea of 'creative destruction': i.e. the idea that crises are inherently good because they revolutionise the economic structure from within, weeding out the excesses and clearing the way for the rise of a stronger, more efficient system ('[T]he buzz is back').

This is also related to the notion of 'social Darwinism', which applies the biological concepts of natural selection and survival of the fittest to sociology and politics, implying that it is natural and thus desirable for the weak to see their wealth and power decrease and for the strong to see their wealth and power increase—and for crises to accelerate this process, by freeing the 'animal spirits' of capitalism ('a new entrepreneurial spirit... has breathed fresh life into the city'; 'the lack of jobs in Greece has actually spurred people into action').

The assumption, which runs through the entire article, is that the pre-crisis Greek economy was fundamentally dysfunctional, with 'big business and big government' stifling individual entrepreneurship and fueling workers' apathy ('[w]hen, in 2008, the financial crisis struck, such enterprises would have been unheard of'). This, of course, is related to what is perhaps neoliberalism's founding myth: the idea that the economy is best left to supposedly self-regulating markets, with the government intervening as little as possible, which harkens all the way back to Adam Smith, the father of modern economics, and to his theory of the 'invisible hand' of the market, which would miraculously guide the economy to equilibrium (hence the term *laissez-faire*, 'let it be', capitalism).

The article is also rife with a number of implicit assumptions which are specifically related to the ideology of austerity: the myth of 'Southern laziness', for example—the idea that the workers of Southern Europe have been lulled by years of excessive salaries and benefits vis-à-vis those of their hard-working northern counterparts, and thus were/are in need of a 'shock therapy' to boost their levels of productivity and entrepreneurship—and more in general the idea, which has become commonplace in Europe from 2010 onwards, that the purportedly state-heavy countries of the European periphery (the so-called PIIGS: Portugal, Italy, Ireland, Greece, and Spain) have been 'living beyond their means' for too long, and that it was/is time for a reckoning. And then, of course, you have the greatest myth of all, which encompasses all the others: the idea that austerity in Greece—and by the same token everywhere else as well, the reader is led to believe, considering that 'Greece implemented austerity programmes faster than any other EU country'—has been a success, and that the countries which have implemented cost-cutting measures are on the road to economic recovery ('the adjustment was a success…the country successfully returned to international capital markets in April [2014] and growth this year is set become positive again').

Now, there is very little, if anything, of what is stated or implied in the article in question that corresponds to Greece's, or to the EU's or Eurozone's, social and political reality. In fact, what it offers is an absurdly biased, grotesquely distorted and almost Disneyland-esque representation of such reality. The truth, macroeconomically speaking, is that 'Greece is and remains in a Great Depression, and is witnessing a full-blown humanitarian crisis, as a result of seven years of precipitous decline in income, coupled with negative investment', as the Greek economist Yanis Varoufakis recently put it to me in an interview.[2] As for the Eurozone as a whole, as of early 2015—hence more than six years after the outbreak of the financial crisis—the currency area is still stagnating (with a number of member states still in outright recession), and its GDP is still below pre-crisis levels.

What this means is that the euro crisis, in purely macroeconomic terms, is far worse than the Great Depression of the 1930s, when it took European countries on average four-to-five years to return to pre-crisis GDP levels.

Moreover, both the EU and euro area continue to register double-digit unemployment rates (10% and 11.5% respectively, as of early 2015)—the highest rates since the signing of the Maastricht Treaty, in 1992 (excluding the 2012 acme), with peaks of 24.5% and 27% in Spain and Greece[3]—and record-level (in modern times) poverty and social exclusion rates, which now affect some 123 million people, or 24 percent of the EU's population.[4] As demonstrated by a number of reports, such as a recent study by the Catholic charity organisation Caritas Europa, hardly a hotbed of left-wing radicalism, this is a direct consequence of the austerity measures, which have 'disproportionately' hit the poor and are responsible for a dramatic rise in inequality and unemployment levels (especially among the youth), suicide, poverty (including child poverty) and at-risk-of-poverty rates, severe material deprivation, homelessness, social exclusion and distress.[5]

If we add to this the fact that austerity has also led to a vertiginous increase in public debt levels across the continent, we can reasonably conclude that 'austerity has been an utter and unmitigated disaster', in both social and economic terms, as Joseph Stiglitiz recently wrote in The Guardian.[6] And yet, to the average reader—and doubtlessly to the Mourby himself—the fairytale-like scenario depicted in the article probably sounds perfectly plausible. And this brings us to the second insight that the article offers us: the way in which ideology is used to conceal reality and ensure the dominance of the ruling class, and why in 21st-century 'liberal democracies' this is a more efficient tool for social control than old-fashioned propaganda (though the two are related, as mentioned).

Obviously, it would be hasty and foolish to assume that the easyJet inflight magazine is part of a big EU-led PSYOP[7] to sell austerity policies to the European public, or that the article's author is on the payroll of some secretive European intelligence agency; yes, corporate control of the major media outlets clearly influences the flow of information to the general public, but in this age of decentralised information distribution and overall 'information glut'—mostly, but not only, attributable to the internet—directly controlling all the media outlets, all the way down to the in-flight magazines of low-cost airlines, would be simply impossible, even for the most resourceful of organisations. In such a context, the political and corporate elites can only hope to indirectly manage the flow of information that is beyond their sphere of control by using mass media and other channels (such as academia), which they do effectively control, to fix the premises of discourse by circumscribing the terms of acceptable debate while excluding the viability of alternative viewpoints, thus manufacturing consent and marginalising dissent, in what Edward Herman and Noam Chomsky have described as a form of propaganda 'lite' (or soft propaganda).[8]

As Augie Fleras from the University of Waterloo, Canada, writes: Media messages constitute potent socializing agents of social control whose representations of reality are constructed and conventional rather than a mirrored reflection of the world out there. The constructedness of these conventions as natural and normal is largely hidden from view as part of a tacitly assumed media gaze but internalized as values, beliefs, and norms without people's awareness that their attitudes are changing'.[9]

Of course, such 'people' include journalists and professionals who work in the media industry in one capacity or another. What this means is that once the elite have succeeded in establishing certain facts, ideas, or myths as 'self-evident truths' through constant repetition—'free markets are a good thing'; 'austerity is working'; 'Greece is recovering', etc.—these will then self-replicate across the board at the hands of well-meaning journalists and bloggers, such as the author of the article in question, who will construct their stories in a manner that is compatible with the 'values, beliefs, and norms' of the dominant narrative (without even being aware of doing so), thus reinforcing such narrative. Add this to the widespread economic illiteracy of the general public and of non-specialists (and of a great deal of specialists as well, for that matter) as well as with the human tendency toward selection or confirmation bias, and the sum amounts to perfect conditions for 'automated', bottom-up, self-replicating, ideologically conforming propaganda.

Coincidentally, the easyJet article offers useful examples of both. As for the problem of economic illiteracy, consider the following paragraph: Massive closures in the years following the 2008 crash led to a lowering of downtown Athens rents. 'Suddenly, you can live in the centre for as little as €250 to €300 a month', says Andria Mitsakos, who runs a PR business in Athens and recently opened Wanderlista Concept Stores, 'and that's for a great apartment in a central location. Low rents also mean low overheads. The diaspora is returning to open businesses'.

Here the journalist makes a common mistake: using common sense to interpret economic data. This analytical approach typically leads to grossly erroneous (albeit conforming to the dominant narrative) conclusions, given the counterintuitive nature of economics. Nowhere is this clearer than when speaking of deflation, defined as a continuous decrease in the general price level of goods and services—a situation which Greece has been in since early 2013, as a result of austerity, and to which the entire eurozone, as of early 2015, is rapidly heading. To the common man, as to the journalist in question, this understandably appears like a desirable thing: cheaper products (or rents, in the article's case), what's not to like? And if this is happening as a result of austerity (as this is so often deduced), it then follows that austerity must be a good thing.

What most people fail to grasp, though, is the reason that prices are falling in Greece and elsewhere, and that is collapsing demand. Simply put, people cannot afford to spend as much as they used to as a result of their income falling due to declining wages and rising unemployment, which forces producers (or home owners) to lower their prices (or rents). This leads to a situation known as a deflationary spiral: a situation where decreases in prices lead to lower production, which in turn leads to lower wages and demand, which leads to further decreases in prices, which leads to growing unemployment, and so on. In other words, there is nothing beneficial about declining prices, as the article misleadingly implies. And they certainly do not provide a solution to the crisis; on the contrary, *they are a consequence of it.*

To return to the example presented in the article: even though the rents in the centre of Athens have declined, they have not gotten 'cheaper' for the majority of Athenians because their income has fallen accordingly. The wealthy is who benefits in post-boom deflationary circumstances such as the one that Greece finds itself in: those who are not affected by the downturn in the real economy and have access to cash, who can scoop up wealth and assets (such as 'a great apartment in a central location') at fire-sale prices. In this sense, boom-bust cycles actually facilitate the transfer of wealth from the working and middle classes to the wealthy. That said, it would be unfair to condemn the author for such a blatant case of 'class blindness': the removal of the issue of class from the public discourse is in fact one of the main features of the dominant ideology (and of the ideology of austerity in particular). The article offers another example of this, when discussing the 'Athens Riviera', an 'all-day beach club, with proper facilities and yacht access', which apparently is doing quite well.

Now, only someone who is completely blinded to the issue of class could take the success of a beach club clearly geared to the wealthiest members of society ('yacht access') as a measure of the overall state of the economy—yet this is exactly what the article implies. This is also a classic demonstration of confirmation bias, of course: you can probably find examples of successful high-end businesses even in the poorest countries in the world. Until now we have used the article as a telling example of the way ideology functions, and how it has been employed—*is being employed*, for that matter—to mask the reality of the devastating effects of austerity on Greece and other countries. But the article says little about the crucial role that ideology has played in shaping the tumultuous events of the past years in Europe.

Conclusion

The fact is that Europeans have been subject to one of the most impressive political marketing campaigns in modern times, which has effectively succeeded in rewriting the history of the financial crisis, and in transforming a crisis of the markets—and more generally of neoliberalism—into a crisis of public spending; and then in using this narrative to push through policies designed to suit the financial sector and the wealthy, at the expense of everyone else, and to re-engineer European societies and economies according to an even more radical neoliberal framework. The left bears a large responsibility: its inability to provide an alternative narrative to the dominant one—or even simply to reach a consensus on the reasons that got us into this mess—was in fact one of the reasons that got me to start my book, *The Battle for Europe*, back in 2012.

What was lacking, in my opinion, was a comprehensive, all-encompassing, critical, accessible explanation of what was happening, capable of linking the various interrelated issues and crises. This wasn't just a purely academic or theoretical problem. It was a thoroughly political problem. The failure of the overwhelming majority of citizens (including myself, to a certain degree) to grasp what was happening, and what appeared to be a problem of overwhelming and daunting complexity, was—I concluded—one of the main reasons that the policies imposed by the European political establishment, which would have been politically unthinkable just a few years earlier, were encountering relatively little resistance.

To a large degree, this is still true today. As a matter of fact, as far as the general public's understanding of the crisis goes, we could almost say that things have gotten worse, since the deepening social and economic crisis in a number of countries and the overall reckless handling of the crisis by the European political elites have rendered the public debate increasingly polarized and crude (see, for example, the increasing popularity of anti-euro and anti-EU propagandists in a number of countries), as well as increasingly framed by national-cultural stereotypes (bad Germans vs. lazy Greeks, etc.). Many of the myths surrounding the crisis have, if anything, grown stronger. This, of course, makes any attempt at challenging the current paradigm and developing a credible, mature alternative—as well as building a transnational resistance movement—increasingly difficult.

At the same time, the growing consensus of left-wing parties and movements in a number of European countries (most notably Spain and Greece) offers reason for hope. In any case, it remains more important than ever to continue developing a convincing alternative narrative of the crisis, capable of showing who the real culprits are and where the true dividing lines of the current situation are actually drawn. To be able to pursue a different path, after all, we first have to understand what went wrong. As financial specialist David Marsh stated, Europe needs nothing less than a Truth and Reconciliation Commission on the model of the one established in South Africa in the 1990s after the abolition of apartheid, to establish the 'crimes of negligence and incompetence' in the ongoing management of the euro crisis.[10] As for me, I will keep striving in that direction.

Questions for Critical Reflection

1. Noted historian and social critic Morris Berman observed that, "An idea is something you have; an ideology is something that has you." Consider Fazi's critique of the language used by Mourby in his easyJet article to frame the purported necessity of austerity measures (paragraphs 6-7). How do Mourby's word choices in the article reflect the ideology of social Darwinism?

2. The author references a pervasive myth about the "South," or the southern regions of the European continent. To what extent in your community, or country, are similar myths about the "South" (wherever that may be)

and its purportedly lazy people reproduced in the larger culture and/or public discourse? To what extent are these sorts of myths used to legitimize the ongoing marginalization or abuse of those from the "South"?

3. How does the "'automated', bottom-up, self-replicating, ideologically-conforming propaganda" (re)produced in mass media camouflage, or conceal, actual economic realities in society?

4. The author refers to Herman and Chomsky's study of corporate media performance and the role that this kind of performance plays in "fixing the premises of discourse," all of which implies the ability of powerful institutions (and people) to assert as truth presuppositions that scarcely ever get questioned or challenged. What presuppositions about the benefits of globalization are (re)produced in your community or country?

References

[1] Adrian Mourby, 'Modern Greek heroes', *easyJet inflight magazine*, September 2014. Mourby is a former BBC producer, and contributes to the *Guardian* and the *Independent*.

[2] Thomas Fazi, 'Varoufakis: "Solo tante menzogne sulla ripresa greca",' *il manifesto*, 29 December 2014.

[3] Eurostat data.

[4] International Labour Organization, *World Social Protection Report 2014-15*, 2014.

[5] Caritas Europa, *The European Crisis and its Human Cost*, 2014.

[6] Joseph Stiglitz, 'Austerity has been an utter disaster for the eurozone', *The Guardian*, 1 October 2014.

[7] Psychological Operation.

[8] Noam Chomsky and Ed Herman, *Manufacturing Consent*, New York: Pantheon Books, 1988.

[9] Augie Fleras, *The Media Gaze*, Vancouver: UBC Press, 2011, p. 107.

[10] David Marsh, 'Euro zone needs a truth, reconciliation commission', *MarketWatch*, 22 July 2013.

Chapter Thirteen

The Cultivation of Fear in the Face of Imports

Daniel Broudy

The goal is a society in which the basic social unit
is you and your television set.
—*Noam Chomsky, 1998*

Introduction

A simple syllogism: Knowledge is a product of sense and perception. As we know by virtue of the senses, whoever controls what can be sensed holds the power to control what is perceived and can, thus, shape much knowledge. The prisoners of Plato's allegorical cave, with their necks constrained in chains, sense the appearances of figures moving on a far wall and perceive, incorrectly, the shadows of people as real. Perhaps nowhere more powerful a place today to shape perception (and opinion) through manipulation of the senses is the living room, where appearances masquerade as realities. This essay looks at a key focal point of our attention, the television, and examines how it is still used to give shape to our understanding, to our ideas, beliefs and fears about others beyond our borders. As with all other living rooms (or caves), this story has a setting.

In the 1970s, Pittsburgh, Pennsylvania was a bustling city built between two wide rivers that met to form the headwaters of the Ohio. The city to me as a young boy was big and imposing and mildly frightening. Steel production never ceased. The blast furnaces, coke ovens, and smelters in towering black mills of metal beams and corrugated sheets dotting the riverbanks would spit steam and smoke and flames into the cityscape. In remote suburban areas outside the city, great mountains of slag, an externality of steel production, grew above the natural green topography over the many decades that Pittsburgh pushed steel into the global marketplace.

The immense machines of heavy industry planted along the rivers, the wide boulevards and avenues merged over time with the rich post-colonial history from which emerged George Westinghouse, Henry Clay Frick, Andrew Mellon, Henry J. Heinz, and Andrew Carnegie, famous industrialists and philanthropists who endowed the citizens with universities, hospitals, museums, concert halls, theatres, public libraries and parks.

It was firsthand experience with this rich mixture of the old and the new, the coarse and the refined that cultivated my view of the wider world. It was also during this time that the city began to see and feel the shock of what's currently called *outsourcing*. Steel production saw rapid declines in Pittsburgh in the late 1970s that produced a spike in the unemployment rate from 1979 to 1983. This rate climbed to over 18 percent as the city saw its population drop dramatically.

Along with the ascent of unemployment and the disappearance of steel manufacturing there also came a rise in Japanese automobile imports to the American market. People whose local manufacturing jobs dissolved and reemerged elsewhere in the broader global economy perceived direct links between the loss of their livelihoods and the growth of Japanese automobile imports. Grief and anger over lost wages grew into contemptuous talk of the Japanese in communities across the city. As stories in newspapers and television appeared to reinforce growing fears that the Japanese were invading, the publicized foreign purchases of prime real estate and symbols of American economic power seemed to confirm those fears. The effect was a public discourse loaded with the weight of collective worry as the impending economic invasion would likely signal the end of American might and sovereignty.

Levels of fear and loathing rose even in the years that followed as media, especially television, stoked anxieties that America was doomed to being bought out. When Rockefeller Center in New York City and Columbia

Pictures in Hollywood were sold, citizens "old enough to remember the 1980s," observed Michael Shuchman, "probably recall how terrified [the country] became about Japan 'buying up' the U.S."[1] Whatever underlying motives the mass media had in casting the Japanese as invaders, the fear it cultivated in the American psyche was real.

The Cultivation of Perception

Like the literal practice of cultivating crops for human consumption, cultivation is also a metaphor used to refer to the practice of cultivating the social mind with the right ideas, beliefs, habits, and behaviors. Whose ideas and behaviors are the "right" ones is one matter that the chapters in this book attempt to address, but success in this communication practice depends upon a powerful and stable system of delivery.

By the 1970s in America, television had already become society's central storyteller and information delivery system. In terms of commanding our attention, it dominated all other media. In observing the extent of this sort of domination and power to mold the public mind, George Gerbner concluded that "television drama presents a largely lawless world in which due process [of law] plays a small part, and that too is self-justifyingly violent. It is also a wild world of many violent strangers, with a mostly violent past and a totally violent future.[2]

Gerbner's extensive study of television drama reveals something profound about how drama in network news also unfolds in news reporting practices. Intentional or not, the dramatic news reporting on unemployment and the importation of foreign cars was seen as compelling proof that we lived in a lawless world where "violent" strangers, it seemed, had taken away our work and presented us with superb facsimiles of what we once made ourselves. The media descriptions used to reinforce this faulty sense of symbolic violence and to prime the minds of the American audience were often loaded with allusions to military actions. When "Japanese carmakers first invaded American shores," reporters wondered, "How far will the trade war escalate?"[3] James Rosenau observed of that era, "American mass media frequently whipped up the American Pearl Harbor paradigm, employing oft-repeated war metaphors in headlines like 'Japan's Surprise Invasion of Hollywood' to refer to Sony's purchase of Columbia Pictures."[4]

It may be no surprise, then, in the context of today's developing trade deficits between China and America that media largely return, as if by reflex, to popular conceptions of war to frame news of trade imbalances, territorial disputes, and related economic strife. Nevertheless, the questions linger: why do mass media draw so heavily upon such emotive language to represent occurrences of the utterly mundane, the tedious transactions of routine commerce in which they themselves take part in such a major way?

One possible reason underlying contemporary methods employed in the manufacture of news drama grounded in concepts of war can be located in an unlikely place: a compelling indictment leveled against big business by a military man who witnessed and took part in the collusion firsthand. In his book *War is a Racket*, Smedley D. Butler, then retired Marine Corps general, wondered "What does [war] profit anyone except the very few to whom war means huge profits?"[5]

Butler railed against the bankers, munitions manufacturers, ship-builders, speculators, and even the meat packers who had vested interests, of which the public at large should be highly conscious. In 1935, when *War is a Racket* first appeared in print, this was certainly the case, as Butler methodically outlines in his book. Those who owned the means of production and controlled capital realized huge profits of millions and billions in the World War, yet the cost to those who fought came in countless mangled bodies, shattered minds, and broken hearts and homes.[6] The parallels in the 1930s between vested business interests and corporate media complicity in the manufacture of consent for war are striking, especially when set beside the narratives offered up for public consumption during the planning stages of the Iraq invasion in the early 2000s.

In striving to produce the necessary "shock and awe" during the information campaign promoting public fear undertaken by elites, submissive mass media are crucial to generating widespread public support. Of that time in the wake of 9/11, for example, Noam Chomsky reflected on the...massive government-media propaganda campaign...starting in September 2002..., [which drove] a large part of the U.S. population completely off the international spectrum."[7] "The United States," noted Chomsky, "was the only country where a large population was genuinely afraid of Saddam Hussein because of his weapons of mass destruction and his links to terror."[8] Pervasive fear turned out to correlate strongly with public support in America for undertaking preemptive military action against Hussein.

Communicated through the power of the visual, the dreadful images of the collapsing twin towers came to form the key iconography of violence enacted against the American homeland and to serve as the core imagery cultivating in viewers an abiding sense of fear and loathing. Following suit, so as to reinforce the visceral outrage, were Hollywood cinema, songs, and news, which assisted at the same time in reinforcing the cultural significance of these images and "winning the hearts and minds" of any portion of the public resisting Administration plans for Iraq. Like then, media today appear to operate with predictable underlying aims.

Mass media, it bears repeating, are corporate by nature and so remain, on one hand, engaged in the monotonous pursuit of perpetual profits while, on the other, focused on meeting the expectations of their shareholders. As the principal aim remains, which is to increase market share, the stories and images emanating from these dominant sources of information naturally reflect the interests of power, the unholy associations that General Butler sought to disclose and inscribe in an indelible public record. While mass media are central to the successful production of public consent in free societies by means of propaganda and mythmaking,[9] so too are they central to the public's consumption of products, perspectives, ideas, or ideologies—all of which can elicit a range of emotional reactions.

Cultivating Concepts and Practices of Consumption

Responses to mass media images can be explained, in part, by Emotional Arousal Theory (EAT). As content can stimulate our appetites for edible things, it can also arouse acute states of emotion exhibited in a willingness and enthusiasm to act. "Emotional arousal," notes Dolf Zillmann, "is... seen as an essential component of such experiences as pleasure and displeasure, sadness and happiness, love and hate,...rage and exultation,... merriment and fear, anger and joy...."[10] This is, perhaps, one reason why visual feasts of celluloid violence elicit such powerful emotions.

In signifying the destruction of a major organ of American economic vitality, the twin towers, captured in cinematic free fall, were framed for weeks on television as vulgar exhibitions of violence that might engender optimum levels of public outrage, anger, and fear. This period of the outrageous media spectacle reveals how political leaders effectively directed the heightened public emotions toward productive social objectives. To underscore the essential importance of consuming what we wished on our terms was President George W. Bush who reminded us all of the imperative to go shopping, to demonstrate to the "evildoers" they could not suppress the nation's will to engage in its daily routines.

The sickening outrage of the attacks was reduced and distilled in the expressed importance of maintaining the flow of capital and commerce. The President's effort to calm the public's sense of fear and vulnerability was part of a "…persuasive mode of social coercion, [which] c[ould] also function as a mode of consumption."[11] Joe Lockard further explains:

> Preventative consumption is a fear response that seeks to avoid the consequences of unpreparedness or inaction. Consumption itself becomes a defense against fears, rational or irrational.[12]

As part of an emotional reaction, our general compliance with the President's proposition for how best to recover normalcy reflected our willingness to consume (so to speak) the idea that the Administration's directions for appropriate national responses were satisfactory or, at least, not to be questioned. A noted journalist and longtime critic of power abuses in Washington, Dan Rather demonstrated this depth of compliance with the dictates of consumption on the *Late Show with David Letterman* shortly after 9/11 when he observed that President Bush, "makes the decisions, and…wherever he wants me to line up, just tell me where, and he'll make the call."[13]

While we consume foods to gratify our gastronomic cravings and curiosities, we consume, as well, to satisfy our emotional and intellectual ones. That is, as the consumption of new ideas or perspectives may satisfy our intellectual tastes (if they aren't "rammed down our throats"), we may "take the bait," "get hooked," or "swallow a new idea whole." As regards the heightened distress provoked by rampant fear-mongering in the post-9/11 period, the largely uncritical corporate media served elite plans to condition the public's fear response and build a broad consensus for a foreign war over "rogue" leaders.

The only viable responses to this scary and mean world manufactured in the black-and-white discourse of mass media were military action and our "patriotic" duty to "line up" and follow the leader. The alternative for refusing to mount the Bush bandwagon for war was public chastisement from media that incessantly forewarned citizens of the likely consequences of inaction. For example, Bill O'Reilly of Fox News, the right-wing automaton of Rupert Murdoch's global media empire News Corp, disciplined as "bad Americans" those "who publicly criticize[d] [the] country in a time of military crisis [while reminding everyone of] "our duty as loyal Americans to shut up once the fighting begins."[14]

Concerning the war, evidently, the public's relative ignorance of the facts—created and controlled (ironically) by the very information system instructing us to 'shut up'—was not sufficient grounds to contest what many suspected to be a military campaign based on false pretenses. Indeed, the logic employed by the corporate media reprimanded anyone with a critical opinion to suspend the practice of thinking[15] and to wait patiently while "the facts [would] be known after Saddam [was] deposed and we [might] find out exactly what he'[d] been hiding, if anything."[16] The grandfatherly advice (however reckless) dispensed by Bill O'Reilly (and other ideologues) pitted "good" against "bad" by recasting critical thinking as a moral violation. This helped exalt the validity of the emotional response over thoughtful circumspection.

Maybe this Manichean rendering of the world is not entirely surprising in view of the close symbiotic relations developed over time between militarism and globalization. It is certainly far easier to understand and deal with a world divided neatly into two opposing halves—into "forwards" (globalization protected by a strong military) and "backwards" (localization supported by local citizen interests). Perhaps, also, this mean world predicted by Gerbner's study, multiplied by our general embrace of the military option over all other competing possibilities, speaks of our implicit expectations and acceptance of violence as a coherent reaction.

If fear does, indeed, engender general anxieties that can be best subdued by consumption, then it is certainly worth discussing the effects of these seemingly distinct processes of social endeavor. We must ask whether fear really is the much sought after response to frightening media stimuli presented for public consumption. Are these powerful stimuli part of a larger system of manipulation at work in higher levels of the social pyramid where elites, like those identified by Butler, ostensibly manage the public agenda and the message? Steven Staples, Chair of the International Network of Disarmament and Globalization, provides some perspective in observing that militarism and globalization:

> ...should be seen as two sides of the same coin. On one side, globalization promotes the conditions that lead to unrest, inequality, conflict, and, ultimately, war. On the other side, globalization fuels the means to wage war by protecting and promoting the military industries needed to produce sophisticated weaponry. This weaponry, in turn, is used, or is threatened to be used, to protect the investments of transnational corporations and their shareholders.[17]

In the case of the Iraq invasion, it is especially easy to discern, in hindsight, how neoliberal elites have managed the messages for preemptive war and defended the ventures of transnationals in seeking control not just over particular territories but a whole world economy and global markets.[18] At present, the public discussion of globalization's seeming self-evident intrinsic value to the world reflects the interests of the "ascendant transnational capitalist class"[19] and proceeds as if it were an indisputable presupposition we are expected to receive without question. Were it so, we may come to believe falsely through media, especially in reports on the state of business and the marketplace, that globalization is a conclusive state of certainty, that we, painted though we are as mere consumers, are locked into by virtue of our purported shared interests with other citizens of the world. Nonetheless, in opposition to the mythologies constructed and

> ...circulated by the corporate media, globalization does not...bring about the conditions for political harmony or economic stability [nor]...furnish mutual economic growth to those nations, particularly Third World countries, who are forced to participate in the global economy under the leadership of the United States.[20]

Thomas Friedman, an early apologist for the neoliberal project for Iraq, crystallized an image of the great chasm of power that separates global interests and local: "[t]he hidden hand of the market will never work without the hidden fist—McDonald's cannot flourish without McDonnell Douglas, the designer of the F-15."[21] Friedman seems to evoke, here, the words of General Butler who confessed his complicity, as a U.S. Marine, in making "Mexico safe for American oil interests in 1914...Haiti and Cuba...for the

National City Bank[ers]...Nicaragua for the International Banking House of Brown Brothers...the Dominican Republic for American sugar...and China [for] Standard Oil."[22]

If it is true that the military is the hidden fist of the free market, just as it is the middleman between public subsidy and corporate profit,[23] Woodrow Wilson captured these facts well in his observations:

> ...the flag of this nation must follow [the manufacturer], and the doors of unwilling nations...closed against him must be battered down. [...] even if the sovereignty of unwilling nations be outraged in the process. Colonies must be obtained or planted, in order that no useful corner of the world may be overlooked or left unused.[24]

What we would likely see in governing systems hastening to encroach on the dominion of foreign powers are plans and policies that mirror the dominant class as well as structures of global politics, economics, and militarism all of which represent the dominant global system. In the early 20th century, Wilson drew upon common metaphors for farming and harvesting where the storehouses of a state's natural riches, guarded by geo-political borders, supplant the sovereignty of nations whose land and resources might be exploited by newly planted colonies. These metaphors of agriculture must have resonated with the masses as America has since grown into the world's number one consumer. The broad distribution of American military men, women, and weaponry over the past decades since the end of WWII, to every useful corner of the world, testifies also to the dominance of the system that Wilson had identified and supported in his early twentieth-century public address.[25]

Conclusion

In the Cold War years, when Pittsburgh was a global center of industrial power, citizens keenly aware of the preceding world war could sense the pervasive, if remote, peril of potential nuclear annihilation. Periodic "air raid" drills that began in kindergarten and continued from elementary to high school obliged pupils to duck and cover beneath their desks to escape the flying shards of shattered glass that would surely follow an atomic detonation over the city. The social import of these public acts of obedience to the civil authorities was reinforced at home by the elite programmers and managers of official information. "Television," notes Chomsky, "drums certain fixed boundaries of thought into your head, which dulls the mind,"[26] and makes thinking outside the box, so to speak, more challenging.

Aided by the ubiquitous wonder of radio and television technology, the Federal Communications Commission neverfailed, as well, to remind nationwide audiences, routinely over the decades, that tests of the CONELRAD (1951-1963) and the Emergency Broadcast System (1963-1997) were fundamental components of living in a "free and democratic society."

It was a simple yet effective communication act. By inserting the solemn voice of a government official, announcing another routine test of the National Broadcast System, these occasional breaks in daily TV programming could create quite an air of seriousness that could return viewers, if briefly, to the sober realities of the Cold War raging just outside the nation's borders. Following that statement, two dissonant tones (highly unpleasant to the human ear and intersecting one another at 853Hz and 960Hz) sounded for twenty seconds and animated in the imaginations of viewers the unseen and unpleasant dangers of the cold, mean world. The brief announcement and aural signal demanded everyone's attention. This auditory sign that tested telecommunications in the face of impending doom during the Cold War era re-emerged in the post-9/11 discourse as a visual sign.

It was in this time, during the rhetorical attacks unleashed on Iraq by the Bush team, that National Security Advisor Condoleezza Rice effectively laid the conceptual groundwork for the literal invasion of Iraq: "We don't want the smoking gun to be a mushroom cloud,"[27] she cautioned in an interview with CNN's Wolf Blitzer. Images of the menacing nuclear flash and bang that herald the coming ominous cloud of radiation prepared viewers of the Rice discussion to envision a homeland beset again by the diabolical aims of legendary Middle Eastern madmen. Following this metaphorical assault on the public's sensibilities was Secretary of State Colin Powell who, in a United Nations televised broadcast, warned the world shortly afterwards of the calamity in store for those who would waver both in confronting and in blocking "the Butcher of Baghdad" in his purported bid to dominate the region.

There can be no doubt that Saddam Hussein has biological weapons and the capability to rapidly produce more, many more. And he has the ability to dispense these lethal poisons and diseases in ways that can cause massive death and destruction. If biological weapons seem too terrible to contemplate, chemical weapons are equally chilling.[28]

As Colin Powell's words served to fortify the sense of fear citizens were induced to feel, it is also equally chilling to ponder how the world's most prolific designer and supplier of weapons, backed by a colossal lobby of corporate banking and industrial interests, has managed to supervise and (re)shape so much of the world's affairs through its global empire of military garrisons (more than 1,000 at last count).

One wonders how could such an unsurpassed complex of global influence really fear the very systems of destruction it trades in so exhaustively? Today's principal expression of globalization, notes Paul Treanor, with its firm embrace of the unregulated market represents an "ethic in itself, capable of acting as a guide for all human action, and substituting for all previously existing ethical beliefs."[29] If this is so, how might thoughtful human beings rewrite the scripts that cast us as thoughtless players expected to act on our fears and to "shut up" and consume what we can in this mean world?

Questions for Critical Reflection

1. The author refers to fear and anger aroused by American mass media in the 1970s and 1980s when Japan (and the Japanese) became the scapegoat for what then seemed to be clear signs of declining U.S economic power. To what extent is national pride and patriotism invoked in your community (or country) when transnational corporations, spurred by globalization, export jobs to "cheap" foreign labor markets?

2. The author suggests that striking parallels exist between big business interests and media complicity during the planning stages for wars in the past century and in the present century. Discuss the businesses that appeared to profit the most from the latest wars in Iraq and Afghanistan.

3. The essay includes a discussion of how stories of events in mass media can be manipulated to incite fear among audience members. Discuss any recent example of how media have portrayed people and/or events to create a sense of fear.

4. Television, the author argues, remains the central storyteller in today's public discourse. It is the primary medium through which the programmers manage and deliver the messages and images we are supposed to absorb as obedient consumers. Discuss any competing media that appear to be challenging, or might replace, the television as the dominant device of social control.

5. What details presented in the essay best exemplify the mass media's subservience to established power?

References

[1] Michael Schuman, "Will Asia 'buy up' America?" *Time.com* http://business.time.com/2011/08/30/will-asia-buy-up-america/

[2] George Gerbner, "Dimensions of Violence in Television Drama" unpublished study for *Mass Media Task Force on the Causes and Prevention of Violence* (1968), 50. Also worth referring to are Edward Said's *Orientalism* (1977) and Jack Shaheen's *Reel Bad Arabs* (2003)—exhaustive surveys of the scary Other in Middle Eastern culture as portrayed in Western art, media, literature, and cinema.

[3] Paul Eisenstein, "US Auto Industry Welcome Tough Car Talks with Japan." http://www.csmonitor.com/1995/0511/12081.html

[4] James Rosenau, *The Oxford Companion to Politics of the World* (ed. Joel Krieger, 2001), 453.

[5] Smedley D. Butler, *War is a Racket* (New York: Revisionist Press, 1974 [reprint 1935]), 9.

[6] Butler, *Ibid.*, 3.

[7] Noam Chomsky, Interview http://www.chomsky.info/interviews/20040102.htm

[8] Noam Chomsky, After the War, http://www.chomsky.info/talks/20031120.htm

[9] Walter Lippmann, *Public Opinion*. (New York: Free Press Paperbacks, 1997 [reprint 1922]) 157-8.

[10] Dolf Zillmann, "Emotional Arousal Theory," *The International Encyclopedia of Communication*. v. 4 (2008), 1521-1525.

[11] Joe Lockard, "Social Fear and the Terrorism Survival Guide," In *The Selling of 9/11: How a National Tragedy Became a Commodity*, ed. Dana Heller (New York: Palgrave

Macmillan, 2005), 226-27.

[12] Lockard, *Ibid.*, 227.

[13] Brent L. Bozell, "Media coverage at its best," *Washington Times*, September 25, 2001, p. A-18.

[14] Bill O'Reilly, "I made a mistake," *The Talking Points Memo*. (3 March 2003). Retrieved December 7, 2014 at http://www.foxnews.com/story/2003/03/03/made-mistake/

[15] In the usual way, Chomsky writes, "Almost every society I've ever heard of…treats these we call dissidents, people who depart from the established consensus, pretty harshly…Another interesting thing about our culture is that we are very outraged by the harsh treatment of dissidents in enemy states." In *Power Systems*, Barsamian, p. 145.

[16] O'Reilly, *Ibid.*

[17] Steven Staples. "The Relationship Between Globalization and Militarism," *Social Justice*. (2000), 18.

[18] Ellen Meiskins Wood, "Kosovo and the New Imperialism," in *Masters of the Universe?* ed. Tariq Ali (New York: Verso, 2000), 199.

[19] Michael Schwartz, "Military Neoliberalism: Endless War and Humanitarian Crisis in the Twenty-First Century," *Societies Without Borders*. (2011), 197.

[20] Peter McLaren and Ramin Farahmandpur, "Critical Revolutionary Pedagogy at Ground Zero: Renewing the Education Left after 9-11," in *Education as Enforcement: The Militarization and Corporatization of Schools*, eds. Kenneth J. Saltman and David A. Gabbard. (London: Routledge, 2003), 307.

[21] Thomas L. Friedman, *The Lexus and the Olive Tree* (New York: Farrar Straus Giroux, 1999), 304, 373.

[22] Smedley Butler on Interventionism, "Excerpt from a speech delivered in 1933, by Major General Smedley Butler, USMC," accessed December 16, 2014 at http://fas.org/man/smedley.htm

[23] Noam Chomsky, interview by Jerry Brown, *Spin Magazine*, August 1993.

[24] quoted in Michael Parenti, *Against Empire* (San Francisco: City Lights Publishers, 1995), 22.

[25] For further reading, refer to *The Latin American Revolution Part II: Latin American Presidents Address the World Social Forum* (2009); William Blum, *Killing Hope: US Military & CIA Interventions Since World War II* (London: Zed Books, 2003), 383.

[26] Noam Chomsky, *Power Systems: Conversations on Global Democratic Uprisings and the New Challenges to U.S. Empire* (New York: Metropolitan Books, 2010), 7.

[27] Condoleezza Rice, interview by Wolf Blitzer, "Search for the 'smoking gun'," *CNN. com,* January 10, 2003.

[28] Full transcript at http://www.theguardian.com/world/2003/feb/05/iraq.usa

[29] Paul Treanor, "Neoliberalism: Origins, Theory, Definition" accessed December 16, 2014 at http://web.inter.nl.net/users/Paul.Treanor/neoliberalism.html

CHAPTER FOURTEEN

EVO MORALES AND BOLIVIA: ELECTION COVERAGE IN THE *TORONTO STAR*

Parma Yarkin & James Winter

Introduction

For centuries, the people of Latin America have been exploited, oppressed, and subjugated. While word gradually has leaked out about the terror perpetrated, for example, by General Augusto Pinochet in Chile beginning in the 1970s, few of us have been made aware of the systemic extent of the murderous repression everywhere else. The conquistadors began this terror with their policies of "extermination," but it continues to this very day under the practices of the American empire, and the pretense of spreading 'freedom and democracy.'

No Latin country has escaped this repression, which has taken the form of economic pressure, trade embargoes, mined harbours, coups, military occupations, takeovers and, when necessary, even outright wars (see Appendix A for an elaboration). Through all of this, the Latin American people have fought tenaciously, died bravely, and struggled on, temporarily defeating the oppressive governments imposed upon them and protected by the U.S. In credible (non-mainstream) sources, one can pick any country and review this kind of history over the past century. The U.S. "saving" the Cubans from Spain in the Spanish American War, for example, only to occupy Cuba for its own purposes, virtually uninterrupted until the 1959 Revolution freeing Cuba from oppression under Fulgencio Batista, the dictator effectively appointed and supported in the usual ways by the United States. These direct and indirect occupations have provided unrestricted access to valuable natural resources and cheap, largely untroublesome labour, kept in line by each country's own particular version of Haiti's Tonton Macouts, the Duvalier regime's thugs.[1]

Beginning in the 1980s, these Latinos and Indigenous peoples were subjected to devastating neoliberal policies, which have extended the stages of neo-colonialism beyond the rape of the people and their resources. Largely through economic blackmail by the International Monetary Fund (IMF) and the World Bank, this has entailed restructuring—primarily the privatization of public resources, sold into private hands for a small fraction of their worth. Hydro, water, banking, communications, every sector has been ravaged in this way, in a largely futile effort to ostensibly cure hyperinflation and debt. Whatever name one uses, from Milton Friedman or Jeffery Sachs, to neoliberalism or Chicago School economics, to the Washington Consensus, the results have consistently proven to be colossal social disasters, but a very successful means of siphoning public monies into private profits.[2]

Cuba was the first country to obtain its independence from America, and its people have been severely punished and blackballed ever since, in an attempt to prevent this freedom virus from spreading. This policy worked until Venezuela under Hugo Chavez in 1998 became the second country to secure its freedom, and like Fidel Castro, as a result, Chavez was vilified in the North American media and around much of the world. In what has been called the Latin American Revolution, over the past decade or so, numerous countries accounting for about 70 percent of the South American population have successfully thrown off the shackles of American oppression. The next country was Brazil, under Lula da Silva, in 2002. While the U.S. tried to take back Venezuela in a 2002 coup, in an unprecedented move the people stormed out onto the streets in the millions and demanded the return of their president.[3] Honduras was not so fortunate when, in 2009, a U.S. supported coup against President Manuel Zelaya reversed their democratic revolution.

In this chapter, we will briefly tell the story of one of these countries: Bolivia, the country where Che Guevara went to fight and was executed on the instructions of the C.I.A. for his efforts, in 1967. In addition to weathering the Spanish conquest, Bolivia was the site of neoliberal exper-imentation. As Naomi Klein explains in *The Shock Doctrine*, Bolivia is the country that launched U.S. economist Jeffrey Sachs' career as a develop-ment specialist in the business of economic turnarounds.

Bolivia was experiencing hyperinflation of 14,000 percent, collapsing currency and economic chaos in 1985, just three years after the last mili-tary junta was forced from power. U.S. President Ronald Reagan's policy of coca eradication triggered this tragic situation the previous year when U.S.-funded military operations destroyed thousands of hectares of coca production. Sachs' plan was described by Naomi Klein as Chicago School "shock therapy." His plan called for a radical restructuring, including the firing of thousands of mining workers, deep cuts in government funding, and other actions amounting to 220 separate laws covering most economic activity in the country. It reduced inflation, but threw tens of thousands of people, already among the poorest in the hemisphere, into deeper pov-erty; eliminated hundreds of thousands of jobs with pensions; and greatly reduced spending on education, health, and other essential social services. In elite financial circles, Sachs was regarded as a "superstar," and he subse-quently found work advising economies in crisis around the world.[4]

Evo Morales Ayma won the presidency of Bolivia in 2005 with 56 per-cent of the vote, in the first election decided by voters, rather than the par-liament, since the end of military rule. He is the first person of indigenous descent to rule Bolivia in 500 years. Born in 1959 into a poor llama-herd-ing family near Oruro at an altitude of 4000 meters, Morales lost three of his seven siblings to early deaths due to a lack of health care.[5] The isolated area also lacked electricity and drinking water. Morales recollects walking with his father and their llama herd to Cochabamba, a month-long trip, and seeing a modern motorbus, his first inkling of developments in the 20th century. The family eventually moved to Cochabamba, the capital of Bolivia's coca growing region. U.S. drug wars were already in effect in the region and the child Morales once saw soldiers douse a coca farmer in gas-oline and set him ablaze because he refused to admit to illegal trafficking. This event moved him to become active in the coca growers union.[6]

After his first election, Morales embarked on an activist agenda that restored state dominance over natural resources, redistributed wealth, greatly reduced poverty and inequality, and rewrote Bolivia's constitution. Achieving economic growth amid a worldwide recession won Morales ku-dos from the International Monetary Fund (IMF), among others.

The re-election of President Morales to a third term in October 2014 signaled continuity for a socialist program that has attracted the highest level (relative to the size of Bolivia) of foreign investment in Latin America. But readers of the *Toronto Star* were not to learn of Morales' successes or the reasons for his third electoral victory. Instead, like many mainstream media outlets, the *Star* opted to run an AP wire story that trotted out tired stereotypes, invoked Fidel Castro and Hugo Chavez, *les bêtes noires* of the establishment press, and while belittling Morales' achievements assured readers that Bolivia's real strength comes from "pragmatic economic stewardship."[7]

Pragmatic economic leadership is not socialism. This chapter examines the *Star's* story in light of Bolivia's recent history, the accomplishments of Evo Morales, the mainstream press environment in which the AP story appeared, and a survey of alternative press articles. Using Herman and Chomsky's Propaganda Model (PM) and Critical Discourse Analysis (CDA), the chapter indicates that the narrow focus of mainstream stories omits meaningful and important information while reinforcing negative stereotypes and perpetuating an elite, pro-business point of view. The alternative media and selected scholarly works, on the other hand, offer a more complete and nuanced picture of the situation.

The region has established stable trading relationships that back up domestic investments and enable economic stability even though the rest of the world is undergoing a major downturn. As Klein explains, the key to this arrangement is that it is a barter system in which the countries decide among themselves what the commodity is worth rather than being forced to yield to a world price. By freeing themselves from international markets and sudden price movements, Bolivia and its allies have "created a zone of relative economic calm...a feat presumed impossible in the globalization era," she concludes.[8]

The picture of Bolivia that emerges from the literature is one of massive social change over the past half century. Herbert Klein attributes this change, in part, to two periods of hyperinflation, which destroyed much of the power of the traditional white economic elite,[9] but it is clear from Naomi Klein's analysis as well as those of Lehman and Bottazzi & Rist[10] that neoliberal shocks and the US drug war reinvigorated grassroots movements among peasant farmers and indigenous communities. Bottazzi & Rist focus on the centrality of land reform to the growth of politically active peasant and indigenous communities and economic restructuring that has occurred during Evo Morales' presidency. Whatever domestic pressures led to change, Bolivia is part of a regional movement that has rejected the "Washington Consensus" and, with popular support, taken back control over resources and implemented social welfare programs. The presidency of Evo Morales must be understood in this context.

Evo Morales

Evo Morales rose to the presidency through the Confederation of Coca Producers of the Tropics of Cochabamba.[11] Starting in the 1990s, Morales' party, which eventually became the Movement Toward Socialism (MAS), began to win seats throughout the coca growing regions in the Department of Cochabamba.[12] Using peasant *sindicatos* as his base, Morales was elected to the National Congress in 1997 along with three other indigenous representatives. By 2002, MAS won one-third of the seats in the Congress while Morales came in second in the presidential race. Pivotal events for the growth of MAS and Morales were the Water War of 2000, in which the water system in the Cochabamba Valley was privatized and sold to Bechtel, and the Gas War of 2003, a pipeline protest that eventually led the president, the notorious neoliberal Gonzales Sanchez de Lozada (Goni) described in *The Shock Doctrine*, to resign and flee the country.[13] Goni's vice president led the country until Morales was elected by majority vote in 2006.

Evo Morales: Accomplishments

Reduction in poverty: Under Morales, through 2012, the poverty rate dropped from 63 percent to 45 percent. Extreme poverty dropped by 43 percent.[14] This was partially achieved through the provision of pensions for all persons aged 65 and older regardless of whether they had contributed to a retirement plan.[15] In addition, the Morales government provided cash transfers to families to keep their children in school and payments to pregnant women. The payments, which go to hundreds of thousands of Bolivians, are substantial, amounting to 10 percent of GDP in 2010. Unlike previous governments, the Morales government pays for these transfers with royalties from nationalized industries.[16] The minimum wage was raised 20 percent in 2013.[17] In addition, the United Nations declared

Bolivia free of illiteracy in June 2014.[18] The effect of this reduction in poverty and increase in minimum wages has been a decline in inequality as measured by per capita household income growth.[19] Thus, the poorest households saw gains of almost 15 percent in their annual income during the past eight years while the incomes of the richest 10 percent grew by a mere .1 percent during the same period. In contrast, most countries around the world, particularly in North America, experienced unprecedented growth in economic inequality in the context of neoliberal economic policies.

Land reform: Under legislation enacted in November 2006, the government requires land to be used in certain ways specified by law if it is to stay in private hands, whether individually or communally held.[20] Under the law, some 10 million hectares were reclaimed by the government since 2006, with 3.8 hectares redistributed to 50,000 peasant families.[21]

Environment: In 2011, Bolivia enacted the Law of Mother Earth, which enshrined eleven legal rights for nature, including the right to life and existence, the right to continue vital cycles and processes free of human alteration and the right to be free from pollution.[22] Morales has also been critical of Western countries that have done nothing to combat climate change. Bolivia's glaciers are melting and, it is predicted, will be gone below 5000 feet by 2020.

Nationalization of major industries: On May 1, 2006, shortly after he took office, the Morales government nationalized all gas and oil deposits.[23] The complex arrangement permits foreign companies to continue to operate, but they are entitled to only 18 percent of the total receipts. The remainder is used to support various state oil and gas enterprises and to pay royalties to the treasury. At least one commentator is hesitant to call this restructuring by the term "nationalization."[24] However, the sector has grown from 10 percent of GDP under neoliberalism to 35 percent under socialism, and the royalties have paid for an ambitious program of infrastructure development as well as poverty reduction.[25] The Morales government also nationalized the telecommunications and electricity industries, bringing to 12 the total number of foreign companies nationalized through 2011.[26]

International change: The Morales government has moved away from the U.S. sphere of influence. In May 2007, Bolivia withdrew from the World Bank because the bank was too friendly with multinational corporations.[27] In 2008, Morales expelled the U.S. Ambassador and the Drug Enforcement Agency.[28] In 2013, the U.S. Agency for International Development (USAID) was expelled.[29] Morales has also defied U.S. cocaine eradication programs and banned the U.S. militarized aproach to control. militarized approach to control.

2009 Constitution: The new constitution was written in 2008 and approved by referendum in 2009. The document recognizes the rights of indigenous people across the country, both highland and lowland communities, and specifies rights for Afro-Bolivians who had been brought to the country to work in the mines.[30] Gender parity in the national legislature is mandatory. The Constitution recognizes Spanish and 37 indigenous languages as official, requiring all regional governments to conduct business in at least one other local language. Civil rights are very extensive, including the rights to privacy, intimacy, honor, self-image, and dignity. This includes recognition of same-sex marriages. It also includes a range of human rights, including the right to unionize and the right to a safe environment as well as the right to education, health care, housing, pensions, food and water. Voting is compulsory for all persons over the age of 18. Finally, it specifically prohibits the establishment of foreign military bases in Bolivian territory.[31]

AP News Service

The *Toronto Star*, Canada's largest and ostensibly most progressive daily newspaper, ran two stories regarding the election of Evo Morales. The first, an extended "think piece" by the *Star's* feature writer Oakland Ross ran on October 6, 2014 in advance of elections later that month in Brazil and Uruguay as well as Bolivia.[32] Ross comments on two flavours of left-wing presidents in the region, exemplified by the "amiable septuagenarian Jose Mujica of Uruguay" on one hand, and, on the other, the "mustachioed former bus driver Nicolas Maduro" struggling to hold Venezuela together after the premature death of "the bombastic populist" Hugo Chavez. The article provides an occasion for the *Star* to resuscitate Chavez to bash any leaders contemplating similar policies. However, elections in Bolivia are breezily dismissed because "incumbent President Evo Morales faces no real opposition and is likely, if not certain, to win handily on the first round."

For its reporting on the re-election of Morales, the *Star* relied on an AP story by Carlos Valdez. In this, the *Star* was hardly alone. The CBC ran the same AP story as did media sites as broad-ranging as Time.com, CBS News, the *Huffington Post*, *The Daily Mail* (UK), and Fox News: all ran the Valdez story. The widespread use of the AP story rather than their own reporters' or stringers' work reveals corporate changes in the media over the past decades.

An Analysis: The *Toronto Star* and the Re-Election of Evo Morales

The *Star*'s preference for the AP story reflects the PM's prediction that media corporations are profit-making enterprises and will not undergo the expense of sending their own journalists to cover a story when a cheaper alternative is available. The AP story's quoted sources include the leading opposition candidate (who won 25 percent of the vote), the executive director of the Democracy Center (based in Bolivia and San Francisco), and the president of Inter-American Dialogue, a Washington, DC, think tank. The quoted comments, even from the "left-leaning" Democracy Center, serve to support the story's general thesis, that Morales has used the accident of prosperity to build up his own power but this is neither desirable nor sustainable. In the AP story, then, we learn that Morales won with 60 percent of the vote, beating out his nearest rival who had 25 percent. In the very first sentence, however, his victory is attributed to his "delivery" of political and economic stability to a country known for the opposite. This point, that despite the talk, Bolivia is still safe for capital, is reassuring to establishment readers in Toronto and frames the rest of the story. Although this point is made at the level of giving Morales agency by "delivering" economic success, the world market is the real agent of Morales' success, the story implies.

The remainder of the story pivots between information meant to reassure the establishment reader and what Huckin calls "insinuation": comments that are "slyly" suggestive.[33] The format of the story is to juxtapose the "pragmatic" side of the Morales' government with his dictatorial aspirations. But it should be noted that the very first quotation goes not to the winner of the election but the loser, who is allowed to utter the platitude that he will "keep working to make a better country." Morales' speech, on the other hand, is introduced by the comment that he credited

Fidel Castro and Hugo Chavez for his victory. One need hardly mention that Castro and Chavez are synonymous with opposition and resistance to North American elite points of view. Morales is quoted as saying, or rather "booming," that the election is a "triumph of anti-imperialism and anti-colonialism," and "[w]e are going to keep growing and...continue the process of economic liberation." These are the only words Morales speaks in the article, and, the article states, they were delivered from the "balcony of the presidential palace." In other words, like dictators and kings in a tired stereotype, President Morales speaks to his people from a palace. The speech, delivered from the palace, cannot really be about socialism, unless it is dictatorial socialism forced on people, the story insinuates.

As regards the CDA term "presupposition," the news story's attribution of Morales' success to the "boom in commodity prices" recurs throughout the article. Listing a few of Morales' accomplishments, the story suggests that Bolivia's performance regarding traditional economic indicators, such as accumulated international reserves, are the result of high commodity prices as is the drop in poverty. Significantly, the article does not admit that the drop in poverty as well as the increase in treasury reserves came from nationalization and redistribution policies. In other words, the article implies that economic success was linked to commodity prices, which, perhaps, "trickled down" to eliminate poverty for half a million people.

The story expresses concern that Morales and the MAS party are using personal popularity to break constitutional restraints on staying in power. Thus, early in the story, it is reported that victory festivities were "dented" by the failure of MAS to win two-thirds of the parliament, because now the party could not "push through" a constitutional amendment lifting the two-term limit on the "presidential mandate." A few paragraphs later, the story explains that Morales wanted to top his previous win of 64 percent in 2009 in order to "lift term limits." Acknowledging that Morales has not said he would seek a fourth term (in 2019) but only that he would abide by the constitution, the story points out that the supreme court ruled that he could run for a third term on a legal technicality. Toward the end of the story, Morales' "image-makers"—otherwise anonymous—are accused of building a "cult of personality" by naming a range of facilities after him.

In addition, unattributed sources are quoted as accusing Morales of using "tens of millions in government money on his campaign, giving him an unfair advantage." First, this statement could only be true if the redistribution programs enacted under Morales are considered to be spending money on his campaign—a presupposition that should be disclosed, and second, if the statement were true, "unfair advantage" would be an understatement. In fact, such conversion would be a sign of corruption and likely criminal. This statement, in other words, seems to be an overstatement by an opponent of Morales, and should have been identified as such.

The concern, of course, is not the length of Morale's presidency—Stephen Harper has been in power for a similar length of time, without ever having majority support—but rather, his ability to challenge the accepted world order. Many U.S.-supported dictators have remained in power for decades. Although the U.S. is only mentioned at the end of the story, it is to clarify that the U.S. considers Bolivia to be "uncooperative in the war on drugs and has halted trade preferences."

The list of omissions in this story is long. A few include the complete absence of discussion of the social movements that gave rise to the MAS and the Morales presidency, the devastating effect of U.S.-imposed drug eradication and neoliberal economic reforms, and the land reforms and nationalizations that funded the government's social programs. Although commenting on his huge margin of victory, the story doesn't mention that Morales was the first in a long line of presidents, whose victory was not decided by the parliament. Nor is Morales' popularity (84 percent) compared to Obama's (44 percent) or to Stephen Harper's (26 percent). The biggest omission is the fact that Morales' nationalization and redistribution policies, described above, along with regional trade agreements with fellow leftist leaders in the region, effectively shielded Bolivia from the greatest world economic slowdown since the Great Depression.

Interestingly, the AP story avoids the use of the word "nationalization" to describe the basis for Bolivia's current economic success. Instead, Morales is credited with "pragmatic economic stewardship that spread Bolivia's natural gas and mineral wealth among the masses." A reader might wonder about the neutral-sounding verb "spread" in that sentence. There is no logical link between this sentence and the statement later in the story that Morales "long ago" used his popularity to exert control by "splintering the opposition, nationalizing key utilities and renegotiating gas contracts to give the government a greater share of the profits." There is a deliberate vagueness to the description of Morales' actions as well as a sense of "that was then" thinking. Again, are the *Star's* readers being told that pragmatic stewardship is synonymous with nationalization?

The article opens with a sentence describing Morales as "coasting" to victory. This term insinuates that Morales did not have to work too hard for the victory, and, sure enough we learn that his win is due to economic and political stability in the country. Thus, the use of the verb "to coast" accomplishes the purpose of dismissing Morales' agency in achieving victory, not to mention the economic turnaround that led to his popularity as expressed by the voters. According to Huckin, CDA also has an ethical purpose. Negatively stereotyping Morales as a power-hungry dictator rather than the thrice-elected choice of a majority of voters in a country with a troubled history of failed presidents undermines rather than celebrates the democratic process.

Conclusion

This chapter has indicated that the mainstream media's reporting on Bolivia and its president is narrow, full of tired stereotypes, and supports policies of the elites rather than the society at large. The alternative press, in contrast to the mainstream media, brings a fuller picture of Evo Morales, the significance of his presidency, and the role Bolivia plays in its region and the world. The strengths and weaknesses of Morales and his MAS party are discussed, absent the hysteria over his departure from neoliberalism, and his outrageous promotion of nationalism and socialism, tools of the people.

Questions for Critical Reflection

1. The authors cite America's 'salvation' plan for Cuba during the Spanish American War. Discuss any military actions (or other wars) that have been undertaken in the name of "salvation," or "freedom," or any other similar abstractions.

2. The authors summarize five key changes to Bolivian society that President Morales has managed to enact during his tenure. Which of these is, arguably, the most momentous?

3. Why do you suppose both so-called progressive media as well as corporate media in North America frame news of Evo Morales in such negative language? What details do the authors provide in the essay that create a negative image of Morales?

[24] Petras, James, "Latin America and the Paradoxes of Anti-Imperialism and Class Struggle." *Global Research*. N.p., 3 Sep. 2014. Web. 15 Nov. 2014.

[25] Johnston, Jake, and Stephan LeFebvre, "Bolivia's Economy in 10 Graphs." *Global Research*. Global Research, 1 Nov. 2014. Web. 20 Nov. 2014.

[26] Herbert S. Klein, p. 288-9.

[27] Herbert S. Klein, p. 288.

[28] Carlos Valdez, "Evo Morales Wins Third Term as Bolivia's President." *Associated Press* 13 Oct. 2014: N. pag. *The Toronto Star*. Web. 25 Oct. 2014.

[29] Lauren Carasik, "Evo Morales' Incomplete Legacy." *Al Jazeera America*. Al Jazeera, 21 Oct. 2014. Web. 20 Nov. 2014.

[30] Herbert S. Klein, p. 291.

[31] Herbert S. Klein, p. 291.

[32] Oakland Ross, "Latin America Elections: Is the 'Pink Tide' Washing Away?" *Toronto Star* 6 Oct. 2014: N. pag. *The Toronto Star*. Web. 25 Oct. 2014.

[33] T. N. Huckin, "Critical Discourse Analysis." *Functional Approaches to Written Text*. Ed. T. Miller. Washington, DC: US Department of State, 1997. N. pag. *US Department of State*. Web. 30 Nov. 2014.

PART IV

SURVEILLANCE AND SECRECY IN THE SECURITY STATE

CHAPTER FIFTEEN

JOURNALISTS AND THE SECRET STATE

Richard Lance Keeble

The Personal and Political

Since I became a journalist and active trade unionist in my home city of Nottingham, England, in 1970, the personal and political have always somehow been connected in my life. In the late 1970s, my pacifism led me to being involved with the Peace Pledge Union, the Campaign Against the Arms Trade and then—on the outbreak of the Falklands conflict in 1982—with the wider peace movement. I edited a trade union newspaper for four years before moving into higher education in 1984. And all my teaching and research over the last thirty years has continued to be inspired by my political commitments.

Indeed, as I delved deeper into the history of international politics since 1945, I became increasingly aware of the centrality of the secret state to any understanding of media/political relations. Yet the notion of the secret state was almost completely missing from any media discourse—both in Britain and beyond. My Ph.D., completed in 1996, looked at the corporate press coverage in the US and UK of the Gulf conflict of 1991 and was titled *Secret State, Silent Press: New Militarism, the Gulf and the Modern Image of Warfare* (1997) when published by John Libbey, of Luton. Its main argument was that, given the close ties between corporate journalists and the intelligence services in both the US and UK, a myth of "necessary, clean, precise, humane warfare" had been manufactured (partly in order to "kick the Vietnam syndrome") when, in fact, an estimated 250,000 Iraqis had been slaughtered in a series of secret massacres. The thesis drew, critically, on Herman and Chomsky's propaganda model (1994) to help explain the trans-Atlantic warmongering media consensus—with Iraqi President Saddam Hussein, the ideal enemy, being represented as "mad, bad, Butcher of Baghdad and global menace, complete with a nuclear arsenal."

Since 1997, I have attempted to theorise journalists' relationship to the secret state in more depth, to analyse its structure and operations—and to track the involvement of certain individual journalists with the intelligence services[1] George Orwell (1903-1950) has been a constant source of inspiration—given his political engagement as a journalist and the wonderful literary qualities of his reportage. And yet Orwell had an extremely complicated relationship with the spooks: on the one hand, he was closely followed—by British, Soviet and Belgium intelligence—while later in his life (as a result of his friendship with David Astor, editor of the *Observer* and deeply enmeshed within the Special Operations Executive) he probably worked for them.[2]

So this chapter will aim to explore various elements of the secret dimension of globalisation—and the crucial role of the alternative media in challenging it.

Secret Warfare

Every year since 1945 the US and UK have deployed forces—largely far from the gaze of the mainstream media.[3] For instance, Jeremy Scahill reported in *The Nation* that the Obama administration has deployed special forces in up to 75 countries.[4] Major frontlines for military action were in Somalia and Yemen—though these rarely make the headlines. The American empire (with military bases in 150 countries at a cost of $250 billion annually) is, in fact, the largest the world has ever seen.[5] The covert deployment of drones (on the Afghanistan/Pakistan border, in Yemen, Somalia, Mali) only intensifies the secrecy of wars.[6]

Globalization of the Surveillance State

Edward Snowden's revelations about mass US surveillance of the globe (with the collusion of British, German and Australian intelligence) confirmed what I had analysed and predicted in *Secret State* almost 20 years ago.[7] The US investigative journalist James Bamford (2008) had also previously highlighted the extent of NSA global surveillance.[8] Yet Snowden's revelations did serve to highlight the essential clandestine, anti-democratic, illegal features of the state. Significantly, in the UK, members of the Cabinet were even unaware of the reach of the secret state into the most private aspects of the individual's life such as their emailing, telephone and social media activities.[9] And the Big Brother obsession with surveillance is not confined to just the major Western powers: it is a global phenomenon. As Greenwald stresses:

> Surveillance unites governments of otherwise remarkably divergent political creeds. At the turn of the twentieth century, the British and French empires both created specialized monitoring departments to deal with the threat of anti-colonialist movements. After World War II, the East German Ministry of State Security, popularly known as Stasi, became synonymous with government intrusion into personal lives. And more recently, as popular protests during the Arab Spring challenged dictators' grasp on power, the regimes in Syria, Egypt and Libya all sought to spy on the internet use of domestic dissenters.[10]

Similarly Bahrain, China, Russia, Pakistan, and Saudi Arabia are among a host of other countries which can all be defined as hyper-surveillance states.[11]

The Role of Corporate Media in Promoting the Secret State

Alongside the 'democratic' state in Britain there exists a secret and highly centralised state occupied by the massively over-resourced intelligence and security services (MI5, MI6 and GCHQ, the Cheltenham-based signals spying centre), secret armies and undercover police units. As Anthony Sampson highlighted, MI5 and MI6 and their many competing factions are only part of a much wider intelligence community: "This includes private companies, often employing ex-MI6 officers, which have their own interests in cultivating mystery and which rapidly expanded in the 1980s and 1990s, benefiting from the global market-place."[12] The radical historian E.P. Thompson, in an early, seminal paper on the emergence of the "secret, unaccountable state within the state" said it had been, paradoxically, "aided by the unpopularity of security and policing agencies":

> Forced by this into the lowest possible visibility, they learned to develop techniques of invisible influence and control. It was also aided by the British tradition of Civil Service neutrality; this sheltered senior civil servants from replacement or investigation when administrations changed, and afforded to their policies the legitimation of 'impartial, non-political' intent.[13]

Significantly, in their analysis of the contemporary secret state, Dorril and Ramsay gave the media a crucial role. The heart of the secret state they identified as the security services, the Cabinet office and upper echelons of the Home and Commonwealth Offices, the armed forces and Ministry of Defence, the nuclear power industry and its satellite ministries together a network of senior civil servants. As "satellites" of the secret state, their list included "agents of influence in the media, ranging from actual agents of the security services, conduits of official leaks, to senior journalists merely lusting after official praise and, perhaps, a knighthood at the end of their career."[14] Indeed, because of its closeness to dominant economic, cultural and ideological forces, the mainstream, corporate media function largely to promote the interests of the military/industrial/political/entertainment complex[15] and the secret state. As Roy Greenslade, Professor of Journalism at City University London and media commentator on the *Guardian*, comments bluntly: "Fleet Street is the plaything of MI5."[16]

Divisions within the Secret State—and the Importance
of the 'Necessary Mavericks'

Yet divisions within the US/UK secret states mean that there are openings for critical journalists. Hence, beyond the managed distribution of tidbits about the operations of the secret state, certain "maverick" journalists (such as Russ Baker, James Bamford, Carl Bernstein, Tom Bower, Ian Cobain, Nick Davies, Tom Engelhardt, Seymour Hersh, Phillip Knightley, Paul Lashmar, John Pilger, Robin Ramsay, Nick Turse) work with whistleblowers and dissenters. These have included:

- 1971: Daniel Ellsberg who, in the Pentagon Papers, as report ed in the *New York Times*, reveals the secret bombing of Cam bodia and Laos.[17]
- 1975: Philip Agee exposes the activities of the CIA in his book *The Company.*[18]
- 1976: The secret signals spy base, GCHQ, revealed for the first time in *Time Out:* leading to the trial and acquittal of Crispin Aubrey, Dave Berry and Duncan Campbell (ABC).
- 1983: Sarah Tisdall jailed after releasing information 1985: Senior civil servant at the Ministry of Defence Clive Ponting claims "public interest" and so the jury acquits him after he revealed secrets about the sinking of the Argentinian war ship(with the loss of 323 lives) during the Falklands conflict of 1982.[20]
- 1986: Mordechai Vanunu reveals Israel's secret nuclear weapons programme in *The Sunday Times.*[21]
- 1988: former M15 officer Peter (Spycatcher) Wright reveals plot to oust Prime Minister Harold Wilson in 1968.
- 1997: David Shayler exposes British attempt to assassinate Col. Gaddafi, President of Libya, in 1996; later jailed for six months in 2002.[22]
- 2003: Katherine Gun, translator for GCHQ, discloses US intimidation of states before UN discussionsover attack on Iraq.

Yet the case of "Deep Throat," the whistleblower at the heart of the Watergate scandal, proves how important it is for both reporters and media consumers to remain sceptical about all matters relating to secret warfare and the secret state. The source for the series of reports by the *Washington Post* duo Carl Bernstein and Bob Woodward that helped topple the US

President in 1974—and the subject of the book (1974) and Hollywood blockbuster, *All the President's Men*, featuring Robert Redford and Dustin Hoffman as the intrepid sleuths—was not a high-minded public servant appalled at White House corruption and the lies over the secret bombing of Cambodia. Rather, it was Mark Felt, the deputy director of the FBI, angry that he had been overlooked for promotion by Richard Nixon with the top job going to L. Patrick Gray.[23] Yet mystery surrounds Felt's revelations. Why was *Vanity Fair* chosen as the outlet in which Felt revealed all? Why were the "Woodstein" duo not informed before publication? Was it not strange that the revelation had to be written by Felt's lawyer (Felt was seriously ill and died soon afterwards). And could there not, in fact, have been a number of "Deep Throats"—as investigative reporter Russ Baker argues.[24]

Spooks—and the Epistemological Implications

The problem with intelligence is that it can rarely be double- checked. By definition, it remains secret and exclusive. It could all be fiction (and often is). As Dorril commented:

> The reality is that intelligence is the area in which ministers and the M16 info ops staff behind them can say anything they like and get away with it. Intelligence with its psychological invite [*sic*] to a secret world and with its unique avoidance of verification, is the ideal means for flattering and deceiving journalists.[25]

Another problem with intelligence is that anyone attempting to highlight its significance is accused of lacking academic rigour and promoting "conspiracy theory." Yet given the close links between politicians, corporate journalists, and the intelligence services[26] some conspiratorial elements have to be acknowledged to be behind mainstream media coverage of domestic and international politics. Moreover, with the emphasis on intelligence, the focus of journalism shifts from objective, verifiable "facts" to myth: in effect there is a crucial epistemological shift.[27] As the historian Timothy Garton Ash stressed: "The trend in journalism as in politics and probably now in the political use of intelligence, is away from the facts towards a neo-Orwellian world of manufactured reality."[28]

How the Alternative Media Exposes the Secret State

Conventional studies of conflict reporting have tended to marginalise or ignore altogether the non-corporate media. This should not come as a surprise: the essential ideological function of the dominant political and cultural spheres is to silence the voices of progressive and revolutionary social movements.[29] Yet the role of the activist, alternative media (linked to the global peace, environmental, feminist, trade unionist, anti-racist, progressive left movements) both historically and today in the formation of a counter or oppositional public sphere and in exposing the activities of the secret state is considerable both in the UK and internationally.[30]

Conclusions

There are, indeed, reasons for optimism. Beyond the gaze of the elite, a global counter-public sphere (though full of internal tensions) is bursting with people constantly challenging the lies and mystifications of the powerful and their propaganda media, bravely protesting (through the alternative media and in so many other imaginative ways) against the warmongers—and for peace.

Questions for Critical Reflection

1. Isn't the secret state all around us: in movies (James Bond and Co.) and in the media (constant revelations from WikiLeaks, Edward Snowden and so on). How then can we call it "secret"?

2. Why is the notion of the secret state largely absent from analyses of the corporate and alternative media?

3. To what extent does the notion of the secret state (and the close ties between corporate journalists and the intelligence services) problematise dominant ideas about democracy and freedom of the press?

4. George Orwell depicted the Big Brother society in his dystopian novel *Nineteen Eighty-Four* (1949) as all-powerful. What can journalists and citizens do to counter the growing power of mass surveillance?

5. How important is it to see secrecy (in international politics, finance, diplomacy, military strategy and surveillance policy) as a crucial (though usually either ignored or marginalized) element of globalization?

References

[1] Richard Lance Keeble, "Hacks and Spooks—Close Encounters of a Strange Kind: A Critical History of the Links between Mainstream Journalists and the Intelligence Services in the UK." In *The Political; Economy of Media and Power* (edited by Jeffery Klaehn) (New York: Peter Lang, 2010), 87-111. And Richard Keeble, "Information Warfare in an Age of Hyper-militarism." In *Reporting War: Journalism in Wartime* (edited by Stuart Allan, Stuart and Barbie Zeliger) (London/New York: Routledge, 2004), 43-58.

[2] Richard Lance Keeble, "Orwell as War Correspondent: A Reassessment." *Journalism* 2. no. 3 (2001), 393-408. And Richard Lance Keeble, "Orwell, *Nineteen Eighty-Four* and the Spooks." In *Orwell Today* (edited by Richard Lance Keeble) (Abramis: Bury St Edmunds, 2012), 151-163.

[3] Ian Cobain, Ewen MacAskill, and Katy Stoddard, "Britain's 100 Years of Conflict." *Guardian*, February 11, 2014. http://www.theguardian.com/uk-news/ng-interactive/2014/feb/11/britain-100-years-of-conflict.

[4] Jeremy Scahill, "Obama's Expanding Covert Wars." *The Nation*, June 4, 2010. http://www.thenation.com/blog/obamas-expanding-covert-wars.

[5] David Vine, "The Lily-Pad Strategy: How the Pentagon Is Quietly Transforming Its Overseas Base Empire and Creating a Dangerous New Way of War." Tomdispatch, July 15, 2012. http://www.tomdispatch.com/archive/175568/. And Catherine Lutz, "US Bases and Empire." DMZ Hawai'I Legacy Website. October 1, 2009. http://www.dmzhawaii.org/?p=4272.

[6] Bureau of Investigative Journalism, "Covert Drone Wars." 2014. http://www.thebureauinvestigates.com/2014/10/26/naming-the-dead-visualised/.

[7] Glenn Greenwald, *Edward Snowden, the NSA and the US Surveillance State* (McClelland & Stewart: Toronto, Canada, 2014). And James Ball, "GCHQ Views Data without a Warrant, Government Admits, Guardian." October 29, 2014. http://www.theguardian.com/uk-news/2014/oct/29/gchq-nsa-data-surveillance.

[8] James Bamford, *The Shadow Factory: The NSA from 9/11 to the Eavesdropping on America* (New York: Anchor Books, 2008).

[9] Nick Hopkins and Matthew Taylor, "Cabinet was Told Nothing about GCHQ Spying Programmes, says Chris Huhne." *Guardian*. October 6, 2013. http://www.theguardian.com/uk-news/2013/oct/06/cabinet-gchq-surveillance-spying-huhne.

[10] Greenwald.

[11] Privacy International, *Global Surveillance Monitor*. 2013. https://www.privacyinternational.org/campaigns/global-surveillance-monitor.

[12] Anthony Sampson, *Who Runs this Place? The Anatomy of Britain in the 21st Century* (London: John Murray, 2004), 151.

[13] Edward P. Thompson *Writing by Candlelight* (London: Merlin Press, 1980).

[14] Stephen Dorril and Robin Ramsay, *Smear* (London: Fourth Estate, 1991), x-xi.

15 Edward S. Herman and Noam Chomsky, *Manufacturing Consent: The Political Economy of the Mass Media* (London: Vintage, 1994 [orig: New York: Pantheon Books, 1988]). And James Der Derian. "Virtuous War: Mapping the Media-Industrial-Entertainment Network." *Third World Quarterly* 26, no. 1 2005, 5-22.

16 Seamus Milne, *The Enemy Within: The Secret War Against the Miners* (London: Pan, 1995), 262.

17 Andy Greenberg, *This Machine Kills Secrets: How WikiLeakers, Hactivists and Cypherpunks Aim to Free the World's Information* (London: Virgin Books, 2012), 11-46.

18 Duncan Campbell, "Whistleblowing: From Xerox Machine to WikiLeaks via Ellsberg, Agee and Vanunu." In *Investigative Journalism: Dead or Alive?* edited by John Mair and Richard Lance Keeble, (Bury St Edmunds: Abramis, 2011), 223-229.

19 David Caute, *The Espionage of the Saints: Two essays on Silence and the State* (London: Hamish Hamilton, 1986), 97-212.

20 Richard Norton-Taylor, *The Ponting Affair* (London: Cecil Woolf, 1985).

21 Adrian Quinn, "All Roads Lead to Assange: WikiLeaks and Journalism's Duty of Care." In *Investigative Journalism: Dead or Alive?* (edited by John Mair and Richard Lance Keeble, (Bury St Edmunds: Abramis, 2011), 230-243.

22 Richard Lance Keeble, "Targeting Gaddafi: Secret Warfare and the Media." In *Mirage in Desert? Reporting the "Arab Spring."* edited by Richard Lance Keeble and John Mair, (Bury St Edmunds: Arima Publishing, 2011), 281-296.

23 See Matthew Ricketson, *Telling True Stories: Navigating the Challenges of Writing Narrative Non-Fiction* (Sydney, Melbourne, London: Allen & Unwin, 2014) and Max Holland, *Leak: Why Mark Felt Became Deep Throat* (Lawrence, Kansas: University of Kansas Press, 2012).

24 Russ Baker, *Family of Secrets* (London: Bloomsbury, 2008).

25 Stephen Dorril, "Spies and Lies." (*Free Press* April, 2003).

26 Keeble, "Hacks and Spooks."

27 Keeble, "Information Warfare in an Age of Hyper-militarism."

28 Timothy Garton Ash, "Fight the Matrix." *Guardian*, June5, 2003.

29 Richard Keeble, *Secret State, Silent Press: New Militarism, the Gulf and the Modern Image of Warfare* (Luton: John Libbey, 1997).

30 See, for instance, Chris Atton and James F. Hamilton, *Alternative Journalism* (London: Sage, 2008); *Contesting Media Power: Alternative Media in a Networked World*, edited by Nick Couldry and James Curran, (Lanham, Maryland: Rowman & Littlefield Publishers, 2003); John Downing, *Radical Media: The Political Experience of Alternative Communication* (Boston, Massachusetts: South End Press, 1984); Susan Forde, *Challenging the News: The Journalism of Alternative and Community Media* (Basingstoke: Palgrave Macmillan, 2011); Tony Harcup, *Alternative Journalism: Alternative Voices* (London: Routledge, 2013); Clemencia Rodriguez, *Fissures in the Mediascape: An International Study of Citizen's Media* (New Jersey: Hampton Press, 2001) and Mitzi Waltz, *Alternative and Activist Media* (Edinburgh: Edinburgh University Press, 2005).

211

Chapter Sixteen

Anonymous and the Left

Garry Potter

Whether we know these people personally or not, Anonymous has proven we
don't give a fuck about borders. We don't care for your petty racial prejudices,
your sexism, your religious ideology, any of it. We are all one. ONE. Singular.
Divided by no mother fucker. One solid force standing as a beacon of light,
a pillar of hope, in this bleak dark world. These people are our brothers. Our
sisters. Our friends. One love. We stand, because the rest can't walk yet. We
speak, because they have not found their voices. Our voice resonates around
the globe. One voice screaming PEACE! COMPASSION! JUSTICE! And if
you fuck with us, with ANY of us, for all downtrodden people are our brethren:
Expect us! Expect us like a mother fucking storm.
Expect us like a force of nature.
—*Bad Rum Pete*
(Million Mask March Facebook page 2013)

Introduction

"Communism is evil. Fuck off and die you faggot!!" was the first reply
to my Facebook post about poverty reduction in Venezuela. This
was on one of the pages where I was "debating" Anonymous' Operation
Venezuela. It marked a very crucial intellectual/political moment for me:
when speaking of Anonymous I began to say "we" instead of "they."

I had been studying Anonymous as an object of knowledge for sociological research for about two years before the late February violent street protests against the Maduro government of Venezuela. Operation Venezuela was Anonymous' response to these protests, in support of them and against alleged government interference with people's Twitter accounts. It involved, among other things, mainly DDoS (distributed denial of service) attacks on Venezuelan government websites. These attacks I thought to be a very, very bad idea. I believed Anonymous was being tricked into operationally supporting American covert operations against Venezuela and the Far Right and the old economic elite's struggle against the Bolivarian Revolution.

But long before I began to say "we" with regard to Anon-ymous, I had a definite side with respect to the political battles "they" fought. They had been in support of Occupy, the Arab Spring, Wiki Leaks and Julian Assange. They had taken down the websites of Visa, Mastercard and Paypal. They attacked the FBI and declared a cyber war against the US government… and many other governments around the world. Thus, when I began my social scientific study of them, my approach was by no means attempting that of a value neutral researcher. I was already something of a self-declared Anonymous "cheerleader."

As I learned more about Anonymous, I discovered many of their flaws, their weaknesses. This was not difficult. Peer into any Anonymous Internet Relay Chatroom and the vulgarity and childishness and ignorance will be right in your face immediately. Anonymous has a culture that still exists today, which derives from their 4Chan roots. The original "membership" of Anonymous was drawn nearly exclusively from the ranks of the /b/tards. 4Chan was primarily an imageboard site where participants could discuss anything from anime to knitting; /b/ was their non-specific topic site.

The posts used "anonymous" as the default setting for a posting handle. This became a social norm. The forum was by turns intimate, irreverent, mutually supportive and hostile. The collective sense of humour that emerged I would characterize as "juvenile shock." It was very much anti-political correctness, so the odious terms "nigger," "bitch," and "faggot" were ubiquitous. It would be easy to write the lot of them off at a quick glance as simply kiddie racist, sexist homophobes. This would be, however, a mistake. Racism, sexism and homophobia certainly float around in the Anonymous world even to this day, but against that there is also a powerful anti-racist, anti-sexist and anti-homophobic discourse often supported by action. For example, Anonymous uses the term "fag" constantly but usually with some irony, as Chelsea Manning is supported and seen as a hero.

Leaving aside this, there is also their ignorance on a broader scale. Many Anons believe in an illuminati plot to cull the earth of billions of people. Many of them believe in chemtrails and, *à la* David Icke, reptilians or aliens in the highest levels of government…and in the American version of this nonsense, believe the government is preparing FEMA camps to intern millions of people. Many Anons are believers in Ron and Rand Paul's depictions of the American Federal Reserve as the principal institutional problem and creator of inequality. Others articulate their notions of freedom through the concepts used by groups such as the Oathkeepers. Some form or another of libertarianism or ill thought out and spontaneous anarchism or even the two combined is the most common political overview of Anons.

One might well wonder then, why I, a professed Marxist, would move from merely studying Anonymous—they are without a doubt a most fascinating complex phenomenon—to considering myself one of them. And I have an answer, which will form the central argument of this chapter.

Anonymous has already done a lot, though their achievements have largely been symbolic. Taking down Mastercard and Visa did not disturb their business. Nonetheless, their targets have been big; their actions have been dramatic and documented with prolific flair. Go to YouTube and key in Anonymous; you will find hundreds and hundreds of extremely creative videos featuring incredibly dramatic exhortations, exaggerations, and pervasive threats to governments and corporations. And some of these threats have been successfully acted upon. But it is not their achievements thus far, impressive though they are, which have motivated me to align myself with them. No, it is their future potential and my hope for it: Anonymous, *with your help,* is going to change the world!

Quarrelsome Quackery and Anonymous' Adolescent Coming of Age

At one point in their history it would have been fair to say that the population of Anonymous could be divided into two groups: purists and moralists. As said before, Anonymous grew out of the /b/tards (as they called themselves) of 4Chan. Posts were anonymous and, perhaps because of that, were raucous, irreverent, and frequently quarrelsome. People involved with

/b/ spontaneously organized themselves to undertake Internet raids (which later became the "ops" of Anonymous). The guiding principle of these raids was that they were done for the "lulz." While there is considerable depth to the notion of lulz, an oversimplification of the concept is nonetheless revealing: lulz is the cruel humour to be found in a provocation inciting an impotent anger. The "purist" faction of Anonymous wished to retain that as the primary focus.

The "moralist" faction in Anonymous developed out of their war with Scientology. Scientology became a target for Anonymous when its leadership tried to prevent the YouTube circulation of a Tom Cruise video clip. Cruise is one of their highest profile celebrity supporters and his YouTube rant, they decided, did not present the face of Scientology the way they wished; hence, they wanted it taken down and YouTube obliged. But it was immediately put back up…taken down and put back up again and again and again. According to mainstream media accounts (Wikipedia actually provides a good example of such—see Project Chanology,[1] online), Scientology's litigious nature and attempts to control "free speech" were an affront to Anonymous' unconditional commitment to Internet freedom of speech. Well, perhaps there was some of that, but mainly it was about the lulz. Anyway, they DDoS attacked Scientology's website and demonstrated physically outside Scientology headquarters in many cities. Scientology obliged the lulz seekers with appropriate impotent rage. The media portrayal of Anonymous as self-appointed defenders of freedom just put the icing on the cake. But there were some who took the role seriously.

The freedom fighter role crystallized around support for the Arab Spring, WikiLeaks, and Occupy. The concept of Lulz was certainly still there, as ops were frequently carried out with elements of dark humour, but now there was something else: a commitment to social justice. The "purist" faction felt that "moral fags," as they were labelled, were taking all this freedom and justice stuff far too seriously. But Anonymous changed over time. New people became involved who lacked a 4Chan history and who never saw Anonymous as anything else other than a political actor. Others of the purist persuasion left Anonymous entirely or simply gave it less of their time. And probably, simply through the people getting older, pranks held less appeal. The moral fags began to dominate. Perhaps, it was simply that the image of selfless crusader for justice held more appeal than did that of class clown. But regardless, the purists' hope for a return to their prankster roots has become increasingly obvious as a futile one. Anonymous, in one way or another, is now a serious political actor. While elements of humour are certainly retained, in their declarations of war against the United States and many other governments and corporations for example, there is a seriousness of purpose to it as well.

This represents one of the strings to my argument about Anonymous' potential. Anonymous is changing in terms of the background and age of its participants. There are more women now in Anonymous, and the prevalence of sexist humour is accordingly in decline. There are older people involved with Anonymous, as well as those from the group's infancy who are simply growing up. I don't know, and there really is no way of telling for sure, just how unusual my involvement with Anonymous is. I certainly did not come out of 4Chan; and while I have never had any sympathy for Scientology, Operation Chanology did not capture my imagination; there are bigger political fish to fry. No, it was the potential to engage with a serious politics of the Left in Anonymous that excited me. To some extent, the direction Anonymous goes in the future is up for grabs.

As the number of my Anon Facebook friends proliferated (by my conscious agency on the one hand and accident on the other as there is a Facebook friendship snowballing effect), I noticed an interesting phenomenon. I was already trying to use Facebook for political communication purposes and had a large number (nearly 2000) of friends from the Far Left (mainly from the English speaking world but to some extent beyond it). My Facebook friends were friends of friends of friends in this linkage of common interest. My FB friends' political selection was not at all party specific or even school of thought specific. Many, but by no means all, were Marxists (of a great many variations!), but there were also anarchists and left wing social democrats and, perhaps sad to say, some liberals. But after acquiring a fair number of Anonymous friends as well, I noticed that there was almost *no overlap at all* between them and my other friends. I looked closely at the friends of my Anonymous friends and found that there seldom was any connection to what could be in any way called "traditional leftwing political activism." And yet they were certainly politically active. They were certainly thinking and questioning the status quo of the existing worldwide political order. But they just weren't doing it within the circles of the traditional political Left.

This brings me to one of my principal points in this essay. I believe Anonymous has enormous potential beyond what it has thus far achieved, and I believe I can demonstrate at least a glimpse of the vision underlying this potential. Secondly, I believe Anonymous' future political development and direction are to some extent up for grabs. To a considerable extent, this will depend upon the number and quality of new people becoming involved. Anonymous wants you!

Anonymous' future will be determined by the collective actions of its participants. Part of their political potential derives from their unique participatory democratic "non-structure structure."

Democratic De-Centralism, Do-ocracy, and the Hive Mind

It is not that there is no structure to Anonymous; there is. Though I am not a Deleuzian, it is the term "rhizone" which perhaps comes closest to describing Anonymous' structure; but even that is inadequate. Jean Paul Sartre famously used the example of people at a bus stop to clarify the notion of a political group. Such a grouping is precisely *not* a political group; their gathering together is purely contingent; they are bound together only by the minimally shared partial project of wishing to catch a bus by which they will be traveling for a time in the same direction. That is all clear and obviously serves well to make Sartre's point about political identity, groups and contingency, except that it is *exactly* this metaphor that Anonymous has used to describe itself:

> You cannot join Anonymous. Nobody can join Anonymous. Anonymous is not an organization. It is not a club, a party or even a movement. There is no charter, no manifest, no membership fees. Anonymous has no leaders, no gurus, no ideologists. In fact, it does not even have a fixed ideology. All we are is people who travel a short distance together—much like commuters who meet in a bus or tram: for a brief period of time we have the same route, share a common goal, purpose or dislike. And on this journey together, we may well change the world.[2]

There are many levels of involvement in Anonymous. Some people's whole lives are consumed by it and have been for a decade or more. Others occasionally take part in an IRC discussion or put an Anonymous mask on their

Facebook page but do little else. Some have taken part in a DDoS attack on…someone or something…but likely never will again. And anonymity itself takes place on a sliding scale. Many, far more than it is likely the public imagines, use their real world identities without concealment. Some rather foolish people have even done so while publicly advocating illegal operations and even participated openly in the planning of such. Others, of course, use encryption, to varying levels of expertise. Tag-name identities are maintained over long periods of time (years) or used for a purpose for a brief time and then abandoned. The point here is that Anonymous involvement is quite varied in kind and scale.

There are many groups within Anonymous, autonomous and closely bounded collectives that have their own agendas and who carry out their own activities. These groups either often or seldom bring these under the Anonymous banner. Anonymous is international with Anonymous groups in non-English speaking countries sometimes put together by mono-lingual Americans or Australians or English. Anonymous is still, to some extent, Anglo/Amero-centric, though this is changing. There are also many national Anonymous groupings put together by the people of these countries (and the phenomenon is now in virtually every country in the world).

There is no central authority but that does not mean there is no hierarchy. Some voices carry further than others. This is so for a variety of reasons, including Facebook algorithms. But it is also because of respect based upon certain cultural values. Quite naturally, those with a longer association with the movement, feel they deserve and often receive greater respect than those who are new to the movement. Hacking skills, of course, very much command respect. In part, Anonymous' immediate springing to the defence of Julian Assange came about because he was already well known to many Anons as a hacker. But this deference to computer skills, while of course still present, is shifting somewhat in relation to a growing awareness of the importance of historical, political and sociological knowledge (I will come back to this point later).

Democratic centralism as the dominant form of political organization amongst the world's far left has both come into practical hard times and intellectual dissent in recent years. Many people have gotten excited instead about the "horizontal" organization/non-organization of groups like Occupy, while others have stressed the limitations. I do not wish to carry this debate any further here; instead, I wish to stress the special conditions which pertain to Anonymous' horizontal/rhizomatic form of organization.

Two conditions set it apart from all other groupings, which might proceed similarly. First, there is anonymity. Second, while Anonymous can, and does, move into the "real world," its essence derives from the Internet. These two conditions make it a hitherto unprecedented political phenomenon.

Or rather, these two conditions in combination with one another make it an unprecedented political phenomenon. There have been many political groupings in history organized around anonymity and secrecy. A cell structure whereby members only know as few as two other members—the person who recruited them and the person they recruited—has frequently been used by underground revolutionary groups. And, of course, on the other hand, there are all kinds of political groupings to be found on the Internet. No, it is the Internet and anonymity that make Anonymous unique.

People log into IRCs as and when they choose with respect to some; but also sometimes only when they are invited and given the proper login instructions with respect to other IRCs. People use real world identities. Or they may be completely anonymous. They often use self-created nicknames. This last is also true on Facebook and Twitter where, of course, you need some kind of identity to get an account. But that identity can easily be hidden. So, there is some lasting structure, a kind of a structure anyway, for continuity in discussions, whereby there are groups of groups, crossing over different social media, with considerable overlap between one another. Ideas, thus, interpenetrate these different domains, cross over and are spread, more or less successfully, throughout the whole "community," dependent upon how popular they are, dependent upon how often posts are shared or re-tweeted etc.

But there is one particular sort of idea at the core of Anonymous' functioning: proposals for ops. Many, many ops are simply decided and acted upon by small groups, which later claim the Anonymous banner. Sometimes this is hotly disputed. For example, Operation Last Resort, a revenge attack upon the FBI for the suicide of Internet activist Aaron Swartz, was one of Anonymous' most flamboyant and technically skilled actions. It was not simply a DDoS attack taking down a website temporarily. No, they actually took over the website:

> When visitors went to ussc.gov, the website appeared as
> normal. However, on various social media outlets, ac-

counts claiming allegiance with Anonymous published "Konami" code, a series of keystrokes with which any visitor to the site could use to turn their keyboard into video game controls...shooting the U.S. Sentencing Commission's website text caused the original image of the site to slowly shrink, revealing a dark Anonymous face (the iconic "Guy Fawkes" mask).[3]

However, controversy arose when other Anonymous groupings asserted that this was not an Anonymous action but itself part of some nefarious FBI plot.[4]

The bottom line is that no one "owns" or absolutely controls the Anonymous identity and basically anyone can claim it. But the claims and the disputes can go beyond intellectual debate. For example, the Facebook group "Anonymous Robin Hood Movement" was recently taken over by other Anons because of their support of American anti-immigrant militia groups (see the messages on their site[5] for examples of both Anonymous support of social justice and anti-racism and the still prevalent juvenile crude humour).

Some ops are participated in by thousands and thousands of people. A rather unusual example (for Anonymous that is) nonetheless illustrates the working principle: the Million Mask March (MMM). The MMM is an unusual example for an Anonymous activity because though organized online (primarily through Facebook) it was a real world event. The Anonymous mask is becoming more and more ubiquitous at political protest events but these are usually events organized by other groups or complexes of groupings; Anons at these events are just another face in the crowd so to speak. But the Million Mask March (MMM) was entirely theirs. MMM events took place in over one hundred countries and in more than four hundred major cities around the world. The vast majority of these had under one hundred participants, but some, like those of London and Washington D.C., had several thousand people participating. All together, conservatively estimating, probably somewhere around one hundred thousand people were involved. While this figure perhaps does not confirm the boast of one of Anonymous' most famous memes—"We are Legion"—it nonetheless is a lot of people, and with an impressive international distribution.

So, what is the democratic principle of organization for ops that the MMM demonstrates? It is very simple: get involved if you approve, spread the word, participate; if you don't approve, don't get involved. It is as simple as that. Most of the ops proposed by people, and there is a constant stream of submissions, never go anywhere. In fact, most Anons do not even get to hear about most ops proposed, for the simple reason that some measure of approval and/or agreement with the op proposed is required for the proposal to even be disseminated beyond a very small number of people. This is where hierarchy and respect come in. People with a huge number of followers on Twitter, for example, can obviously have their proposal reach a larger number of people than those who do not. But this is no guarantee that it will be taken up. Conversely, the suggestion of an unknown with few followers might be. The suggestion might strike a nerve and catch on, in a similar process to a YouTube video going viral. The bottom line is this: ops get carried out by more or fewer people, or none at all, by a simple process of "do-ocracy." This is the core of Anonymous operations; and as such, I would argue is also the core of the Anonymous identity. Anonymous is what Anonymous does.

And herein lies the problem and the hope and the potential for the future. What Anonymous does or does not do will be determined by who does or does not participate. One could say that the world's intellectuals and Leftwing activists have, thus far, consistently not voted in the Anonymous operational "elections." Their voice has not been raised beyond a whisper. This, I would argue, can be, and should be, changed. Anonymous represents enormous potential to change the world!

Anonymous and the Left, Commodification, and the Internet

There is a battle over water on the planet. It manifests itself, as political battles do, on both conceptual and practical levels. We have, on the one hand, Peter Brabeck-Letmathe, Chairman of Nestlé, asserting that there is no such thing as a human right to water.[6] Water is a commodity to be bought and sold like any other, and justice and need will be balanced out according to the laws of the market. And, just as one example among a myriad of others on a practical level, there was the Bechtel corporate water consortium's attempts to own and control Bolivia's water supply.[7] But, on the other hand, there is also resistance to exploitation. The indigenous people of Cochabamba united in protest at water rate increases and Bechtel control, and they blockaded the roads to demand justice.[8]

Underlying such struggles is a wholly different conceptual schema for understanding water: the water of the earth belongs to us all and access to it is a basic human right. From the point of view of Anonymous and increasing numbers of others, Facebook and the Internet are like water.

Facebook is not an international social media platform designed to facilitate online communication and creativity amongst the human species. It is not a research institute expressly designed to further understanding of the human condition. No, it is a publicly traded corporation that exists solely to create wealth for its shareholders. But there are different levels to reality; and while this last statement is true, it merely expresses a shallow legal and economic and present day reality, corresponding to the dominant features of the "capitalist condition." But our human condition has a reality to it in Facebook that transcends shareholders' legal claims and the existing legal framework for publicly traded corporations. Facebook is so big now, and so intertwined with our lives, millions and millions of our lives, that it has become something like water.

Water can be, and is, commodified and legally owned…but millions of us know this to be wrong! We know that water belongs to everyone, that it is a fundamental human right. Facebook is becoming something like that. It is an international communications platform whose usage is so important and widespread that it is wrong for it to be owned and commodified. Millions of people are beginning to feel this way. People are NOT thinking: "I chose Facebook; it is my market-selected, social media platform of choice…and thus, it is perfectly all right for Mark Zuckerberg to set whatever conditions he likes as to how it works…because we all click-signed something in the pages of small font that we quickly scrolled through when we joined it." If we have a problem, can we simply say we will choose another company's product? No! Facebook is ours. We make it what it is!

We use FB because it is there; we feel like it should be ours; and one day we are going to take control of it! That is the revolutionary objective, not to attack Facebook or take it down or boycott it; but for us all to collectively take control of it…permanently! This will be a big part of the Internet future we need to fight for. Facebook is merely one of the many social media platforms of the Internet and what was just said above about it also applies to the Internet as a whole. People do not want its commodified form; they accept it for the moment because they must.

But there is a continual struggle to create spaces where the rules and values of capitalism do not apply; witness the open source movement and the development of shareware; witness the fact that you can simply post a technical question, virtually any technical question, to Google or Yahoo and receive answers—frequently very knowledgeable, thoughtful and helpful answers. This is done by people from motivation deep within our nature as social beings. There are the continual attempts by the various corporate powers to subject all of this to commodification…but there is also resistance; witness for example Pirate Bay.

Then there is surveillance. The Internet has greatly extended the gaze of the panopticon. There are a variety of traditional forms of resistance to this, the Electronic Frontier Foundation, for example, is a politically liberal form of such. But where is the more radical Left with regard to this? The importance of these issues is acknowledged politically by a great many intellectuals of course, but where is the active resistance?

Enter Anonymous: the would-be hero and protector of Internet freedom. One of their recent memes shows, in part, both exaggeration and the potential reality of their protector and liberator role: there is a picture of a pair of sinister eyes with the caption, "They are watching us," and then below that there is the familiar Anonymous mask, "Keep calm. We are watching them." Like many Anonymous memes, this one is clever but also contains exaggeration and truth in nearly equal measures. Many Anons work for the corporations that spy on us. Many are involved in Internet security and even run their own security firms. Edward Snowden was surely not alone in the NSA. The possibility of government or corporate hack by day, Anonymous hacker by night, is likely manifest in considerable (though, of course, impossible to measure) numbers.

But it also works both ways. Anonymous is probably *the* most infiltrated political grouping in human history. At one time perhaps, a certain naivety concerning this existed. But if Anons needed a wake up call concerning corporate shills, law enforcement and intelligence service infiltration, the short-lived history of LulSec (an independent but related group to Anonymous) provided it. The infamous Hector Xavier Monsegur (alias Sabu), a key member of LulSec, was first arrested and then turned into an informer by the FBI and his informing led to the arrest of most of the rest of the group.[9] So now, political discussions and even operations, are discussed in the awareness that not only monitoring but even participation by intelligence groups is of near certain probability.

But Anonymous has continued to be relatively successful in its various attacks upon corporations and government (of a great many different governments) agencies *in spite of corporate and intelligence agency monitoring and infiltration.* Calls to (virtual) arms go out on Facebook and Twitter, even as the knowledge of their open cooperation with the NSA has become near universally known in the Anonymous world. Ops are planned in IRCs in the full knowledge that in spite of (unevenly distributed) encryption skills, an NSA agent may well be lurking, or even joining in the active planning. There have been high profile arrests (e.g. Jeremy Hammond and Barret Brown) and innocent newbies have been picked up for relatively low-level participation. But, in spite of this, Anonymous has been able to carry on relatively successfully.

Nevertheless, while Anonymous has been able to *operationally* deal with infiltration, the *political* effects of infiltration are a more complicated story. Anonymous is sometimes used as an unwitting weapon by various governments and intelligence agencies. Among other things that I was claiming in my debates with Anons was the assertion that such was precisely the case with Operation Venezuela.

I was by no means alone in this claim; the operation was hotly debated in terms of both justification of the Bolivarian revolution and condemnation of US covert foreign policy actions. The *ad hominem* attack that I quoted to open this chapter was by no means unusual; the flames burn very hotly in Anonymous flame wars. But there is also quite measured rational discussion over a presentation of evidence and insight. Anons can be, and often are, persuaded by such. Which brings me again to intellectuals and the Left.

Anonymous Needs You

Anonymous, as I hope this essay has made quite clear, is nothing if not contradictory in just about every respect. Anonymous provides a terrain for discussion and debate that most intellectuals would find pure hell. There are no rules, even those of rudimentary politeness. Or rather there are, precisely those of civilized discourse and intellectual generosity, except they can be ditched at the drop of an ad hominem. Ad hominem attacks flow in abundance. Worse still, behind them there is always the threat and real possibility of attack. No, most Anons are not hacker geniuses, but some are. Facebook pages, for example, are continually being hacked and are even subject to hostile takeovers.

Anger enough of the wrong people and you could find yourself subject to a life destroying attack. For example, Aaron Barr,[10] at the time CEO of the security firm HBGary, publicly threatened to expose the real world identities of many anons to the FBI. He was hacked; thousands of email addresses and files of his company were dumped online and myriad private emails of his and the company's were made public on social media sites. Effectively HBGary and Barr's career were both destroyed.[11]

And then, of course, there is the ignorance, the overwhelming, depressing ignorance. As said earlier, quackery abounds. There is racism and sexism and homophobia. If there is an Anonymous cultural rule about political correctness, it is that PC must be harshly violated at all times. There is a lot of humour and playfulness on the Anonymous turf, but it is a rather rough playground.

But in some ways, it is also every professor's dream as well. The vast majority of Anons are students. No, I don't mean students enrolled in school or university, though many of them are that as well. No, I mean students in the best sense. Most Anons are on a learning quest.

I spend enough time talking with my colleagues to know that my experiences with the students in my classes are scarcely unique; indeed, they are close to a very sad norm. The careful presentation of just about any idea from the world's greatest thinkers will be greeted with yawns; extraordinary facts—the distribution of wealth in the world for example—appears to be far less interesting than what Cindy wore to the party last Saturday. Huge numbers of Anons are the exact opposite of this. They may sometimes be aggressively and ignorantly opinionated, but they are engaged and interested. Very interested! Interested enough to do independent research; interested enough to act upon their knowledge; and always wanting to find out more. And they do respond to logical argument, appeals to reason, and presentations of factual information.

Intellectuals, most particularly leftwing intellectuals, can feel depressingly impotent. We understand the world, but nobody is listening to us; nobody wants to listen to us. We do not have much effect upon events. Well, here is an arena where your words can be causal. It is a very rough and ready arena, but one where a lot of the academic jargon is stripped away. You can affect events.

Operation Venezuela took place. Venezuelan government websites were DDoS attacked somewhat successfully. But this was certainly not an operation that the whole community was behind. There is a tendency within Anonymous to over-simplify. Protest, any protest, is good; government, any government, is bad. Nonetheless, the community, or part of it anyway, is receptive to argument. I attempted to parse the Venezuelan situation in a somewhat nuanced fashion. Maduro is not Chavez; populism has serious problems; some corruption undoubtedly exists; food and other shortages, though caused in large part by hoarding, are still real problems. But in spite of this, the Bolivarian revolution still needs to be defended against attacks upon it by the old political economic Caracas/Miami elite and the US. I was by no means alone in making such arguments. The result was that though an op took place it was a weak operation that would have been much stronger but for the internal opposition. The Anonymous community, or a part of it anyway, is now much better educated concerning both Venezuela and US foreign policy.

Just to be clear here, I am not calling for an academic leadership and takeover bid in Anonymous. Anonymous has shown itself to be very resistant to leaders. Its "structure" makes the emergence of such very difficult. No, I am simply calling for greater participation. The battle for control over the Internet is a crucial one, and Anonymous is likely to be at the heart of it. But Anonymous has also been expanding its range of activities to environmental activism and the pursuit of social justice.

I really don't think it will happen, but Anonymous could simply fizzle out. More likely is the possibility that it will develop in such a way that my "we," in referring to them, will go back to a "they." They might easily become less relevant to the struggle for a better world. On the other hand, it *could* go the other way. Anonymous could become an incredibly powerful force for international justice and liberation. Their future, our future, will depend upon you, upon us. Perhaps the most fitting final thought here would be the well known Anonymous meme: "The corrupt fear us, the honest support us, the heroic join us."

Questions for Critical Reflection

1. Some people believe it cowardly to hide behind a mask or behind computer anonymity? Do you agree with this? If so, why? If not, why not?

2. Do you think that some much more regimented and hierarchical form of political organization is required to effect political change, as opposed Anonymous' unstructured anarchy? If not, why not? If so, what form of organization would you suggest?

3. We live in what some social critics have characterized as a very narcissistic society. Anonymous' very anonymity goes against this societal trend. Do you think this is a good thing? Why or why not?

4. Anonymous' attacks sometimes cause considerable monetary damage to corporations. Do you think this kind of damage is acceptable as a form of political protest?

5. Does the idea of Anonymous excite your imagination? If so, why?

References

1 "Project Chanology," last modified January 6, 2015, http://en.wikipedia.org/wiki/Project_Chanology.
2 "YourAnonMedia 2012 'How to join Anonymous—A beginners guide'" *YouTube*, accessed July 6, 2014, http://www.youtube.com/watch?v=ZdL3aUOyZBE
3 Violet Blue, "Feds stumbling after Anonymous launches 'Operation Last Resort'" *ZDnet*, (2013), accessed January 30, 2014, http://www.zdnet.com/article/feds-stumbling-after-anonymous-launches-operation-last-resort/
4 Curt Hopkins, "Anonymous claims it wasn't behind Operation Last Resort' *The Daily Dot*, (2013), accessed February 1, 2014, http://www.dailydot.com/news/anonymous-operation-last-resort-hoax/
5 "Anonymous Robin Hood Movement," *Facebook*, accessed July 6, 2014, https://www.facebook.com/groups/ARHMgroups/
6 Andrew G. Marshall, "'Human Beings Have No Right to Water' and other Words of Wisdom from Your Friendly Neighborhood Global Oligarch," *Andrew Gavin Marshall*, (2013), accessed July 7, 2014, http://andrewgavinmarshall.com/2013/04/22/human-beings-have-no-right-to-water-and-other-words-of-wisdom-from-your-friendly-neighborhood-global-oligarch/
7 William Finnegan, "Leasing the Rain," *The New Yorker*, accessed April 8, 2014, http://www.newyorker.com/archive/2002/04/08/020408fa_FACT1
8 *Ibid.*, Marshall.
9 For one account of this – there are many – see Andy Greenberg, "Was Anonymous' Hacker-Informant a Tool of FBI Entrapment?" (2012) at http://www.forbes.com/sites/

andygreenberg/2012/03/07/was-anonymous-hacker-informant-sabu-a-tool-of-fbi-en-trapment/

[10] Matt Sledge, "Aaron Barr, Cybersecurity Analyst Who Was Hacked By Anonymous And Infiltrated Occupy Wall Street, Gets Fired," Huffington Post, (2012), accessed January 20, 2014, http://www.huffingtonpost. com/2012/01/20/aaron-barr-cybersecuri-ty-anonymous-occupy-wall- street_n_1219328.html

[11] The story has been recounted in numerous outlets but see Sledge (2012) for a more recent take on the continuing repercussions of Barr's battle with Anonymous.

CHAPTER SEVENTEEN

THE GLOBALIZATION OF WHISTLEBLOWING

Brian Martin

Introduction

In the late 1970s, I collected evidence that several environmental scientists and teachers had come under attack, for example being censored, denied tenure, or dismissed. In those days, environmentalism was considered quite radical. My assessment was that these researchers and teachers were seen as threatening to the status quo. I called the phenomenon of attacking dissidents "suppression of dissent."[1]

Not long before this, the first important writings about whistle-blowing appeared in the US.[2] A typical whistleblower is an employee who speaks up in the public interest, typically about fraud, abuse of process, or hazards to the public. Whistle-blowers frequently suffer reprisals, including petty harassment, ostracism, reprimands, assignment to onerous or trivial duties, referral to psychiatrists, compulsory transfers, demotion, dismissal, and blacklisting. Bosses are usually responsible for reprisals, but co-workers sometimes join in, due either to fear of being targeted themselves or to a wish to ingratiate themselves with management.

For the whistleblower, this sounds pretty bad, and it is. Many whistleblowers suffer a great deal, often with damaging effects on their careers, finances, health, and relationships. Many whistle-blowers are conscientious employees who make reports, believing that problems will be investigated and rectified. Instead, they are shocked to their core when they are treated as the source of the problem. The result is that they can lose their faith in society, specifically their faith in systems ostensibly designed to supply justice.[3]

The phenomenon of group members speaking out in the public interest has been occurring as long as groups and abuses have existed. However, the label "whistleblower" only gained currency beginning in the 1970s. Before then, some people might have known about it but had no name for it—as in the cases of other things such as sexual harassment, bullying, and nonviolent resistance.

Few whistleblower stories are documented. Probably most are known only to the whistleblower and relatively few co-workers. The cases reported in the media are just the tip of a large iceberg. Because relatively few cases are revealed to wider audiences, it is impossible to catalog a full history of whistleblowing. All that can be done is to extrapolate from what is known.

After I started writing about the suppression of dissent, people started contacting me to tell me about their own situations, often asking my advice. In this way, I heard about ever more cases, including different types. Prominent whistleblowers and dissidents are frequently contacted by others who have similar experiences.

For example, Clyde Manwell was Professor of Zoology at the University of Adelaide in the early 1970s. After he and his wife Ann Baker spoke out about the possible risks of spraying pesticides, there was an attempt to dismiss him from his tenured position, eventually involving inquiries, court cases, and student protests. As a result of the publicity, he was contacted by dozens of scientists and scholars recounting similar problems. Later, Clyde, Ann and I, along with another dissident, Cedric Pugh, edited a book about the suppression of dissent.[4]

Whistleblowers Australia

In the early 1990s, Whistleblowers Australia was set up to provide information, advice and contacts to whistleblowers. Most of the group's members were whistleblowers. I remember one early meeting of the national committee in which members introduced themselves, telling their stories, sometimes at considerable length. The common pattern was one of reprisals from employers and the failure of appeal bodies such as boards of management, ombudsmen, auditors-general, parliamentarians and courts.

In Sydney, there was a weekly meeting of the state branch of Whistleblowers Australia at which people were invited to share their stories and receive support and advice from experienced members. I was able to attend a few of these meetings and was impressed by how valuable it was for whistleblowers to share their experiences with others who understood what it was like.

Many would start off by saying "I'm not a whistleblower, but..." or "I don't like the term word whistleblower." At that time, many members of the public saw whistleblowers as dobbers (an Australian term for snitches) or traitors. But these were loyal employees who reported problems to their bosses. They said they were just doing their jobs. They were shocked by the reprisals. Sometimes, someone said to them, "You're a whistle-blower." They looked up "whistleblowers" in the telephone directory, and later on the web, and discovered Whistleblowers Australia. But they still carried derogatory connotations of "whistleblower" in their heads, so they disliked or disowned the label and said "I was just doing my job."

Over the years in Australia, the term "whistleblower" has gradually acquired more positive connotations. Media coverage has played a big role in this, with stories about whistleblowers often portraying them as courageous critics of wrongdoing. In a typical story, "a whistleblower"—sometimes named, sometimes anonymous—is reported as making allegations about fraud, pedophilia, or health hazards, while managers say there is no problem. In many of these cases, later investigations vindicate the whistleblower. This sort of media framing has improved the image of whistleblowing.

From 1996 to 1999, I was president of Whistleblowers Australia. Everyone thinks the person at the top has more knowledge and power, so I heard from more whistleblowers than ever. Their stories became predictable: speaking out, reprisals, reports to watchdog agencies such as anti-corruption agencies (usually without success) and serious damage to careers, finances, and sometimes relationships and health. I felt I was repeating my standard advice so often that I decided to write a book summarizing it, now in a revised edition.[5]

Meanwhile, I took on the role of international liaison, trying to find out what was happening in other countries. Whistleblower laws were introduced in Australia, Britain and other countries, but there was little evidence they were effective (on whistleblower laws, see Vaughn, 2012[6]). In a few countries, there were organizations to support whistleblowers. In the US, there were several important groups, most prominently the Government Accountability Project. In Britain, there were Public Concern at Work and a more activist group, Freedom to Care, which was similar to Whistleblowers Australia in mainly being made up of whistleblowers.

I occasionally heard about cases in other countries, such as Norway, Germany, and New Zealand. However, it seemed that initiatives to support whistleblowing—both at the government level and at the level of grassroots organization—were far more common in English-speaking countries. One possible explanation builds on ideas about community and solidarity.

Solidarity and Dissent

In traditional agricultural societies, there is a great deal of solidarity within groups, such as extended families, religious groups, and work groups. Indeed, members may not even think of themselves as individuals: their identity derives from group membership. In such societies, betraying the group is almost unthinkable. (It is unwise to romanticize traditional groups, because they harbored all sorts of abuses: think for example of slavery and violence against women.)

As societies industrialized, this traditional group membership weakened, especially due to capitalism. In search of jobs, some people leave their families and their usual occupations and religious groups. Employers try to rely on commitment to the organization, but workers are more atomized and alienated.

Whistleblowing can be seen as a violation of traditional loyalty to the group. However, in societies with high individualism—notably the US—groups are no longer as integral to life as they were before. Furthermore, individuals are more likely to think and act on their own volition and values. This possibly helps explain why whistleblowing became recognized and supported earlier in English-speaking countries, where individualism and the breakdown of traditional groups tend to be greater.

Whistleblowing can be seen as analogous to a body's immune response against disease: whistleblowers point to problems in an organization that need to be fixed. The more corrupt the organization, or the less accountable, usually the more hostility to whistleblowers.

The Leaking Option

Government spy agencies are among those especially hostile to whistleblowers, because these organizations, by virtue of their secret work, are seldom accountable to the public and, hence, often involved in disreputable or criminal activities. When WikiLeaks was set up in 2006, it provided a way for whistleblowers within the national security apparatus to raise their concerns without as much risk as before. The success of WikiLeaks, in collaboration with mainstream media, in revealing secrets is reflected in the extraordinary campaign by figures within US government circles to demonize WikiLeaks founder Julian Assange and to encourage companies to withdraw financial services from WikiLeaks.[7]

WikiLeaks' most important source was Bradley Manning (now Chelsea Manning), who might never have been identified except for revealing his identity to a hacker, Adrian Lamo, who turned the information over to the US government. The impact of WikiLeaks, and its record in never revealing the identity of its informants, points to the potential power of anonymous whistleblowing, which can also be called public interest leaking.

Most whistleblowers today continue to speak up, commonly assuming that their concerns will be investigated and any problems fixed, and they are often dismayed by the reprisals they suffer. Meanwhile, most of their co-workers, who are more afraid, cautious or cynical, remain quiet about festering problems. Worst of all, few whistleblowers are able to bring about change in their organizations. In this context, the option of anonymous whistleblowing has several advantages.

By remaining anonymous, whistleblowers can usually avoid reprisals. Another advantage is that they can remain on the job, collect more information and continue to leak. This overcomes the problem of employers marginalizing the whistleblower and cutting off access to information.

Online leaking services such as WikiLeaks are suitable for certain kinds of public interest leaking, especially large-scale revelations, but for the more common sorts of problems, other leaking outlets are often better. The key thing is to get information to audiences who care about it and who have the capacity to take action. A traditional option is to provide information to a trusted journalist; media stories can alert a wider public and put pressure on employers to fix problems. Often just as effective is to establish a connection with an action group, for example an environmental, human rights, or financial responsibility group.

It can be very powerful to build alliances between insiders, typically employees, and outsiders, such as journalists or campaigners. While employees have information about what is happening inside an organization, it is often risky for them to openly voice dissent. Whereas outsiders are relatively safe from reprisals, they often lack the most precise information about how best to target their campaigns.

As more corporations undertake global operations and as international organizations play larger roles in the execution of those ventures, the opportunities for corruption and abuse increase and the need for whistleblowing increases worldwide.

Two Routes

There are two main routes for whistleblowers. The first is to use official channels, such as reporting problems to the boss, higher management, internal grievance committees, boards of management, professional associations, ombudsmen, and other oversight bodies. Reporting to the boss can be effective when the problems are minor and no one in power is threatened by addressing them. However, when bosses are either part of the problem, for example receiving payments, or have tolerated the problem, then the whistleblower will be seen as a threat and likely subject to reprisals, small or large. An important skill for potential whistleblowers is to figure out when and how safe it is to make disclosures.

The second main route is to take concerns to wider audiences. This is the route of publicity and mobilization of support. The wider audience could be other workers, other businesses, the general public or international audiences, among others.

Potential whistleblowers considering the route of publicity and mobilization need a variety of skills. They need to understand the organization and how senior managers will react to disclosures. They need to understand the thinking of other workers and how to win some of them over. They need to understand channels for communication to wider audiences, and how to craft messages that will stimulate shared concern and action. They need to understand their own capacities and vulnerabilities, so they can develop an effective personal strategy and acquire the knowledge and skills to pursue it. If they leak information, they need to maintain appearances, including continuing to do their job well.

This sounds like a very high expectation for whistleblowers, and it is. Great skills are needed to be effective. After all, owners and top managers have extensive powers, and most other workers are likely to be unwilling or unable to take risks to their jobs and careers.

Conclusion

The globalization of whistleblowing can be reconceived as globalization of knowledge, skills, networks and alliances among workers and outside activists. However, this sort of globalization will not occur quickly or automatically. In many parts of the world—indeed in most parts of nearly every country—it is still exceedingly risky to speak out against corruption and abuses, especially when it involves those with the most power. It is unwise to encourage workers to become whistleblowers unless they are aware of the risks and there is a reasonable chance their actions will make a difference.

Previous forms of solidarity, in small communities, have been co-opted by governments and managers, through what is called patriotism and corporate loyalty. Commitment to rulers and bosses allows abuses to occur, so there needs to be a new form of loyalty. In the labor movement, this was to the working class and to co-workers, but unfortunately this has allowed new venues for corruption, in unions and in political parties ostensibly siding with workers. Whistleblowers within unions and political parties are treated as traitors, just as they are within corporations and government departments.

Rather than unthinking loyalty to any group, citizens and workers need to be able to understand the world and make independent judgments about right and wrong. Then comes the harder part: acting strategically, with like-minded others, to bring about change.

The globalization of whistleblowing should be seen as part of an ongoing struggle between unrestrained and unaccountable power holders and grassroots challengers. A whistleblower has information, and often believes this is enough on its own, with the strategy of "speaking truth to power." Unfortunately things seldom work this way, which is why whistleblowers so seldom make a difference. Information needs to be used to support collective action, and that means taking it to wider audiences. The globalization of whistleblowing will involve the spreading of skills and the willingness to act openly or anonymously in the public interest.

Questions for Critical Reflection

1. The author points out that the phenomenon of whistleblowing had no name, at least until the early 1970s. Why do you suppose it has taken many hundreds of years for human societies to evolve enough to name and define this practice?

2. Why do support groups for whistleblowers emerge sooner in some countries than in others?

3. What are the advantages and disadvantages of remaining anonymous when revealing information?

4. The author recommends that potential whistleblowers have the right knowledge as well as the right skills. Discuss how any of the recommendations might be useful to problems you have witnessed.

5. The author refers to the ability of the powerful to rebrand concepts such as 'patriotism' and 'loyalty'. Discuss examples of other words that have been redefined to protect power and privilege.

6. Discuss any reasons why you feel it is useful to act in ways that align with the public interest.

References

[1] Martin, Brian. 1981. "The scientific straightjacket: the power structure of science and the suppression of environmental scholarship," *The Ecologist*, 11 (1): 33–43.
[2] Nader, Ralph, Peter J. Petkas, and Kate Blackwell, eds. 1972. *Whistle Blowing: The Report of the Conference on Professional Responsibility.* New York: Grossman; Peters, Charles, and Taylor Branch. 1972. *Blowing the Whistle: Dissent in the Public Interest.* New York: Praeger.
[3] Alford, C. Fred. 2001. *Whistleblowers: Broken Lives and Organizational Power.* Ithaca, NY: Cornell University Press.
[4] Martin, Brian, C. M. Ann Baker, Clyde Manwell, and Cedric Pugh, eds. 1986. *Intellectual Suppression: Australian Case Histories, Analysis and Responses.* Sydney: Angus and Robertson.

[5] Martin, Brian. 2013. *Whistleblowing: A Practical Guide.* Sparsnäs, Sweden: Irene Publishing.

[6] Vaughn, Robert G. 2012. *The Successes and Failures of Whistleblower Laws.* Cheltenham, UK: Edward Elgar.

[7] Assange, Julian, with Jacob Appelbaum, Andy Müller-Maguhn and Jérémie Zimmermann. 2012. *Cypherpunks: Freedom and the Future of the Internet.* New York: OR Books.

PART V

ENERGY POLICIES, EXTERNALITIES,
AND RESISTANCE

Chapter Eighteen

From BP to Bhopal: Migrant Practices of Cultural Translation for Equitable Development in the Global South

Renu Pariyadath

Introduction

I have been a Non-Resident Indian (NRI) almost all my life. As children, my sister and I partook in journeying to India in the summer where I got to meet my grandparents, cousins, aunts and uncles. My mother would always have a gift for each of them that she would carefully pick from supermarket aisles and clothing stores in our host city, Muscat, in the couple of weeks leading up to our India trip. Male relatives would receive fabric cuts for shirts or trousers, perfumes, and deodorants while women got 'foreign' chiffon or polyester-blended saris, perfumes, lotions, soaps and Yardley talc. Children would receive bars of chocolate or toffee, clothing and toys. My grandparents received appliances for the home and kitchenware such as blenders and tea sets.

The giving ritual was an important part of our visit and always included the domestic helpers who would receive hand-me-down clothes from our family at our ancestral home. Perhaps, in showering gifts on the family, we subconsciously sought to assuage the power differential that we'd assumed existed as a function of our lives in a more "developed" or "modernized," oil-rich nation. Looking back, much of our relating in those months of summer was founded on the idea that consuming was power and that sharing the power of consumption with less-privileged kin in India was good citizenship. All this, of course, was in the 1980s and early 1990s, the pre-liberalization period in India after which stores in Muscat and other parts of the world began to appear with a "Made in India" tag, making it increasingly difficult to find suitable foreign made gifts to take back home.

My story of giving is typical of other migrants from India. Academic and policy researchers have taken great interest in mapping and envisioning ways in which the diaspora of a nation, especially nations of the Global South,[1] contribute to the development of the 'home nation'. A search on the web for the phrase 'diaspora and development' will reveal numerous reports on the topic by migration policy think tanks, allied organizations of the United Nations, other international funding institutions, and national and state governments. India's diaspora occupy a place of pride in these reports, earning the top position among nations receiving economic remittances. The $70 billion remittances received by India in 2013 trumped the $65 billion that the country earned from its software service exports.[2] India's diaspora, then, is often hailed as the model for other "Third World" or "Developing" nations. The economic remittances and Foreign Direct Investment (FDI) that diaspora bring to the home nation are strategies that promote neoliberal development in countries like India.

Neoliberalism, or the practice of liberalization as it is known in India, is a form of economic liberalism characterized by free trade, deregulation and open markets. In this form of liberalism, private entities ultimately take over social and economic sectors that were once the responsibility of the state. More recently, diasporic contributions in the form of non-monetary remittances have been acknowledged. These social and cultural remittances encompass the "ideas, values, identities and social capital," or "social remittances"[3] that migrants bring back with them to the home nation. These are cultural and social skills that migrants mediate and help circulate between the home and host nations, in effect hybridizing the home nation's cultural practices. A closer examination reveals that the notion of social remittances also carries forth many attributes of the development discourse with the host nation portrayed as the provider. The value addition always happens in nations of the Global North even if goods are produced in the Global South.

The "ideas, values, identities and social capital," counted among resources for development, usually function to cultivate and sustain a steady flow of export-ready labor migrants. When we closely examine these discussions on how to engage the diaspora, we see that the diasporic actor is party in these conceptions to a monolithic idea of development, in which the establishment of neoliberalism in the home nation takes priority over the needs of the ordinary person. Above all, this discourse in which scholars, policymakers, international funding organizations and governments participate, lays the groundwork for an industrialized, capitalist society. Members of the diaspora contribute to this set up through their philanthropy to the home nation, economic and social remittances, and FDI, easing the entry of multinational corporations into developing nations. In addition, the diaspora are envisioned as caretakers of the neoliberal nation, increasingly assuming responsibilities that were previously shouldered by the welfare state.

One of the arguments I make in this essay is that in participating in this monolithic discourse of diasporic contributions to the home nation, scholars, policymakers, international funding organizations and government bodies, align with the neoliberal construct of development. In this construct, social, cultural, and economic contributions made by migrants service the transnational workforce and market. The neoliberal discourse of diaspora and development and the concept of remittances downplay benefits to transnational corporations, the non-human migrants that benefit from the kind of development envisioned in policy and research reports. Missing from the equation is the role-played by less privileged migrants and their labor, and various others affected along the global supply chain that makes possible the neoliberal project. It is in this context that I first began to take seriously the activities of the diaspora organization Association for India's Development (AID). The volunteer-run movement AID was started in 1991 by Indian graduate students at the University of Maryland. The movement, which today has 39 chapters across the United States, works to raise funds for grassroots and community-led interventions on social issues in India, focusing on sustainable development rather than top-down development.

The group also supports various people's movements in India with local actions in the United States such as protests at consulates and rallies, in order to put pressure on the Government of India and make demands on behalf of partner groups in India. The International Campaign for Justice in Bhopal is one such campaign that has received continued support from AID. Diaspora support for grassroots movements like that of the Bhopal struggle highlight a different way in which diaspora contribute to the home nation's development. This chapter specifically takes interest in the die-ins performed by diaspora activists at the Austin chapter of AID to mark the anniversary of the Bhopal gas disaster. This mode of diaspora contribution destabilizes the previously mentioned provider status of the host nation through the scrupulous work of cultural translation, making apparent for a fleeting moment, the dependence of the host upon the home nation. In this way, the case points to alternative diasporic practices of relating with the home nation in which migrants bring back to the United States cultural ideals or a different "interpretations of needs"[4] of the people from the "developing" India.

AID-Austin's annual Bhopal die-in not only points to alternative modes of contributing to the home nation that are neglected in the 'diaspora and development' discourse, but it is also an action that challenges corporate greenwashing and the double standards of the US government. These and other acts of transnational activism that stand in direct opposition to the neoliberal understanding of development need to be counted among the diaspora's nonmonetary contributions to the home nation. The die-ins that I discuss in this essay have been staged every year since 2008 but, in order to elucidate the diaspora's work of cultural translation, I focus specifically on the protest marking the 26th anniversary in 2010, the year that the BP oil spill occurred in the Gulf of Mexico. These die-ins provide some insight into the modes through which privileged migrant and diaspora activists can make visible, rather than erase, the Third World within the Global North. In addition to the capacity to physically move to the US, migrant and diaspora communities acquire multiple social and linguistic mobilities that enable them to contribute to the home nation in a different way from that imagined and documented by policy and academic researchers.

The Bhopal Gas Disaster and the Campaign for Justice

Many know of the gas leak in Bhopal as *The World's Worst Industrial Disaster*. In 1934, Union Carbide Corporation India Limited became one of the first US companies to set up shop in India. In the 1970s, Union Carbide built a pesticide plant in the central Indian city of Bhopal with the goal of ushering in the nation's green revolution. Severe cost-cutting measures at Union Carbide meant poor maintenance of the Sevin- and methyl isocyanate-producing plant in Bhopal. Safety systems required by US regulatory bodies for a facility producing toxic chemicals were thus not functional at the plant in Bhopal. This failure to secure the production of toxic chemicals led to the leak of 40 tons of methyl isocyanate on the night of December 2, 1984, killing an estimated 7000 to 10,000 people in the three days immediately following the incident, permanently disabling about 3900, and injuring over 550,000[5].

Today, 30 years later, half a million people continue to suffer from ocular, respiratory and mental health illnesses, immune system impairment, neurological and neuromuscular damage, cervical and breast cancers, and gynecological disorders. Children born in the gas-affected areas of Bhopal are seven times more likely to have a congenital deformity than children born in other parts of Bhopal.[6]

From the time the disaster first occurred, the campaign for justice in Bhopal has had international support. In the immediate aftermath of the disaster, activist and survivor groups in Bhopal demanded that Union Carbide pay $3.3 billion in compensation but as it became clear that effects of the gas were long-term and ongoing, the amount demanded was changed to reflect this new information. In 1989, Union Carbide and the Indian government settled the case outside court for $470 million, without consulting the survivors. The amount agreed on by the two parties was only about 15 percent of the compensation sought by the survivors, and each survivor received approximately $500 for permanent health damages caused by the disaster. In 2001, The Dow Chemical Company (Dow) acquired Union Carbide, assuming no responsibility for the disaster in India.

A transnational campaign to bring justice to the survivors of Bhopal, The International Campaign for Justice in Bhopal's (ICJB) demands include getting Dow to assume responsibility for cleaning up contaminated groundwater in Bhopal and facing criminal trial in India. It aims to hold the Indian central and state governments accountable for establishing an empowered commission to address the health, environmental, and economic issues in Bhopal.[7]

The ICJB also demands that the US government extradite the company's then CEO, Warren Anderson to face trial in an Indian court of law. AID is a coalition partner of the ICJB. Through the annual die-in, the Austin chapter attempts to spread general awareness about the Bhopal disaster on the University of Texas (UT) campus and also informs people about the funding that UT-Austin receives from Dow. The die-in in 2010 was staged to garner signatures for a petition to UT's president, William Powers Jr. The petition pointed out that despite the UT student government's and the Graduate Student Council's passing non-cooperation resolutions against Dow in February 2006, the university had not taken a stance on the issue. The student resolutions demand that UT publicly call on Dow to clean up former Union Carbide sites in Bhopal to US Superfund standards. The resolution also pledges that the university "as a symbolic and a moral gesture," would not accept money from Dow, as it "could be better spent providing safe drinking water and a clean environment to the survivors of the Bhopal tragedy."[8]

AID-Austin's Bhopal Die-in

On the day of the protest, AID-Austin volunteers occupied the West Mall in UT with "corpses" covered in blood-speckled white shrouds, representing the 25,000 odd victims who had died over the years. Other protestors shouted, "Corporations lying by the hour, what do we do? Fight the power!" The volunteers had the task of translating a disaster from another time and space to the citizens of Austin city. To make an impact, the volunteers had to not only raise awareness about the disaster but to also get the citizens of Austin to act in solidarity with the people of Bhopal. A die-in is a civil disobedience tactic that has historically been used by politically left-leaning groups to challenge injustices. Causes represented at die-ins have ranged from anti-war activism to human rights, LGBT rights, disability rights, animal rights and political causes such as Justice in Palestine. In itself the die-in is a powerful performance that brings the immobile and voiceless subaltern other from Bhopal, represented by the corpses, into the space of the city. However, AID-Austin's die-in protest also engaged local knowledge of the BP oil spill at the 26th anniversary of the Bhopal disaster, which came barely six months after the BP oil spill, and engaged in cultural translation work that allowed audiences to make connections to a forgotten and silenced story of corporate negligence in the Third World.

The BP Oil Spill

One of the most publicized instances of corporate migration gone wrong, British Petroleum (BP) was held accountable for the 2010 Deepwater Horizon oil spill. This was not the first time that a migrant corporation had violently transgressed into the environmental bounds of the host nation. Arguably, more human and environmental costs have been borne by areas affected by rogue corporations such as Dow Chemical, Monsanto, ExxonMobil, and Chevron. But the publicity accorded by national and international media to BP's environmental disaster and to the ensuing public outrage was spectacular. Through constant media coverage, the Obama government narrated in meticulous detail, the disaster, its causes and impact on people and the environment, leading to an unprecedented crusade by the state for corporate answerability. In 2012, BP pleaded guilty to 14 criminal charges and agreed to pay $4 billion in criminal fines for the oil spill that killed 11 people and released millions of barrels of oil into the Gulf of Mexico.[9] More recently, a federal judge ruled that BP was guilty of "willful misconduct" and "gross negligence" for which the corporation could be liable for civil penalties to the tune of $18 billion.[10]

In BP's case, President Obama responded rather swiftly to the oil spill when compared to similar acts of corporate negligence, especially outside the borders of the US. When the President spoke of the disaster in terms of "the battle we're waging against an oil spill that is assaulting our shores and our citizens" and discussed his "battle plan," which involved the deployment of 17,000 National Guard members, it became clear that BP's mistake was unforgivable, for it was a crime against the American nation. The oil spill began to be described in superlative terms as "the worst environmental disaster America has ever faced." Noticing the differential attention given to manmade environmental disasters occurring within the borders of the United States and those without, AID-Austin activists rightly invoked the BP spill to draw attention to a similar disaster by a migrant corporation from the United States.

Volunteer activists in the Indian diaspora seized the opportunity presented by the framing of the BP oil spill as a "limit case,"[11] having no historical parallel and positioned at the very boundaries of representation. In drilling into public consciousness, the image of BP as a company that had overstepped into the pristine territory of the United States, the Obama government and the media instilled in the people a paradigm for evaluating the citizenship practices of migrant corporations. The expeditious dissemination of the new standards for corporate accountability and citizenship to the US public were noticed and adopted by AID-Austin as a way of translating the Bhopal disaster from a different time and space to the residents of Austin.

A Work of Cultural Translation

Performance studies scholar Diana Taylor's work on the limit event is useful in analyzing the work of cultural translation performed by AID-Austin. According to Taylor, the "limit event" is a case that occupies "the outer edges of intelligibility" and stands at the "very boundaries of representation."[12] In other words, the limit event is an exceptional one that is difficult to make sense of because there is no parallel to compare it with and no language to describe it. The limit case, Taylor explains, is a paradigmatic event that has no historical precedent and the only way to connect many such disparate but similar cases is "only by illustration."[13] The BP oil disaster is, to many people in the United States, an event of catastrophic proportions and a paradigmatic exemplar of what happens when good and profitable corporations become bad citizens.

Using a discourse of "incommensurability and exception" de-contextualizes events and counters "broader emancipatory politics," according to Taylor, preventing the public from making the necessary connections between events that are thematically identical.[14] Taylor's solution to the limit case is to place such events side by side in a loose episodic relationship with each other so that we may be able to see the obvious links between the two.[15] And this is also how AID-Austin activists related the BP oil spill to Bhopal.

Activists at the die-in used their knowledge of both 'local' and 'global' events to deconstruct the BP limit case and essentially connect the local catastrophe to a global one. BP is a larger catastrophe affecting Austinites, constituted as the foreign corporation's destruction of the nation's healthy body the largest environmental disaster that the United States has faced. The disaster was a prime opportunity for activists to help unfold the episodic nature of the supposed limit case. On a poster displayed at the die-in, photographs from the Bhopal tragedy and the BP oil spill were placed side by side with the captions describing a loose timeline of both events. A banner headline that ran across the poster proclaimed "It Started Long

Before the BP Oil Spill." While the left side of the poster had an image of the oil spill with a blazing red fire and black smoke against the blue sea, on the right side, Bhopal's black and white pictures provided a stark contrast.

The first picture of Bhopal alongside BP's blazing fire, was one of the Union Carbide factory emitting a thin plume of smoke, presumably the toxic gas. On the far right was another black and white picture of men and women with cotton gauze pads across their eyes. Although the event took place in 1984, there was no dearth of color pictures, so the contrasting images were a deliberate choice. This choice highlighted the considerable passage of time between the two events and the time taken to bring justice to the people of Bhopal. Both pictures were captioned with date stamps and a brief one-line description of the event. On the left, below the first image of BP, was a picture of dead, slick-covered birds with the captions: "5 months later," "oil-well sealed," "$20 billion in compensation." On the right, instead of more ghastly pictures of Bhopal victims, was an image of rural Indian children smiling into the camera, flaunting an Obama "Change" poster with the words "Change the Double Standard—Justice for Bhopal."

The accompanying captions read: "26 years later," followed by "25,000 lives lost," "Groundwater contaminated," "347 metric tonnes of hazardous waste," "500,000 suffering from exposure related illnesses," and finally, the measly $470 million in compensation. Another poster nearby headlined "Austin and the Bhopal Struggle" listed how University of Texas and Austin had been involved in the campaign over the past few years and outlined "How YOU can help."

The Corporation as a Migrant and Citizen

AID-Austin's unfolding of the episodes in this limit event brings to the fore actors that were previously invisible in the diaspora and development narrative invoking the tropes of corporate citizenship and migration. To the activists and their immediate audience at the West Mall, the corporation, like any other migrant, has responsibilities to citizens and environments of the host nation that both BP, and Union Carbide failed to fulfill. In using the familiar BP oil disaster to segue into their cause, AID-Austin essentially made the claim that the Bhopal gas tragedy was a palimpsest or a manuscript whose earlier inscriptions had been effaced and reused to write another text. It did not matter, the activists showed, if the corporation in question was BP, Union Carbide, or Dow Chemical.

What was important was to understand the work to erase the history of "irresponsibility" by presenting the BP oil spill as the new superlative with no parallel. Lives were also replaceable. The lives of silenced others in remote corners of the world were interchangeable with the lives of voiceless birds and animals affected by the oil spill. Morris has discussed the "transgressive potential of embedding original, perhaps unconventional and dangerous, material into the layers of an established text."[16] What seems like the established text here, the failure of a multinational corporation to be a good citizen across borders is re-inscribed with the history of another failure of citizenship.

Reminding audiences of the Bhopal disaster, erodes the construction of BP as a limited case by exposing another corporation, one that was a citizen of the United States, as a migrant citizen and a bad one at that. As in the case of BP, citizenship had failed in Bhopal's case, not only because of the corporation's indifference to securing lives that are interchangeable but also the failure of the state(s) and its citizens to hold the migrant corporation accountable.

In performing the presence of missing links in the corporate supply chain and of workers and others affected by its operations, AID-Austin activists reveal that the relation of privileged migrants/citizens to subaltern populations is better described in terms of complicity rather than dependence. Those who have privilege can transgress rules without repercussions, cross national borders with relative ease, and choose to remain uninformed and unaware about how their way of life compromises the security of subaltern groups. By furnishing information about the Bhopal disaster and making Bhopalis visible locally, the protestors made Austinites aware of their complicity in the disaster as US citizens but they also offered the spectators a way out—Change. With the immediate and lateral placement of the images of the dead birds with that of the "transgressed" Change poster in the hands of the children, AID questioned the United States' double standards in valuing lives. The picture in itself is interesting.

Rather than having angry protestors hold the change poster, smiling children, presumably symbolizing the future and hope, appear to mock and taunt the Obama administration's "Change you can believe in" slogan. Change for whom? What about Change for Bhopal? Does "Change you can believe in" stop at the shores of the United States? With the "Change" poster, AID invoked, on the one hand, a sense of dissonance in Austin citizens but on the other, also showed them that they had the power to alter the double standards of the state. The remaining posters at the die-in venue pointed to change that Austinites could effect. Austin citizens were told that they could help by simply signing the petition to get their university to instigate action against Dow Chemical and, perhaps, eventually get the US state to extradite Warren Anderson.

Other ways to effect change were to sign the Austin City Council Resolution support sheet and the Student Government (SG)/Graduate Student Association (GSA) Resolution support sheet. Finally, citizens could join AID in their campaign to pass the SG/GSA UT Austin resolution, clean up the factory site, provide medical relief for the survivors, clean drinking water to communities, and ensure economic compensation for all victims. At the end of the three-hour period for which the die-in was staged, AID-Austin activists were able to garner 54 signatures towards its cause by making visible Bhopal survivors across time, space, and national borders.

Conclusion

While any discussion surrounding the migration of people is politically provocative, even more so is the movement of people from the Global South to the North. The exodus of laborers of various skill levels from countries such as India in the "developing" South to the United States in the "developed" North has resulted in nested pockets of the "Third World" within the "First World" and vice versa. As a British colony, India made significant contributions to the global migrant labor pool by supplying indentured laborers for colonial plantations when the British empire ended slavery in 1833.

Scholars such as literary theorist Gayatri Spivak[17] and historian Vijay Prashad[18] have pointed out that colonial modes of extracting labor persist in the neoliberal model of development. Along with the westward movement of labor, multinational corporations, the empire builders of our time,[19] have also been migrating. Motivated by higher profit margins, they often retrace the routes traveled by the colonial East India Company, the first-ever multinational corporation.[20] Justifications for postmodern migrations by corporations, usually from the Global North to the South, echo imperial narratives of development and beneficence for the receiving country.

For instance, a Union Carbide Corporation print advertisement from

1962 sports an illustration of Indian women in the foreground carrying a pot and an umbrella, looking on as a farmer tills the soil.[21] In the backdrop is a river and the Gateway of India monument flanked by a sprawling industrial plant. The headline, "Science helps build a new India" is followed by the text "Oxen working the fields…the eternal river Ganges…jeweled elephants on parade. Today these symbols of ancient India exist side by side with a new sight—modern industry." The ad boasts about the new chemicals and pesticides facility near Bombay, alluding to Bhopal's plant, and of its role in "bring[ing] the promise of a bright future" to 400 million people with "technical knowledge from the Western world."

Ironically, the tagline accompanying the company logo proclaims "A hand in things to come." Narratives such as these voiced by corporations, receiving state governments, and academic and policy research reports on 'diaspora and development', highlight the improvement in the availability of jobs, economic benefits to communities and the nation, downplaying the restructuring of lives and mass displacement of people caused by these migrating, non-human legal persons. Instead, in the "developing" world, and in the Indian context, the transnational corporation's access to cheap labor has almost always trumped the improvement of the lives of the indigenous people it depends on for this labor.

I have tried to illustrate how AID-Austin's die-in for Bhopal challenges this very discourse and practices of neoliberal development by making visible two prime actors in this narrative—the transnational/migrant corporation and millions of others who suffer various injustices due to the widening global supply chain, such as the survivors in Bhopal. Without these actors, the story of development in the 'Third World' remains incomplete and grossly misrepresented. Contributions by members of the diaspora in such cases are invaluable but not necessarily in the way imagined by the diaspora and development nexus.

Activists located in the Global North could help represent people excluded from the narrative of diaspora and big development by telling the story from the perspective of the affected, providing context where necessary, to gain support from citizens of the host nations. Today, while corporations have serpentine supply chains that extend across cities and nations, juridical scope for activities at the numerous links in this chain has not been similarly globalized. In redressing corporations' acts of transgression, nation-states of the Global North continue to exercise sovereign control.

While legal apparatuses play catch up to the reach of multinational corporations and their exploits in foreign terrain, transnational activism by diasporic actors in the Global North have a prominent role to play in making visible the people and environments variously affected by the migration of a corporation's activities. Through their medium, those who cannot migrate acquire a fleeting presence in cities of the Global North and, are enabled to informally participate in the politics of that land.

Dow's official line has always stressed that the Indian subsidiary, UCIL, was separate from the parent organization that it acquired despite company records confirming the US corporation's lead role in the design and operation of the plant. The Carbide factory's brainwave, Solar Evaporation Ponds lined with polyethylene, were devised to hold factory effluents, which would miraculously leave the environment unharmed. But these ponds have been leaching 10,000 tons of toxic chemicals into the soil and ground water.[22] Meanwhile, Dow continues to proclaim its commitment to the environment in the United States and worldwide. In March 2014, the company announced that it had devised a breakthrough technology that would "help deliver a more sustainable water supply to the world, addressing global water scarcity in a very tangible way."[23] The transnational campaign for justice with supporters such as the activists in AID-Austin, has been working relentlessly over the last three decades to dismantle Dow's attempts at greenwashing, exposing the company for its deceptive self-portrayal as the paradigm of environmental sustainability.

Questions for Critical Reflection

1. What is the author's main argument against the discourse of diaspora and development that academic and policy scholars participate in?

2. According to the author, how does the Bhopal case study offer a more nuanced version of the Indian diaspora's contributions to the home nation?

3. Are there similar instances of invisible corporate actors and workers in other globalized industries that the media have recently covered? In the author's example, diaspora of the affected nation work to make these actors visible. Who works to make these actors visible in these recent examples in the media?

4. According to the author, non-globalized juridical scope requires actions such as the Bhopal die-ins in the United States. What other alternatives may be available to similarly affected groups seeking justice?

References

[1] The Global North is a widely used term to describe "developed" countries in North America, Western Europe and parts of East Asia, and roughly maps over what used to be known as the First and the Second World. The Global South, meanwhile, refers to the "developing" or Third World, including countries in Africa, Central and South America and Asia.

[2] "Remittances to Developing Countries to Stay Robust This Year, Despite Increased Deportations of Migrant Workers, Says WB." *World Bank Group.* accessed September 14, 2014, http://www.worldbank.org/en/news/press-release/2014/04/11/remittances-developing-countries-deportations-migrant-workers-wb

[3] Peggy Levitt, "Social Remittances: Migration Driven Local-Level Forms of Cultural Diffusion," *International Migration Review* 32(4) (1998): 926-948.

[4] Arturo Escobar, "Imagining a Post-Development Era? Critical Thought, Development and Social Movements," *Social Text* 31/32 (1992): 46.

[5] TThe figures are derived from Amnesty International. *Clouds of injustice: Bhopal disaster 20 years on.* (London: Amnesty International Publications, 2004), The ICJB website (www.studentsforbhopal.org) and numbers quoted by survivor organizations in Bhopal. Union Carbide claims 3,800 deaths, municipal workers who loaded bodies onto trucks for burial in mass graves or to be burned on mass pyres, put the numbers at least 15,000 bodies. Survivors, who base estimates on the number of shrouds sold in the city, claim about 8,000 died in the first week and the official death toll, according to the local government stands at more than 20,000 to date.

[6] "New Abnormalities Seen in third Generation of Bhopal Children." The Bhopal Medical Appeal, accessed September 15, 2014, http://www.bhopal.org/2013/03/new-abnormalities-seen-in-third- generations-of-bhopal-children/

[7] "2013 Mission Statement." International Campaign for Justice in Bhopal, accessed, September 14, 2014, http://www.icjb.org

[8] "26th Anniversary of Bhopal Gas Disaster." AID-Austin Facebook Event Page, accessed September 14, 2014, https://m.facebook.com/ events/130159067042091events/130159067042091

[9] Clifford Krauss and John Schwartz, "BP Will Plead Guilty and Pay Over $4 Billion," *New York Times*, accessed November 15, 2012, http://www. nytimes.com/2012/11/16/business/global/16iht-bp16.html?_r=0

[10] "BP's 'Gross Negligence' Caused Gulf Oil Spill, Federal Judge Rules," Washington Post, accessed September 14, 2014, from http://www. washingtonpost.com/business/economy/bps-gross-negligence-caused- gulf-oil-spill-federal-judge-rules/2014/09/04/3e2b9452-3445-11e4-9e92- 0899b306bbea_story.html

[11] Diana Taylor, *The Archive and the Repertoire: Performing Cultural Memory in the Americas*. (Durham: Duke University Press, 2003).

[12] *Ibid.*, Taylor 263.

[13] *Ibid.*, Taylor 263.

[14] *Ibid.*, Taylor 273.

[15] *Ibid.*, Taylor 275.

[16] Charles E. Morris, "'The Responsibilities of the Critic' F.O. Matthiessen's Homosexual Palimpsest." *Quarterly Journal of Speech*. (84 (3): 261-282, 1998.).

[17] Gayatri Chakraborty Spivak, "Diasporas Old and New: Women in the Transnational World." *Textual Practice*. (10.2, 245-270, 1996)

[18] Vijay Prashad, *The Karma of Brown Folk*, (Minneapolis: University of Minnesota Press, 2000).

[19] Nick Robins has outlined the role played by the East India Corporation in forming the prototype for the modern day corporation in The corporation that changed the world.

[20] Nick Robins, *The corporation that changed the world: how the East India Company shaped the modern multinational*. (London: Pluto Press, 2012).

[21] "Bhopal, India," Chemical Industry Archives: a project of the Environmental Working Group. Image retrieved September 15, 2014, http://www.chemicalindustryarchives.org/dirtysecrets/bhopal/pdf/ bhopalUCCad.pdf

[22] Shahnawaz Akhtar, "94 percent Bhopal Vitims not Propoerly Compensated: Activists." (2008), accessed October 21, 2014, http:// twocircles.net/2011dec20/94_per-cent_bhopal_victims_not_properly_ compensated_activists.html#.VEaTRYvF-5A

[23] "Dow Names Breakthrough to Global Water Challenge." *Dow Chemical*. (2014), accessed October 21, 2014, http://www.dow.com/ news/press-releases/article/?id=6459 news/press-releases/article/?id=6459.

Chapter Nineteen

Turning Carbon into Gold: Globalization and the Emissions Trade

David Layfield

Introduction

Like many people, I first heard about climate change in 1989. This coincided with a run of warm summers and mild winters in England when, for a couple of years, the southern half of England saw neither snow nor frost. Like many people, I also wondered what to do. After all, I didn't own a car, rarely ever ate meat, had never travelled by air, and from my parents I learned to wear warm clothes, rather than to turn up the thermostat for the home heating. As I read more about the science behind climate change and watched the television documentaries that were made about it in the early 1990s, I also wondered what governments were actually doing about the climate problem. Would governments take the science seriously? Would they show the leadership to make the necessary economic changes over the 25 to 30 years that scientists were saying would be crucial?

Through the 1990s a series of meetings and conferences led to the Kyoto Summit in December 1997. At the end of the summit, world leaders presented the Kyoto Protocol, hailed as the solution to climate change in a globalising world. In this chapter I want to take a critical look at the results of the Kyoto Protocol in more detail and at the results achieved, before suggesting alternatives that could be more effective in reducing the carbon emissions that cause climate change.

During my academic research, I discovered that the principal result of the Kyoto Protocol has been to establish a global market for carbon. By permitting governments to trade carbon permits across national borders, Kyoto has created a range of highly complex financial products, many of them controlled by transnational banks and other global financial institutions. The complexity of these financial products and the difficulty in checking their quality mean this global carbon market has not been able to reduce global carbon emissions. This highlights the connection between climate change and neo-liberal globalization. The solution to the problems caused by the growth of global markets has been to create more markets, and for these to rapidly become global in scope.

I also want to suggest that rather than emissions trading, national regulations, as well as local-level initiatives, could offer more effective and democratic ways to reduce carbon emissions. Changing our own lifestyles and working for our cities and states to change theirs, offers a way to participate that could bring deeper changes than buying and selling emissions permits.

What is the Kyoto Protocol?

Before discussing these ideas in more detail, a look back at the development of a global market for carbon might be helpful. The Kyoto Protocol establishes carbon trading as a legitimate means for governments to reach their emissions targets, on average 5% below 1990 emission levels by 2012. The Protocol goes on to establish the Clean Development Mechanism (CDM) as a way for developing countries to participate in a growing global carbon market. Article 12 of the Kyoto Protocol accepts that developing countries do not have to meet reduction targets; instead, the CDM will 'assist Parties not included in Annex 1 in achieving sustainable development'.[1]

Sustainable development can also be used to 'assist parties in Annex 1 in achieving compliance with their quantified limitation and reduction commitments'.[2] Through the CDM, investment, and technology will transfer from Annex 1 (The members of the OECD, plus Russia and Eastern Europe) to non-Annex 1 (developing) countries. To help the CDM attract investors in the richer Annex 1 countries, emissions reductions earned from participating in the CDM can count towards their own reduction targets. Typical CDM projects involve energy and transportation, garbage disposal, land use and forestry, with 80% of current CDM projects located in China.[3]

The Kyoto Protocol sets up a system to trade carbon emissions. Systems based on trading pollution permits have also been used elsewhere. For example, they are a principal part of the United States' acid rain program. In the acid rain program, big utilities operating coal-fired power plants receive a number of permits to emit sulphur dioxide. If a utility emits less sulphur dioxide than its target, then it can sell the permits it doesn't need to those who have emitted more than their target and, thus, need to buy more permits. The number of permits received by utilities gets smaller each year, so they have an incentive to produce less sulphur dioxide. To economists, this system has become part of a familiar method of putting 'prices' on pollution.

The Kyoto Protocol applies this same logic to a range of gasses causing climate change, including carbon dioxide, methane and nitrous oxides, and it also lets governments and large businesses trade permits across national borders. Each government that has ratified the Kyoto Protocol has to maintain a database of all the climate change gases emitted in their nation each year. They then set a national target, (agreed upon between the government and the Kyoto Protocol Compliance Committee) and issue permits (Assigned Amount Units or AAUs in the carbon trade jargon). The permits give power utilities and other large polluters a target each year. If they emit less than their target, then they are free to sell their AAUs to those who have emitted more than their target, and so need to buy more.

Since the Kyoto Protocol was ratified, some rather complex new ways of trading carbon emissions have emerged. The most important include Removal Units (RMUs), which represent carbon 'removed' from the atmosphere through forestry or changes in land use. For example, if a company plants trees, then it is allowed to estimate how much carbon will be absorbed by the trees each year as they grow. It is then allowed to count the carbon absorbed by the trees *as if* the carbon absorbed were a reduction in that company's emissions.

Certified Emission Reductions (CERs) are particularly controversial, and these are earned through participation in the Clean Development Mechanism. In a typical CDM scheme, a European utility will offer investment and expertise to build a solar, wind or other renewable energy project in the global south, *instead of* building a coal or oil fired plant. The CDM rules say that the European utility is then allowed to estimate the amount of carbon that would have been emitted *if* the coal or oil fired plant *had* been built. If a supposedly independent verifier agrees with the evidence presented by the utility, then it is issued CERs, which it can count, or trade, *as if* they were a reduction in its own emissions.

The Carbon Trade

Today, it looks as though trading is going to become big business, and carbon—both real and conceptual—is well on the way to joining oil, food, and metals as a globally traded commodity. But, like other markets for other commodities, the market for carbon emissions is likely to be unstable.

One of the things I discovered during my research on the Kyoto Protocol was that international carbon markets are very complex. Each government is required to maintain a national registry of AAUs, RMUs, CERs, and a record of who owns them, as well as a record of each Unit's identification number. Any international brokerage or market dealing in the various Units is required to keep a transaction log, including seller and buyer details, the national registries involved and the identification numbers of all Units passing through their trading books. There should be a 'virtual trail', that is a network of computer records for every AAU, RMU, ERU, and CER, its ownership history, and all of the trades it was involved in. The vision behind all of this appears to be the creation of a single, global market for carbon, in which every tonne of carbon emitted from any source is represented by a virtual trail of permits, projects, and trades.

I also discovered that carbon trading has attracted new entrepreneurs suggesting it is possible to make millions of dollars from climate change, with less effort than it takes to engage in work on a regular job. One example offers prospective clients the story of Jim Watts, a delivery driver in Los Angeles, who grew tired of the long hours and heavy traffic and decided to quit his job:

> He read everything he could on global warming and how carbon credits could generate large returns, if he invested his time into understanding how market prices were manipulated. He invested $40,000 in a little known [sic] commodity called a CFI (Carbon Financial

Instrument)…He consistently doubled and tripled his
money every year.[4]

This particular website promises that we can all do the same and offers to
sell a set of manuals on carbon trading and how to become a CDM verifier.

Capital markets and financial firms are taking a keen interest in carbon
as well. According to a 2007 news report, for example, 'managing emissions is one of the fastest growing market segments, and companies are
scrambling for talent. Their goal: a slice of a market now worth $30 billion,
but which could grow to $1 trillion in a decade'.[4] Whilst carbon traders do
not yet earn the big salaries claimed by some traders and investment bankers, many large financial firms are opening carbon trading departments
and assembling trading teams. Some noteworthy names in the market include Barclays Capital, Shell, and Price Waterhouse Coopers, along with JP
Morgan and Goldman Sachs.

Despite the fall in carbon prices during the recession, and the difficulties
in negotiating a successor to the Kyoto Protocol, the global carbon market
is here to stay, in some form, despite recent findings that the market for
carbon is now, apparently, declining, with reduced demand pushing carbon prices down.[6] Hidden dangers lurk in such a complex web of financial
flows. There is a great distance between traders and the 'real' environmental
problem they are supposed to be solving, and the 'assets' they trade are
highly abstract. In the well-tailored suits they wear to work in large financial firms, they cannot readily apprehend the remote and yet real effects of
their trades in carbon on the environment. Each AAU, CER, RMU, and
so on, represents a precisely measured and verified quantity of carbon that
is not emitted, or that is supposedly removed from the atmosphere.

As one critical observer put it, 'unlike traditional commodities, which
sometime during the course of their market exchanges must be delivered
to someone in physical form, the carbon market is based on the lack of delivery of an invisible substance to no-one'.[7] This is an important point, as it
cuts to the heart of what investors actually own in the carbon markets. It is
beginning to look as if investors actually own a financial product, a form of
climate-related paper, that is, at the same time, categorically different from
existing financial products.

The most controversial aspect the Kyoto Protocol is checking on the
carbon credits earned through the CDM. This is also a vital issue because
the global carbon market would probably not work without it. As men-

tioned earlier, the CDM was intended to bring developing countries into the Kyoto process, and the CDM should also transfer technology from the rich to poorer countries. Following Kyoto, allowing companies to trade credits from the CDM was a way to introduce private sector finance for low-carbon projects to developing countries.

Once a utility company earned credits for a CDM project, it might then sell the credits to an investment bank or another financial firm. The investment bank could then use a small piece of some of the credits for the carbon not emitted to create part of a security. This is almost the same as what American banks did with mortgages before the 2008 financial crisis. The investment bank might then offer their carbon-based security for sale to another bank or for retail sale to individual citizens. When they buy a security, a bank will act according to the information the market provides to them. This information is purely financial, focused on prices, earnings in the future, whether the security can be sold later, and how risky it might be. It is not information about climate change, nor is it information about whether the security they might buy really does represent real carbon that has been removed from the atmosphere.

Including accurate, up-to-date information about whether the security actually does reduce anyone's carbon emissions appears to be too difficult, and may even have a detrimental effect on the market were these details to be included. One of Mark Schapiro's interviewees noted how 'if credits were revocable,…industries operating under caps would find they did not have the credits they thought they had. And they were afraid that if that were the case, there would be no market'.[8] Schapiro's article says that the need to hold companies to account for the quality of the credits they were putting onto the market 'was dropped in the interests of attracting more capital into the market more quickly'.[9] It seems that the need to make the financial dimensions of the market work took precedence over any question about whether the climate-based financial products being traded were actually reducing anyone's carbon emissions.

This means that there is a risk that markets fill up with what could be called 'sub-prime carbon' leading to a bubble, and then to a crash in carbon markets. Michelle Chan thinks, for example, that sub-prime carbon is likely to originate in the CDM as 'sellers often make promises to deliver carbon credits before the CDM Executive Board (or other crediting body) officially issues the credits, or sometimes even before verifiers confirm how much or even if [emissions] have been reduced'.[10]

If sellers 'overpromise'; or if one or more cannot then deliver the credits that may have already changed hands several times, the market experiences a shock. Such a shock could lead to the questioning of other climate-related paper assets. Next, there would be a sudden fall in prices as investors rush to turn their AAUs, RMUs and so on, into capital or cash.

This is always a danger in a market in which most trades are for short-term profit, rather than compliance with emission targets, something noticed by World Bank researchers.[11] According to Chan, 'a market dominated by speculators may push up prices, create a bubble and spur the development of subprime assets'.[12] This means that complex assets, rushed to the market without proper verification and monitoring become an investment opportunity for short-term profit. They are also a potentially serious threat to market stability and possibly the climate itself in the long term. There is even more risk when the various forms of emission credits are turned into a security or other product.[13]

Were the climate-related bubble scenario ever to play out, then, the fate of the carbon represented by all the various securities and permits would be unknown. Perhaps an event like this would simply turn people away from environmental investment in general, undoing years of environmental campaigning in the process.

I think that these are dangers which have been glossed over in the rush to create trading schemes and to bring new capital into carbon markets. For governments and banks, the priority after the Kyoto Protocol has been to create a market, and to enable trading to take place. They also wanted to attract large sums of capital into the market. Questions about whether the development of a global market for carbon would actually work as way to reduce carbon emissions appear to have been hidden behind a veil of esoteric economic complexity. The great emphasis has been on designing tradable products, rather than on checking and being certain that the assets traded in carbon markets are 'real' carbon.

Results and Alternatives

So far the results of carbon trading have not been good. At least the present market system hasn't led to a reduction in global carbon emissions. In fact, according to the Global Carbon Project, emissions are rising more rapidly than in the 1970s and 1980s (Global Carbon Project 2014).[14] Governments have realised the necessity for regulation and the need to support local projects. In many European cities, for example, local transport and energy initiatives have combined government spending with private sector know-how. The return of efficient, electric trams to several British cities would be a good case study; the reduction of car ownership in continental cities such as Copenhagen would be another.

If the global emissions trade will not reduce emissions, then there is still much that concerned citizens can do:

Information: Keep informed about your local city, region or national government and what they are doing to reduce carbon. Keep informed about the campaigning and non-profit groups working on climate issues.

Political Pressure: In democratic countries, contacting your representative, writing letters to newspapers, starting a local campaign can all make a difference. Using your vote is also the most basic way to influence leaders in a democracy. Going to lobby a city or even national government is a more ambitious way to get involved.

Lifestyle Change: Several website offer the chance for ordinary citizens to calculate the amount of carbon they are responsible for each year. (Although take care, as these are set up with specific climate zones in mind—a German carbon calculator would not work for someone living in the Philippines.) The old green demand to 'reduce, re-use, recycle' meant something and is still sound advice.

For those who are more worried about climate change, and who want to do something more serious to help, then there are two things you can do which come up again and again in the literature on climate change. The first is to give up your car, The second is to stop eating meat, or you can also wear warm clothes instead of turning up the heating.

Questions for Critical Reflection

1. What do you think governments should do to help prevent climate change?

2. What ways can ordinary citizens in countries across the globe work together to help solve climate change?

3. The author presents a thought-provoking analysis of problems inherent in a system that permits trading in a carbon-based market. Summarize this complex problem in simple words.

4. The author refers to a sort of misplaced emphasis in the carbon market, as "tradable products" take precedence over "checking…that the assets are 'real'." How has misplaced emphasis by the government affected its ability to find effective solutions to lingering problems in society?

References

[1] United Nations. 1998. *Kyoto Protocol to the United Nations Framework Convention on Climate Change*. Available online: http://unfcc.int/resource/docs/convkp/kpeng.pdf . Article 12, Paragraph 2.

[2] *Ibid.*

[3] Kapoor, K, & Ambrosi, P. 2009. *State and Trends of the Carbon Market 2009*. Washington DC, The World Bank. Ch.3.

[4] Carbon Ventures. 2009. Carbon Ventures: new global warming secrets revealed [online]. http://www.carbonventures.net [accessed 1 July 2009].

[5] Kanter, J. 2007. Where greed is green. *New York Times*, 20 June.

[6] Linacre, A. et.al. 2011. *State and Trends of the Carbon Market 2011*. Washington DC, The World Bank.

[7] Schapiro, T. 2011. Conning the Climate. *Harper's*, February: 1-15.

[8] *Ibid.*

[9] *Ibid.*

[10] Chan, M. 2009. *Sub-Prime Carbon: re-thinking the world's newest derivatives market*. Washington DC, Friends of the Earth.

[11] Kapoor & Ambrosi. 2009. *op. cit.*

[12] Chan. 2009. *op. cit.*

[13] See, for example, discussions of mortgage-backed securities in Bookstaber, R. 2007. *A Demon of Our Own Design*, New Jersey: John Wiley & Son. Ch. 4 and Lanchester, J. 2009. *Whoops! Why Everybody Owes Everybody Else and Nobody Can Pay*. London: Penguin Books.

[14] Global Carbon Project. 2014. *Global Carbon Budget 2014*. http://www.globalcarbonproject.org/carbonbudget/index.htm [accessed 16 October 2014].

CONTRIBUTORS

DEBAHIS "DEB" AIKAT, PH.D. A former journalist, Debashis "Deb" Aikat has been a faculty member since 1995 in the School of Media and Journalism at the University of North Carolina at Chapel Hill. An award-winning researcher and teacher, Dr. Aikat theorizes the role of social media, international communication, news media and the future of communication in the digital age. Dr. Aikat's research interests range across the media. His research has been published in book chapters and refereed journals such as *First Amendment Studies, Health Communication,* and publications of the Association for Computing Machinery (ACM), and Microsoft Corporation. The Scripps Howard Foundation recognized Dr. Aikat as the inaugural winner of the "National Journalism Teacher of the Year award" (2003). The International Radio and Television Society named him the Coltrin Communications Professor of the Year (1997). Aikat worked as a journalist in India for the Ananda Bazar Patrika's *The Telegraph* newspaper from 1984 through 1992. He also reported for the BBC World Service. Aikat earned a Ph.D. in Mass Communication and Journalism from Ohio University's Scripps School of Journalism in 1995. He completed in 1990 a Certificate in American Political Culture from New York University. He lives in Chapel Hill, North Carolina, USA.

DANIEL BROUDY is Professor of Applied Linguistics and Chair of the Graduate School of Intercultural Communication at Okinawa Christian University. As a former intelligence analyst with the U.S. Army, he draws upon his military experience and doctoral training in psycholinguistics to develop courses in communication and in the rhetoric of the visual. His publications and research critically assess systems and methods of mass manipulation and propaganda. He is the author of *Clearing a Vygotskyan*

Path: Phrase Play from Poetics to Prose (Waldport Press, 2008), co-author of *Rhetorical Rape: the Verbal Violations of the Punditocracy* (Waldport Press, 2010); *Writing Research Papers* (Macmillan 2011); managing co-editor of *Synaesthesia: Communication Across Cultures,* and co-editor of *Under Occupation: Resistance and Struggle in a Militarised Asia-Pacific* (Cambridge Scholars Publishing, 2013).

KRISTIN COMEFORO, PH.D., is Assistant Professor of Com-munication at the University of Hartford, in Connecticut, USA. Her research interests include the representation of the LGBTQ community in mainstream advertising, along with the intersection between brand discourse and public policy. Most recent work includes analysis of audience response on Facebook, to branded discourse in relation to marriage equality. Her work has appeared in edited volumes such as "Queer Media Images: LGBT Perspectives," "Coming out of the closet: Exploring LGBT issues in strategic communication with theory and research," and "We Are What We Sell: How Advertising Shapes American Life…And Always Has …"

THOMAS FAZI is a journalist, writer, documentary filmmaker, activist, and Anglo-Italian translator (of authors such as Christopher Hitchens, George Soros, and Robert Reich). Among other things, he is the co-director of *Standing Army* (2010), an award-winning feature-length documentary on U.S. military bases featuring Gore Vidal and Noam Chomsky; and the author of *The Battle for Europe: How an Elite Hijacked a Continent—and How We Can Take It Back* (Pluto Press, 2014). He is a regular contributor to *Social Europe Journal, il manifesto, openDemocracy, Krytyka Polityczna, Green European Journal,* eunews.it and other printed and online journals. He collaborates with the Italian civil society network *Sbilanciamoci!* and is the coordinator of the European Progressive Economists Network (Europen). His current website is www.battleforeurope.net.

ROBERT JENSEN is a professor in the School of Journalism at the University of Texas at Austin and board member of the Third Coast Activist Resource Center in Austin. He is the author of *Arguing for Our Lives: A User's Guide to Constructive Dialogue* (City Lights, 2013); *All My Bones Shake: Seeking a Progressive Path to the Prophetic Voice,* (Soft Skull Press, 2009); *Getting Off: Pornography and the End of Masculinity* (South End Press, 2007); *The Heart of Whiteness: Confronting Race, Racism and White Privilege* (City Lights, 2005); *Citizens of the Empire: The Struggle to Claim Our Humanity* (City Lights, 2004); and *Writing Dissent: Taking Radical Ideas from the Margins to the Mainstream* (Peter Lang, 2002). Jensen is also co-producer of the documentary film *Abe Osheroff: One Foot in the Grave, the Other Still Dancing* (Media Education Foundation, 2009), which chronicles the life and philosophy of the longtime radical activist.

RICHARD LANCE KEEBLE has been Professor of Journalism at the University of Lincoln since 2003. Before that he was the Executive Editor of the *Teacher*, the weekly newspaper of the National Union of Teachers and he lectured at City University London for 19 years. He has written and edited 29 publications on a wide range of subjects including peace journalism, literary journalism, communication ethics, practical reporting skills, George Orwell, the coverage of US/UK militarism and the links between the intelligence services and Fleet Street. He is also joint editor of *Ethical Space: The International Journal of Communication Ethics* and the winner of a National Teacher Fellowship in 2011—the highest prize for teachers in higher education. He is chair of both the George Orwell Society and Louth Male Voice Choir. In June 2014, he was given a Lifetime Achievement Award by the Association for Journalism Education, the body that links university journalism teachers in the UK.

JEFFERY KLAEHN holds a Ph.D. in Communication from the University of Amsterdam (2007) and recently completed a second Ph.D., in Sociology, at the University of Strathclyde. He serves on the editorial advisory boards with *Studies in Comics*, the *International Journal of Comic Art (IJOCA)*, *ImageText: Interdisciplinary Comics Studies, International Communication Gazette,* and *Synaethesia: Communication Across Cultures.* More information about his work can be found at: http://uva.academia.edu/JefferyKlaehn

REISA KLEIN, PH.D. is currently a course instructor in Communication Studies at Carleton University. Her research applies a critical feminist analysis to beauty and the body as sites of resistance including in the context of Holocaust survivors, fashion blogging and neo-burlesque theatre. Her current area of interest explores the intersection between tattooing, women's bodies, and health discourses and practices.

DAVID LAYFIELD was born and raised in Derby, in the English Midlands. He did a variety of jobs before going to university in his late twenties. He eventually graduated with a Ph.D. in politics from the University of Nottingham, and came live in Okinawa, in 2005. He lives with his wife and son; and is currently an Adjunct Assistant Professor at the University of Maryland

University College, Asia. His main research interests are in international relations as well as international environmental and labor issues. His publications include *Marxism and Environmental Crises* (Arena Books, 2008) and several journal articles. He is currently researching a book on the rise of non-regular employment in the global economy, and hopes to help in developing better international communication between workers affected by the rise of non-regular employment.

NORIKO LAYFIELD holds a degree in international relations from Columbia University and a Ph.D. in political philosophy from the University of York, Great Britain. She has worked in the area of political philosophy, and published articles in the philosophy of language, which draws attention to the feminist debate on sexual objectification, silencing, and reciprocity in communication. She currently works as a translator for public and private organizations, and teaches as a lecturer at Okinawa Christian University in Okinawa, Japan.

BRIAN MARTIN is Professor of Social Sciences at the University of Wollongong, Australia and Vice President of Whistleblowers Australia. He is the author of fourteen books and hundreds of articles on dissent, nonviolence, scientific controversies, democracy, and other topics.

MICHÈLE MARTIN is Professor Emeritus at the School of Journalism and Communication of Carleton University. For the last fifteen years or so she has been interested in the politics of visual representations. She has published critical books and articles on various aspects of this issue from a historical sociology approach.

CHRISTOPHER DANIEL MELLEY is a lecturer in composition and literature at Okinawa Christian University and Okinawa Prefectural University of the Arts. His doctoral work in philosophy at Universtität des Saarlandes investigated healthcare ethics committees and the role of the philosophy in healthcare settings. His writing and research focus on themes within applied ethics.

KATARZYNA MOLEK-KOZAKOWSKA, PH.D., is Assistant Professor at the Institute of English, Opole University, Poland. Trained as a linguist, she specializes in discourse analysis and media studies. She has published articles and chapters on various aspects of mass-mediated political discourse, rhetorical and stylistic properties of journalistic discourse, methodology of critical discourse analysis and critical media literacy. She co-edited a two-volume book *Exploring Space: Spatial Notions in Cultural, Literary and Language Studies* (2010, CSP), and authored a monograph *Discursive Exponents of the Ideology of Counterculture* (2011, Opole University). She co-edits the international open-access academic journal Res Rhetorica (www.retoryka.edu.pl).

CHARLOTTE V.T. MURAKAMI is currently a lecturer at the Language Education and Research Center, Fukuoka University, Japan. She was formerly a Modern Foreign Language teacher in the UK, and then left to teach English as a Modern Foreign Language further afield. She holds two Masters in Philosophy and Linguistics. She was recently awarded a Doctorate of Education from Exeter University, UK, for a thesis that investigated the motives underpinning a conflict between educators and politicians in England as to how language should be constituted as a body of knowledge in the curriculum and taught in classrooms from 1979-1997. She is now working on ways to share her new methodological and theoretical toolbox for understanding motive and conflict across educational history.

RENU PARIYADATH has a Ph.D. in Communication Studies and a minor in Gender, Women's and Sexuality studies from the University of Iowa. Renu researches activism around corporate accountability, non-profit and social movement organizing, and environmental justice, from a postcolonial/transnational feminist perspective.

GARRY POTTER is a filmmaker and Associate Professor of Sociology at Wilfrid Laurier University. He has made two feature length documentary films: *Whispers* of *Revolution* and *Dystopia: What is to be done?* He is also author of the book Dystopia. In addition to it, he is the author of two other books: The Bet: Truth in Science, Literature and Everyday Knowledges and *The Philosophy of Social Science: New Perspectives*, as well as numerous scholarly articles. He was also co-editor of the book After Postmodernism. Currently, he is producing a series of educational films about classical sociological theory for Insight Media.

HINAKO TAKAHASHI is a lecturer of Education and Language courses at the University of Maryland University College in Okinawa. She earned an M.A. in Applied Linguistics from the University of Massachusetts

Boston and a Ph.D. in Language, Literacy, and Sociocultural Studies from University of New Mexico. Her interests include second language education, bilingual education, heritage language, and Vygotsky's Socio-cultural Theories. While living in the U.S. for almost 20 years, she was a lecturer at the New Mexico Highlands University, an elementary school teacher for over 10 years, and worked for a school reform consulting organization as the literacy specialist. She was born in Japan, lived in Spain as a teenager, and in the U.S. as an adult.

JAMES WINTER is Professor of Communication and Social Justice at the University of Windsor, Canada. He is the author of Lies *The Media Tell Us* (Black Rose Books, 2007); *MediaThink* (Black Rose Books, 2002); *The Big Black Book: The Essential Views of Conrad and Barbara Amiel Black* (Stoddart, 1997), with Maude Barlow; *Democracy's Oxygen: How Corporations Control the News* (Black Rose Books, 1996); *Common Cents: Media Portrayal of the Gulf War and Other Events* (Black Rose Books, 1992); and is the editor of *Silent Revolution: Media, Democracy, and the Free Trade Debate*, (University of Ottawa Press, 1990); and *Press Concentration and Monopoly* (Ablex, 1988), with three others. He was the founder of the University of Windsor chapter of Cinema Politica in 2009, and the founding editor and publisher of *Flipside*, a muckraking alternative online webzine, from 1995-2000.

DANIEL XERRI is a teacher of English and the chairperson of the EFL Monitoring Board. After reading for a B.A. (Hons) in English at the University of Malta, he completed an M.A. in English Literature. He subsequently finished a PGCE in English and an M.Ed. in Applied Language Studies. Currently, he is completing a Ph.D. in Education at the University of York. His research focuses on the interplay between teachers' and students' beliefs and pedagogy. His research interests consist of teacher education and professional development. Mr. Xerri has published a string of peer-reviewed articles in international academic journals as well as chapters in books edited by various academics. In 2013, he was awarded the Terry Furlong Prize for Research by the National Association for the Teaching of English in the United Kingdom. In 2014, he was awarded a Research Mobility Programme Award by the World Universities Network. Together with colleagues at the University of Malta Junior College, he was the recipient of the 2014 Innovation in Assessment Prize awarded by the British Council.

PARMA YARKIN is a graduate student in communications at the University of Windsor.

FLORIAN ZOLLMANN holds a Ph.D. in Journalism Studies from the University of Lincoln. His doctoral thesis assesses U.S., U.K., and German elite press coverage of U.S./Coalition 'counter-insurgency' operations in Iraq in the light of Edward S. Herman and Noam Chomsky's propaganda model. Currently, he is contracted to write a follow-up study on international news coverage of human rights issues during a range of contemporary conflicts including Kosovo (1999), Iraq (post 2004), Gaza (2008/2009), Libya (2011), Egypt (post 2011), Syria (post 2011), and Ukraine (2014) for the international publisher Peter Lang (to be published as a monograph in 2016). Additionally, he is conducting research on the ethical implications of surveillance in liberal democracies and press-state relations in the 21st century new media environment.

CPSIA information can be obtained
at www.ICGtesting.com
Printed in the USA
LVHW04s2333290818
588617LV00009B/180/P